THE GODDESS, GODDESS, THE GRAIL & THE LODGE

DEDICATION

I have great pleasure in dedicating this book to my colleagues
and friends, Christopher Knight and Stephen Dafoe.

Copyright © 2004 O Books
46A West Street, Alresford, Hants SO24 9AU, U.K.
Tel: +44 (0) 1962 736880 Fax: +44 (0) 1962 736881
E-mail: office@johnhunt-publishing.com
www.johnhunt-publishing.com
www.0-books.net

U.S. office:
240 West 35th Street, Suite 500
New York, NY 10001
E-mail: obooks@aol.com

Text: © 2004 Alan Butler
Design: Nautilius Design (UK) Ltd

ISBN 1 903816 69 6

A CIP catalogue record for this book is available from the British Library.

Printed in 2004   by Maple-Vail Manufacturing Group, U.S.A.

THE GODDESS, THE GRAIL & THE LODGE

ALAN BUTLER

BOOKS

Winchester, UK
New York, USA

CONTENTS

ACKNOWLEDGEMENTS

It is first necessary to acknowledge the help and support of my wife and best friend Kate Butler. Her constant encouragement and her willingness to travel to so many out of the way places have been invaluable in the creation of this book.

I also want to express special thanks to Stephen Dafoe. Our transatlantic co-operation has opened up many new avenues and Stephen's deep and abiding knowledge of the Templars and Freemasonry have made my work much easier.

It gives me the greatest pleasure to mention a man who has probably done more than just about any other to add to the knowledge base of those of us who look at Templar and Medieval Monastic matters. In my opinion his praises are not sung half enough. His name is John Ritchie, a Scot of great knowledge, significant charm and a peerless wit.

I must also thank Lynn Picknett and Clive Prince, not only for reading this book and writing an excellent Forward but also for their constant friendship and support across the last seven or eight years. Our many conversations, in Scotland and in London opened up new lines of research that proved to be extremely useful.

Doubtless I have failed to mention many people who have contributed to this book in one way or another. In any case it would be impossible to list them all by name. If you are one of them, then please accept my thanks.

FOREWORD

All the most thought-provoking non-fiction is created around a paradox. Although each step of logic is tested and re-tested in the crucible of laborious intellectual research, it can only speak to the reader if it is based on passion and commitment - and a burning desire to add something precious to the world of humanity. This book rings through with the integrity of wishing to make the world a better place through the sharing of time-honoured revelations.

There is nothing faddy or sensational about Alan's work, nothing of the desire to create a furore out of thin air, as so often happens in the only-too-heady milieu of 'alternative history'. He follows the subterranean stream of goddess worship that runs through both time and dreams with equal vitality. It should be known and loved by a much wider audience. It is a secret, but one for everyone who is ready to embrace its often uncomfortable demands on both the psyche and the soul.

It may seem strange in our egalitarian age to suggest that rarely have women been so demeaned and degraded as they are today - but, controversially, Alan sees modern feminism as an attempt not to make every woman a goddess, but to force her into the mould of testosterone-fuelled men. This can only lead to yet more imbalance. It is perhaps no coincidence, as Alan points out, that the early goddess-worshipping cultures were markedly more peaceful and creative than the more dogmatic and unyielding patriarchies.

But how can women learn to be goddesses if they have no knowledge of the old beliefs? This book will show each modern woman the richness of the legacy that is rightfully hers, and each man his powerful role in the divine balancing act.

As a historical detective, following the Golden Thread from the great - and usually misunderstood - Megalithic cultures through the important dynasties he believes arose from the 'Salt lines', Alan Butler vividly presents a compelling picture of the fight for life of a great secret, and one that we 21st-century sophisticates simply can't afford to ignore.

LYNN PICKNETT
CLIVE PRINCE

LONDON
2003

INTRODUCTION

The small Island of Malta lies in the Mediterranean Sea. Malta has a rich and fascinating history, and one that dates back so far it is impossible to know exactly how long our species has had a bearing on that rocky landscape. Malta is where this book ends and so in a way it is also fitting that it should represent our beginning.

Dotted around Malta, and on neighbouring Gozo, there are a number of interesting and deeply mysterious structures. Nobody doubts that these date back six thousand years and many suggest they are older. Most clearly represent 'temples', created with gargantuan stones. Most of these structures have been deliberately shaped so as to represent female reproductive organs. The temples of Malta and Gozo represent the oldest structures of their kind in the world.

What was in the mind of those who created Malta's amazing temples? It is my fervent contention that the proof of their purpose exists in 365 places throughout Malta and Gozo, for this is the number of Christian Churches that exist there. Malta is a deeply Catholic society and practically every Church in Malta and Gozo is dedicated either to the Virgin Mary, or to a female saint. In almost any humble parish Church we find Mary in her guise as 'Queen of Heaven' or portrayed as 'Our Lady of Sorrows'.

It is self-evident to anyone who looks at the situation fairly, that the Maltese have the same reverence for a female deity (The Great Goddess), that their distant ancestors had when they pushed, pulled and hammered those massive stones into place.

The Maltese were not alone in showing reverence to the Great

Goddess in prehistory. It is now a generally accepted fact that most Neolithic Europeans and many Neolithic Asians were also believers in a female deity. Doubtless her praises were chanted and spoken amongst the great uprights of Stonehenge in England or within the chambers of Newgrange in Ireland, and in a hundred thousand other places through far more centuries than we could even contemplate.

In terms of period human beings have lived in closely ordered societies of one sort or another, none of the recognised religions in the world today are anything more than infants. Because religious adherence has played such an important part in our collective cultures, it might appear that our present beliefs are somehow ageless and unchanged but this is far from being the case. However, there is one belief pattern that is clearly as old as our species and which is as real in the world today as it was when the stones of Malta were cut from the living rock.

Come with me on a journey. Let me show you that the most revered of all human religious beliefs not only survived the change in attitude that led to the patriarchal beliefs we know today, but that it was carefully and continually re-invented to suit prevailing circumstances. Allow me to give you a glimpse of a secret knowledge that also survived and which has been carefully preserved by a Priesthood determined to maintain its age-old traditions and beliefs. This is the remarkable 'Grail Knowledge' that has been so important to Western cultures and also to the very building of the United States of America.

What follows is one of the most extraordinary stories imaginable, made all the more remarkable because it is self-evidently true.

CHAPTER 1

Memories of the Goddess

I n an increasingly secular age, very few of us, at least in the western world, spend much time thinking about the origins of religion, or even about the nature of "Godhead." However, the very word Godhead makes a definite assumption – that the creative deity at the heart of everything is a "God" and therefore male in gender.

In the western world at least, most of our grandparents accepted the precepts laid out in the Christian Bible: "In the beginning was the Word and the Word was God." It was what they were taught and they knew that the Bible was a document of extreme age – so presumably it was correct. However, even the very oldest part of the Bible – the Old Testament, was not written down until after 500 BC. We know this to be the case because the Old Testament has been clearly affected by Babylonian myths and legends. Large sections of the Jewish population were captive in Babylon around this period, and since some of the very earliest stories in the Bible, that of Noah for example, are Babylonian in origin, it follows that the written Testament cannot be any older than this period. 500 BC might seem to be a very long time ago, but when compared with the period during which humanity has been on the Earth, it might as well be yesterday.

Judaism, from which Christianity derives, shows itself to be a patriarchal belief pattern – in other words, at least as far as God is concerned, it is male orientated. It shares this quality with the newest of the world's greatest religions, Islam, with which it has common roots. Another of the world's most important faiths, Hinduism, though possessed of goddesses, is also basically patriarchal in nature. Bearing these facts in mind, together with the many millions of devotees involved, we could be forgiven for accepting that a belief in a male Godhead is a natural proclivity for humanity.

Nevertheless, however natural and accepted "God"-centered religion might seem to be in the world at present, there is a wealth of archeological and cultural evidence to show that this was not always the case, and certainly not as far as much of Europe was concerned.

For some decades, a heated debate has existed amongst two distinctly different groups of historians and archeologists. One group makes the assumption that the acceptance of a masculine God is somehow endemic to our species. However, many thousands of distinctly reputable experts disagree and these people are clearly winning the argument. This group was initially championed by the late Marija Gibutas, a Lithuanian archeologist. She, and they, suggest the historical evidence proves conclusively that for tens of thousands of years, prior to the arrival of the Indo-European speaking peoples, during the late Stone Age and Bronze Age, it wasn't God, but rather a Great Goddess who reigned supreme in European religion.

Although we don't know much about the origins of the "original" Europeans, nobody doubts that they were absorbed, or in some cases destroyed, by more warlike insurgents from further east. Balts and Estonians settled along the Baltic Sea, as early as 3000 BC, though they were clearly not the first inhabitants of the region. More Indo-Europeans from Asia, the Slavs, settled around the Vistula, Bug, and Dnieper rivers, probably shortly after 3000 BC. Somewhat later, circa 2600 BC, another group of Indo-Europeans moved as far West as Belgium and the Netherlands. Areas of France and Britain probably held out against the newcomers longer, but we cannot be certain.

Old cultures and religions did not die out immediately and many aspects of religious belief would have passed to the insurgent people. In terms of evidence, those adhering to the theory of early goddess supremacy seem to have an unassailable armory. A huge quantity of effigies have been found across much of Europe, some of which date back as much as 30,000 years. The artistic skill employed varies markedly between locations and the periods they were manufactured. These clearly represent female figures. By far the majority of them have exaggerated sexual parts and many seem to be associated with fertility and childbirth. This, says Gibutas and her allies, is the first proof of more or less universal goddess and fertility worship for tens of thousands of years in Europe, prior to the Indo-European invasions.

However, the statues are only the tip of a very large iceberg. There is no doubt that much of the Paleolithic period and the later Neolithic period were comparatively peaceful times across much of the Continent. Adherents of ancient goddess worship point to the fact that villages in early farming communities were not fortified and that life appears to have been very settled and without undue violence. They also note that burials from the period indicate no existence of a "warrior" class, as would later be the case and that with regard to graves and grave goods, there is little or no differentiation between males and females. This, they suggest, quite clearly points to a feminine gender Godhead and not to the patriarchal society and religion of more recent times.

Another line of research involves the myths and legends of later cultures, such as that of the Egyptians and the later Greeks. Followers of Gibutas and other goddess adherents suggest it is easy to "tease out" from the mythological patterns memories of pre-heroic religion. It is possible, they believe, to see in goddesses such as Isis in Egypt and Demeter in Greece, recognizable manifestations of a much earlier "Great Goddess," who once lay at the center of religious worship across a vast region.

Further to this, and across most of Europe, the early Christian Church swallowed up any number of local female deities, regurgitating them as saints, with manufactured histories and biographies so that reticent devotees would eventually accept Christianity. Nowhere is this clearer than in the case of St. Bridget, who clearly represents a goddess of extreme antiquity, Brigga, who was venerated across large areas of the British Isles and who gave her name to the Brigantes, the largest Celtic tribe in Britain. A similar situation happened in northern France where Rosemerth had been worshiped since time out of mind. In this case, the qualities of Rosemerth were simply attached to the Virgin Mary, a practice on behalf of the developing Christian Church that we will see time and again as the pages of this book unfold.

The superstitious Celts, although amongst the later Indo-European peoples who entered Europe, appear to have retained at least some aspects of the old religion and social order that had existed at their arrival. It might surprise some readers to learn that despite being amongst the most warlike of the Iron Age Europeans, the various tribes of Celts, both in Britain and across what we now know as France, were quite prepared to accept queens as well as kings. Examples of this practice include Cartemandua, queen of the Brigantes, and Boudicca, famous queen of the Iceni. This fact may not demonstrate that the Celts were avowed Great Goddess worshipers but it shows that a certain "equality" of the sexes had survived, perhaps a legacy of the old Neolithic European ways.

So it is suggested that Goddess worship had existed across much of Europe until the arrival of these very different people, who brought with them their own more martial and patriarchal traditions, forming the Indo-European language groups that predominate today. The Indo-Europeans would become known to us as the Celts, the Germanic peoples, the Slavs, and in fact practically all the cultural groups to be found in Europe at the present time.

Though the newcomers certainly were more or less affected by the cultures they conquered, only in very isolated pockets, such as in the case of the Basques of southern France and northern Spain, might we still find remnants of the true, undiluted "original" inhabitants of western Europe. The Basque tongue remains absolutely unique in the world and clearly originated from some very different language base than Indo-European. It is interesting to note that although Basques are generally Christian today, the historical social structure of this people shows women to have been far more emancipated than was the case with their European neighbors, even in comparatively recent times. From their number came powerful priestesses, who had an important contribution to make within society and government.

The theories of Gibutas regarding Goddess worship were to create an echo in terms of my own research, particularly with regard to one group of pre Indo-Europeans that she recognized as being a late survivor of European Neolithic values. This was the culture of ancient Crete, which we now refer to as the Minoans. Gibutas said of the Minoans:

The Old European mythical imagery and religious

practices were continued in Minoan Crete. The Minoan culture mirrors the same values, the same manual aptitude in artistic endeavor, the same glorification of the virgin beauty of life. The Old Europeans had taste and style – whimsical, imaginative and sophisticated; their culture was a worthy parent of the Minoan civilization.

However, before we look at the Minoan culture more closely, it is only fair to point out that the Goddess worship theory for ancient Europe is by no means unopposed. Criticism is forthcoming for a number of reasons. Some archeologists see in the proliferation of "Goddess" statues, with huge breasts and over-emphasized sexual organs, nothing more or less than a sort of early *Playboy* center-fold. With regard to myths and legends, these detractors want to know how it is possible to reliably infer anything about a basically matriarchal social structure from the myth cycles of a series of clearly patriarchal societies?

It is interesting to note that most of the detractors from the European Goddess theory are men, whilst the majority of the adherents are women. There is a great danger, even among scientists, that we may subconsciously allow present values to have a bearing on the way we view the past. I hope my research has been genuinely influenced by the evidence as I have seen it. And to me, there is no better example of how society and religion probably coexisted in much of Europe, prior to the later Bronze Age, than in the case of the people who inhabited the beautiful Island of Crete, before the Mycenaean domination, which took place around 1450 BC.

Crete is a large Island, situated in the eastern Mediterranean Sea. It is now a part of Greece but from as early as 2000 BC, its people represented Europe's first super civilization.

The true nature and accomplishments of Cretan civilization only began to reveal themselves at the beginning of the twentieth century. A wealthy archeologist and scholar, Arthur Evans, negotiated for the right to excavate in various places in Crete, but in particular on a hill, somewhat inland from the present capital of Heraklion, on the Island's north coast.

Here Evans discovered the ruins of the palace of Knossos and within a couple of decades, the prehistory of Europe had to be rewritten. The Cretans were known from Greek myth and legend, particularly in terms of a supposed "king" of the Island, known as Minos. Because of this association, Evans called the ancient Cretans "Minoans" a name that has stuck, though what the Minoans called themselves remains a mystery.

Many of the finds from Knossos, and now from numerous other sites in Crete, are breathtaking in their beauty and also prove the technical skill that went into their production. The Minoans were brilliant artists, creating colorful and delicate pottery, bright and active wall frescos, and buildings erected in a grand style.

The palace of Knossos was huge, covering an estimated 20,000 square meters. It had known numerous phases, the most recent being completed between the sixteenth and fourteenth centuries BC. When built, Knossos was four stories high in places, with light wells streaming the Cretan sun into its deepest interiors. Great staircases were flanked with elegant, tapering pillars. In the heart of the building was to be found a series of rooms that appear to have had a deeply religious purpose. Sophisticated drainage, of a quality not to be seen again until at least the time of the Romans, criss-crossed the site and there is even an example of a flushing toilet. Archeological finds from the palace are literally tens of thousands in number and, together with those from other sites across Crete, offer a tantalizing glimpse of a civilization that looks truly unique when set against the contemporary Egypt of Babylon.

One of the earliest realizations regarding Knossos, and the other known Minoan palaces of Phaistos, Malia, and Zakro, is that there were no fortifications whatsoever. This might be viewed as strange because all the palaces, and Knosses especially, were the repository of every possible product of Minoan ingenuity and craft. Vast magazines held stores of olive oil, grain, wool, pottery, and especially honey. Much of this was destined for export. The Minoans had an excellent navy, both merchant and for defense. Crete lacks metal, which meant that the components to make bronze – copper and tin – had to be imported, sometimes from great distances. So, although the Island was a natural fortress in itself, it certainly was not insular. It kept good relations with Egypt and had colonies all along the Mediterranean, up into the body of Greece and along the coast of the Levant.

Two specific facts about Crete will become increasingly relevant as our evidence unfolds. Firstly, there is the vast number of sheep known to have been raised on the Island in Minoan times. In addition, the huge number of "seal stones" found on Minoan sites is worthy of mention. The seal stones, some of which are very beautiful, had specific designs carved into their hard stone surfaces. They would have been used to create images on clay or wax seals, probably on corn sacks or around the necks of storage jars. Literally tens of thousands of seal stones have been discovered. They are still given to newly married brides and are known as "milk stones," believed to aid in fertility and the feeding of infants. The sheer quantity of seal stones that survive, both inside and outside of museums, gives some indication of how many there must once have been. This leads to a specific inference. The Minoans were involved in "personal trade" and there is a distinct possibility that free enterprise of a type undreamed of in contemporary Egypt for example, existed on the Island of Crete, even in this very early period.

Every piece of evidence unearthed paints the same picture of this truly vibrant society. There is nothing remotely "marshal" about Minoan art. Statues of heavily armed warriors or even kings are non-existent and, as far as can be ascertained, the Minoans had no large, standing army. From before the second millennium BC, on until independent Minoan civilization ceased, after 1450 BC, everything points to a society very much at ease with itself.

The archeological record clearly shows that women were far from being second-class citizens within Minoan society. Indeed, women figure far more prominently in art than do men. And whilst males are usually displayed wearing little more than a loincloth, women wore brightly colored full skirts, under tightly fitted bodices betraying bared breasts. Women also sported elaborate hairstyles, beautifully made hats, and cosmetically enhanced their appearance.

There are many pictorial references to women in what can clearly be only religious settings. It is the considered opinion of the world-famous archeologist, Jaquetta Hawkes, that the scenes depicted on pottery, frescos, and seals clearly show that the women of Minoan Crete were responsible for running and serving the beliefs of the people.[1] So many are the representations available that it is quite possible to recreate the essential features of Minoan religion.

It is now generally accepted that Minoan religious belief centered upon a single, Great Goddess. She had many manifestations, for example Goddess of agriculture, Goddess of birth, Goddess of the dead, etc., though ultimately these were nothing more than alternative manifestations of the primary deity. The creation myth of Minoan Crete is cyclic and perpetual. In this the Goddess, who is eternal, gives birth to a son, who is known as the Young God. The Young God grows to maturity and becomes the consort of the Goddess, at which time he is transposed into the Old God. He conjoins with the Goddess, who produces a new son, the Young God. At this time, the Old God must die and the cycle begins all over again.

So frequently is the Goddess portrayed in Minoan art, in association with trees or crops, that there is little doubt that her presence was seen to be synonymous with the bounty of nature and with rebirth. It has been suggested that some of the ceremonies depicted on pottery or fragments of frescos relate to religious practices associated with veneration of the Goddess. These show processionals, in which devotees carry vessels of one sort or another, perhaps containing libations to the Goddess or her consort.

Minoan religion clearly points to a very 'primitive' origin, which is also to be seen in early Egyptian and Sumeria/Babylonia. In fact, shades of this, our earliest religious beliefs, are to be found everywhere. The Great Goddess "is" the Earth, and through her fertility, she brings forth, every year, new offspring. Symbolically, this is specifically related to grain, such as wheat and barley. The Young God "is" that corn, and he grows to maturity before being cut down, to make bread and beer. But of course, it is "his" seed, now as the Old God, that goes back into the soil to create next year's crop. The Young God cannot be born, except by the death of the Old God. Remnants of such "vegetation myths" can be found in the Greek story of Demeter and Dionysus, the Egyptian fables concerning Isis and Osiris, and in literally dozens of other examples.

In addition to their nature worship, the Minoans were inordinately fond of the "bull games." These appear to have been a forerunner of today's bullfighting, still a regular occurrence in parts of Europe and especially Spain. The difference in the Minoan case is that the bulls were apparently not harmed in any way. Ferocious wild bulls were brought into an arena, where young people of both sexes would perform athletic and extremely dangerous feats, jumping and somersaulting over the back and flanks of the animals. Representations of bulls' horns are to be found everywhere in Crete. They surmounted the flat roofs of Knossos and perhaps the other palaces. It is entirely possible that the power and strength of the bull was seen as a physical representation of the masculine aspect of Godhead. However, the certain presence of female acrobats in the bull games also points to a degree of emancipation within Minoan society that would have appeared incredible to later cultures.

Specifically sacred to the Goddess were double-headed axes. Many hundreds of these, in bronze, silver, gold, and stone, have been found in votive sites up and down Crete. They were often associated with burials. Also closely linked with the Goddess was the spiral, which crops up regularly in Minoan art. Neither of these symbols is unique to Crete but both were widespread across prehistoric Europe.

It is believed by many experts that the "mystery cult" of Demeter, which would eventually be celebrated on the Greek mainland in Eleusis, originally began at the palace of Knossos in Crete. Few deny that Demeter, about whom I shall have much more to say presently, was originally a Minoan deity because tradition from time out of mind asserts the fact. In addition, the linguistic form of her name smacks of some lost language. Even after many centuries, the Greek Demeter retained her close association with nature and kept her position as Goddess of the dead. During the Demeter mysteries, it is thought that devotees went through a form of death and rebirth ritual and it is entirely possible that this first took place in the deepest recesses of the huge palace of Knossos. It may not be too far fetched to suggest that similar practices happened in many of the so-called "chambered tombs, "much further west, in Britain and France. Such ceremonies were never totally eradicated, even though Christianity tried so hard to do so. On the contrary, as we shall eventually see, they are regularly performed in towns and cities all over the world, on almost any day of any week.

How far the Minoans traveled from their island home is not known, though they certainly had settlements in Sicily and possibly in southern Spain. Archeological artifacts discovered in the south of England, particularly in Devon and on Salisbury Plain, close to the enigmatic Stonehenge, might point to the fact that Britain was visited regularly, probably for tin, which was available in Cornwall and was absolutely necessary to Minoan metal workers.

Items such as gold earrings and a fabulous gold cup, known as the Rillaton Cup, have been found by archeologists buried in southern England. Because of their form and craftsmanship it was once suggested that such goods had been traded with the early Britons by Mycanean sailors. It was later shown that the items in question, which had been used as grave goods, had been buried before Mycanea emerged as an independent culture. Since Mycanea was to gain virtually all its artistic prowess from Minoan Crete, which it conquered, the only satisfactory explanation is that the artifacts are genuinely Minoan in origin. This suggests a likely relationship between the contemporary culture of Britain and that of the Minoans and we shall see that there was certainly a commonality in terms of the cultures' understanding of both geometry and physical geography.

In fact, there may well have been regular trading relationships across a large percentage of the coastal fringes of western Europe from a very early date. Every new discovery leads archeologists to realize that late Stone Age and early Bronze Age abilities in seamanship were much greater than was once realized. Trade, even across great distances, was essential to the early farming communities and the sea, particularly in summer, was the easiest highway for carrying bulk products. The Minoans definitely exported vast quantities of olive oil, honey, wool, pottery, and a wealth of other merchandise. How far they took it can only be conjecture.

The Minoans were contemporary with the later stages of a culture in Britain, France, and in many of the Islands of both the Baltic and the Mediterranean that we know as the "Megalithic." The word means "big stones" because many of the people of these regions had been cutting and dragging large stones around the landscape for maybe two thousand years, even prior to the Bronze Age. The way these stones were arranged differs from region to region. In Britain and France, they form circles, avenues, fans, and alignments. Meanwhile, in the Balearics, in Minorca, there are numerous examples of single uprights, topped by one major crosspiece, forming a sort of "T".

In Malta, and especially on the neighboring island of Gozo, we find what could only really be considered as "temples." Dating back as early as 3600 BC, long before the Pyramids of Egypt were even contemplated, the Ggantija complex on Gozo retains the torso of a huge female figure, which we can only surely take to be representative of the Great Goddess.

The absence of statues of the Goddess elsewhere cannot be taken as proof that she wasn't important, or even pivotal. If we were to strip away the frescos, pottery, and seals, together with a few very small statuettes in Minoan Crete, the remaining architecture would say little or nothing about the Goddess. On the contrary, the ceremonial sites of the Minoans, originally caves and then later manufactured structures, carry little in the way of statuary of any religious sort. Meanwhile, the climatic conditions and acid soils in the Far West mean that, in an archeological sense, much more is lost to us than is retained. Nevertheless, it seems fair to suggest that at most Megalithic sites the Goddess was "ever present" but not necessarily depicted. I personally find no problem with this. The Goddess represented the Earth, so she was to be found everywhere.

As a good example, there is strong evidence to show that our ancient ancestors also equated the planet Venus with the Goddess, probably as a direct, physical representation of her presence. Together with researchers and writers Christopher Knight and Robert Lomas, I carried out an intensive study of a Megalithic structure in Wales, known as Bryn Celli Ddu. The structure, which may have been incorrectly described as a burial mound, is built of extremely large stones and contains a central chamber with what was obviously intended to be a carefully created viewing space to the west.

The chamber also has a carefully carved central pillar, which has horizontal lines etched into it. We were able to show that Bryn Celli Ddu was designed to track the movements of Venus when it appears as an evening star, following the Sun down towards the western horizon. In this sense the structure is a sort of observatory and one that is deeply important in terms of Goddess worship, though there is no direct "effigy" of the Goddess to be seen.

All over the Salisbury Plain in southern England, burials from the Megalithic period have been unearthed which amongst their grave goods have sported beautiful, polished double-headed stone axes. In some instances the stone used has come from far away. A microscopic analysis of the faces of these axes shows that they were never used – they are entirely "ritual" in context and they are just as likely to be related to the Goddess as the double axes found in Crete are known to have been.

Perhaps the most persuasive evidence for a Europe-wide period of tens of thousands of years during which the Goddess was venerated would be concrete proof that this veneration never ceased. I intend to show conclusively in the ensuing chapters that to a very important group of people that I have named "The Golden Thread," and as a result of an unbroken tradition, the Great Goddess is every bit as important now as she was to the Paleolithic hunter-gatherers of 30,000 years ago. She also remains pivotal to both the beliefs and practices of many millions of other people in the modern world, even if the people concerned remain totally oblivious of the fact.

Further to this, I dare to make the bold assertion that the very nature of western society as we know it today, economically, politically, and religiously, is directly responsive to a continued recognition of and veneration for the Great Goddess. At all stages in the painful journey toward democracy and the age of reason, people well aware of religious imperatives almost as old as humanity, doggedly stuck to the beliefs of their ancestors. Against prevailing, patriarchal trends this relentless "continuum" patiently, steadily, and secretly stuck to an agenda that is now plain to see. Nor should we be surprised to discover that some of the most apparently male-orientated organizations, for example the Freemasons, is founded directly, squarely, and quite deliberately on Goddess veneration. They, and groups who went before them, like the Cistercian monastic Order and the famous Knights Templar, retained an agenda that has proved absolutely essential in providing us with the freedoms that many of us hold so dear today.

CHAPTER 2

The Web of Demeter

Sometimes adventures begin in most unlikely ways. For me, it was a brief holiday in Crete, fourteen years ago. At the time, I knew little about the Minoan civilization, or indeed about what a major part my growing recognition of the Great Goddess in our common past would play in my life henceforth. To explain much of the evidence that is to come, it is necessary to take a small departure from the theme of the Goddess, though in the end this little trip into calendars and units of length is of the utmost importance because it "proves" what follows.

I was already something of an expert in the history of astrology and astronomy and had spent years studying ancient calendar systems. A wealth of admittedly circumstantial evidence had already made me believe that in the dimmest recesses of our common ancestry, both the measurement of the year and the way we view geometry must have been very different than they are today.

In the western world, we use a very complicated calendar. Like most ancient cultures, we have twelve months in each year, though we squeeze these into a year of 365 days, which means that the months are bound to vary in length, because 12 will not divide into 365. Part of the problem stems from the fact that a "month" is basically a lunar construct. Our ancient ancestors were great Moon watchers. We know this because a number of the Megalithic structures in Britain have been demonstrated to have particular properties for lunar observation, in other words they were built specifically with Moon watching in mind.

Unfortunately, the Moon is not especially co-operative. Its cycles, from full Moon to full Moon, are about 29.5 days in length, which is an impossible number for any "tidy-minded" society. The Sumerians and Babylonians simply rounded the lunar cycle up to 30 days, and had twelve months of 30 days. This wasn't correct, because it only totaled 360 days, instead of the true 365.25 days, but they simply added an extra month every so often to keep things right. This is also probably the reason why they opted for a geometry with 360 degrees to the circle.

Via Ancient Greece, we have retained Sumerian/Babylonian geometry, but in terms of the year, we do things differently. Looking at the year, and the way we split it, had led me to a particular theory, born out of my astrological research, though at the time it could not be anything more than conjecture. Put quite simply, I wondered if, at some very remote time, the year had been considered to be 366 days in length and that the number of days in each month had alternated between 30 and 31 days. (Any reader wishing to follow the various steps my research took can read Appendix 1, in which the situation is explained more fully.)

A quick look at the modern calendar shows the 30 and 31 day pattern still existing to an extent.

> March = 31 days
> April = 30 days
> May = 31 days
> June = 30 days
> July = 31 days

And again:

> August = 31 days
> September = 30 days
> October = 31 days

November = 30 days
December = 31 days

The pattern breaks down in places, but only because of a couple of jealous Roman Emperors. Julius Caesar wished to have a month named after him, which was July. The Emperor Augustus, who came later, was awarded the following month, but since he was considered "greater" than Caesar, he could hardly be expected to have a month of only 30 days. As a result, August was lengthened to 31 days. This meant that February, the last month of the year to the Romans, had to become even shorter than it had formerly been. In addition, the modern year is only 365 days in length and not 366 days.

I did not pursue my idea of a 366-day year with any particular fervor, mainly because of leap years. The fact is that no year with an equal number of days can ever remain correct with the true solar year. It takes the Earth 365.25 days to go around the Sun, so whatever system is used, compromises will have to be made. In modern society, we celebrate a year of 365 days, though we lengthen it to 366 days every fourth year, in order to keep the calendar correct. There are numerous other rules, relating to century years and millennium years but to all intents and purposes, our calendar is now reasonably accurate. It has taken centuries to gradually get to the system we use today and, on occasions in the past, the "civil" calendar has been hopelessly at odds with the real or "solar" calendar.

If life is so complicated with leap years for a 365-day year, how much more difficult might it be to compensate for a 366-day year. The whole contemplation gave me a headache, and since there was really no evidence for a 366-day year, I put the notion on the back burner of my mind.

However, whilst I was in Crete, I came across a facsimile of a very curious little artifact, discovered in the ruins of the palace of Phaistos. The original is in the Heraklion museum in Crete. It dates back to 2000 BC and is a baked clay disc, about 15cm in diameter. Pictures of the Phaistos Disc can be seen in Appendix 1. The disc is double sided and on each side carries an incised spiral. Within each of these spirals, there are hieroglyphic symbols, in groups, pressed into the clay. Nobody knows what these symbols mean, because we have no knowledge of the Minoan language. However, it was not the "meaning" of the symbols, but rather the number of them on each side of the disc that eventually interested me.

In short, it seemed to me that the Phaistos Disc represents a unique little calculating machine, which indicated to a society celebrating a 366-day year, how to bring that year back into synchronization with the true solar year of 365.25 days. Appendix 1 explains the whole procedure, but it turned out to be incredibly simple, utterly ingenious, and far, far more accurate than our own system of leap years.

It next occurred to me that if the year was 366 days in length, it was likely that circles had been split into 366 degrees. This might have been something of a leap in logic but it opened a door that was to change my life forever. It also caused me to recognize a direct connection between the Minoans and the Megalithic people of Great Britain and France.

These were my eventual conclusions: To the Megalithic peoples of probably much of Europe, each theoretical circle, including that of the Earth traveling around the Sun and around its own center, contained 366 degrees of arc, to match the number of days in a year. Each degree could be split into 60 smaller units, known as minutes of arc, and each minute of arc could be split into six smaller units, known as seconds of arc.

Meanwhile, in Britain, a very bright professor of engineering who was born a Scot but who spent most of his academic life at Oxford, had been busy carefully surveying and measuring as many of the British and French Megalithic monuments as he could. This man's name was Alexander Thom and during 50 painstaking years he amassed more concrete evidence regarding the methods of the Megalithic builders than any individual before or since.

Thom's primary discovery remains his most controversial. Against all odds and common sense, Thom began to realize that these late Stone Age and Bronze Age builders had been using a standard unit of length in all their endeavors. Disbelieving his own findings, Professor Thom checked and rechecked his findings but he could not get away from the fact that a linear length of 2.722 statute feet (82.96656 cm) cropped up at every site, from Orkney in the north, to Brittany in the south. He called this unit "the Megalithic Yard" and its discovery was to dog him for the remainder of his life. Science scoffed at the comprehension of a unit of measurement that was somehow kept accurate to at least 1 part in 500 across such a vast area and for well over 2,000 years. Bearing in mind the primitive lives of the people concerned it had to be nonsense. No satisfactory way of passing on such information could be comprehended. Wooden rods would vary with temperature and humidity, or become broken, bent, or lost. Ropes would be even worse. So despite the fact that the Royal Statistical Society scrupulously verified all of Thom's observations, saying there wasn't 1 chance in 100 he was wrong, archeologists did and still do scoff at the mere idea of the Megalithic Yard.

To try and settle the argument once and for all, writers and researchers Christopher Knight and Dr. Robert Lomas, joined forces with me in order to try and work out a way that the Megalithic Yard might have been passed on, intact from site to site and century to century. It took a while, but we eventually came up with the answer. The Megalithic Yard had been ascertained wherever it was necessary, by tracking a rising star passing between two posts, whilst swinging a pendulum. If the posts were 1/366th of the horizon apart, a pendulum that swung 366 times as the star passed between the posts would have to be exactly _ of 1 Megalithic Yard in length.[2] Archie Roy, Emeritus Professor of Astronomy at Glasgow University, validated our findings and called it "a significant breakthrough in our understanding of our Megalithic ancestors."

When the Megalithic Yard is allied with the theoretical 366-degree geometry, and then related to the polar circumference of the Earth, something truly remarkable takes place.

> 1 Megalithic second of arc = 366 Megalithic Yards = 30365.76 meters
> 1 Megalithic minute of arc = 2196 Megalithic Yards = 182.1945 km
> 1 Megalithic degree of arc = 131760 Megalithic Yards = 10931.67 km
> 366 Megalithic degrees of arc = 48224160 Megalithic Yards = 40,009,9 km

This last figure is so close to the generally accepted polar circumference of the Earth that the difference is virtually non-existent. The inference is obvious.

> *Whoever used the Megalithic Yard knew the true polar circumference of the Earth and had designed their basic unit of linear measure to reflect the fact.*

A further proof of the validity of these observations came when I discovered that the Minoans had possessed a linear unit of their own. This was rediscovered by Canadian archaeologist J. Walter Graham, back in the 1960s. From measurements of all the Minoan palaces, he was able to demonstrate that the Minoans had used a unit of 30.36cm, which he called the "Minoan foot."

This turned out to be a simple metrication of the Megalithic system because 366 Megalithic Yards (30365.40 meters) and 1,000 Minoan feet (30,360 meters) are the same thing, to within 99.98% accuracy or 1 part in over 5,000. Graham didn't have as many examples to work with regarding the Minoan foot as Thom did with the Megalithic Yard. The very tiniest error on his part would make this fit absolutely perfect. I took this as proof that the Megalithic peoples of Britain and France and the Minoans on Crete were using the same basic system, based on a knowledge of the size of the Earth and on the 366-degree geometry.

The reason why all of this is crucially important to the Goddess and her survival will be revealed as our story unfolds. My book, *The Bronze Age Computer Disc*, which explained all these facts, was published in 1999.[3] Only a month or so after it appeared, I came across further evidence that was even more controversial and which would change our comprehension of the Neolithic and Bronze Age mind and capabilities for ever.

I had been reading a back edition of a magazine, published in the 1970s. It was named *Unexplained* and one particular feature caught my attention. It was an apparently ridiculous story about a French researcher, by the name of Xaviar Guichard. Guichard was a high-ranking police officer in Paris, who had enjoyed a lifelong fascination with history and with maps, which he pawed over endlessly. As early as the 1920s he had come to a remarkable and apparently absurd conclusion. Guichard declared that when places with specific types of names were joined together on maps of France, they produced long, straight lines. These place names all contained an "al" component, chief amongst them being the many locations named "Alaise."

The first sets of lines Guichard discovered were of what is known as a "compass rose" variety. From a central node, for example the village of Alaise, in the Jura Mountains of eastern France, long lines radiated out, like the spokes of a bicycle wheel, constantly passing through other Alaise or similar place names. Guichard associated the "al" component of the place names with the ancient word "hal," which is present in many languages and means "salt." He conjectured that perhaps these long lines, that sometimes extended hundreds of kilometers across the landscape, had represented paths, over which that all-important commodity, salt, had been traded. Because of the ancient nature of the settlements concerned, Guichard was certain that the lines must be at least Bronze Age in date.

Ultimately, Guichard discovered a different sort of "salt line." These looked very much like modern lines of latitude and longitude on a map. (See figures 1 and 2.) What was particularly interesting was that these lines occurred at almost exactly 1 degree intervals, but not quite. Guichard monitored this fact. He assumed

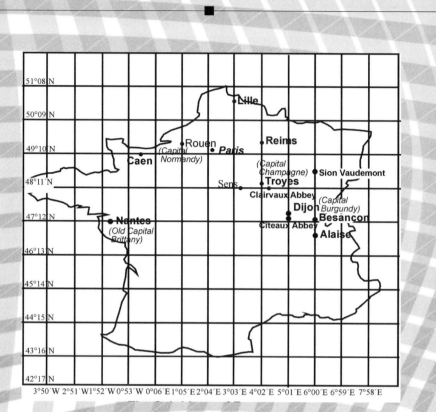

Figure 1

The Salt Lines of France (With places mentioned in the text)

that the lines were "intended" to be lines of longitude and latitude, literally "etched" onto the topography of France, and marked by the "al" place names. However, he surmised that the people who laid out this "spider's web" had not been able to adequately measure the size of the Earth and so had placed the lines very slightly closer together than they should have been.

Guichard may have been of this opinion, but I was not and I guessed immediately what I would find if I measured the true distance between his proposed salt lines of longitude and latitude. I found them to be 59 minutes and 1 second of arc apart. The

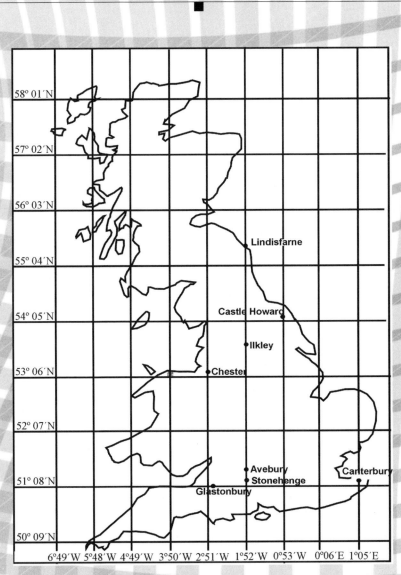

Figure 2

The Salt Lines of Britain (With places mentioned in the text)

people who had created these lines knew "absolutely" what the measurements of the Earth were. Xaviar Guichard did not understand about Megalithic geometry or the 366-degree circle, but whoever had laid out the salt line system clearly had. In any circle of 366 degrees, the degree markers, on a map or on the ground, will be very slightly closer together than in a circle of 360 degrees. Guichard's salt lines fitted an Earth divided into 366 degrees – and to a totally uncanny and disconcerting accuracy.

Guichard wrote a book about his findings. It was entitled *Eleusis – Alesia* and it appeared in 1936.[4] The book is almost impossible to find these days and it is written in French, but I did eventually manage to track down a copy. Very few copies of the book were produced, and about 500 of the ones that were printed were destroyed in a fire in an Abbeyville warehouse. It probably made no difference. To anyone in the scientific community Xaviar Guichard was clearly mad and his theories were not worth a light. However, if that is the case, why do his salt lines of longitude and latitude so accurately fit the Megalithic mathematical model that I had, quite independently, rediscovered? The time scale was the same – at least as early as the Bronze Age, and I was able to exploit Guichard's findings in a way he never had.

Xaviar Guichard had plotted the longitudinal and latitudinal salt lines across much of France, Spain, Belgium, and even Italy. He had also looked for them much further east. What he had singularly failed to do was to check their expected positions in Britain. He maintained that all the lines of longitude commenced in the little village of Alaise, in eastern France, which has a modern longitude of exactly 6 degrees East of Greenwich. It was therefore very easy for me to plot where all the other lines should fall, and so I made the calculations and drew the projected lines onto large-scale maps of Britain.

The first significant fact was how often one of these salt lines of longitude or latitude pased right through, or immediately close to, a Megalithic site of historical significance. (See map, figure 2.) These included Stonehenge, Avebury, Silbury Hill, Brodgar, Callanish, and a host of others. Guichard's observation of the "Al" and "Hal" place names was also as relevant in Britain as it had proved to be in France and beyond.

All of this should rightfully be nonsense, but clearly, and for whatever reason, it is not. Research far beyond the shores of Britain and France has now proved to me beyond doubt that the salt lines are a hard and fast reality. For all I know they are a worldwide phenomenon. It will take decades to check the run of every potential line, everywhere on the planet. It is for this reason I have included the expected location of every single projected salt line of longitude and latitude in Appendix 2, so that interested readers can look carefully at the salt lines in their own region.

Although I called the lines "salt lines" in deference to Guichard's original notion, it is clear that they serve a far more important purpose and that they represent the remnants of a "living map," the implications of which would cause a rewriting of ancient history. How the lines were surveyed and made remains a total mystery, as does any understanding of their genuine purpose. I cannot even be sure if they are a natural or a totally "created" phenomenon, but of their genuine existence I have no doubt.

As we shall see, many of the locations to be found on the salt lines, particularly in France and Britain, are and almost certainly always have been, sacred to the Great Goddess. We shall also discover that this amazing "net," covering the face of the Earth, though generally forgotten to history has clearly been remembered by an important and enduring section of humanity.

CHAPTER 3

The Goddess of Ten Thousand Names

Hinduism, the main religion of India, probably rightly claims to be the oldest existent religion in the world. The most venerable Hindu texts, the Vedas, are known to date back to at least 1500 BC. Judaism also has an ancient pedigree, though even the most venerable parts of the Old Testament did not appear in written form until around the ninth century BC, despite the fact that much of it is based on oral traditions that could be significantly older. Buddhism, a faith followed by many millions, began in either the sixth or fifth centuries BC.

Christianity, as an offshoot of Judaism, obviously came late on the scene, at around 2,000 years ago, whilst Islam sprang from the words of Mohammed, an inspired Holy teacher and Prophet who died in AD 632, making this the youngest of the world's great religions.

We have already seen that a selection of the many female representations found across Europe and beyond are known to date back to at least 7000 BC, but even these come nowhere near to the dawn of religion as far as humanity is concerned. Rock art from the Sahara and also within Europe may be 20,000 or more years old, whilst Australian examples have been found in layers known to date back at least 40,000 years. If these animals, human representations and symbols can be said to have religious significance, and they almost certainly do, the oldest of the world's present belief patterns are infants by comparison. What is more, there are strong indications that our close cousins, the Neanderthals, who emerged 135,000 years ago, had a belief in an afterlife. They certainly buried their dead, with both grave goods and strewn with flowers. Since *Homo Sapiens*, our own branch of the hominid tree, only emerged 120,000 years ago, it might reasonably be suggested that religion actually "predates" our species.

Scientists from Duke University Medical Center, Durham, N.C. in the United States, claim that nerve canal sizes in the fossil skulls of Neanderthal Man indicate that he could talk, which, bearing in mind other evidence is probably not too surprising. The idea of burying the dead with ritual and with grave goods seems unlikely without the emergence of story-cycles leading to some form of religious practice.

The first true writing known is that from Sumeria, dating back to around 3500 BC, though arguably there may have been symbols from earlier periods that carried specific meanings. Writing came to Egypt soon after. It follows, nevertheless, that we have been speaking for an incredibly long period, but writing for only a very short time. To put this in perspective, if the 120,000 years of Homo Sapiens was considered to be a single year, our ability to talk was probably present on 1 January, whereas writing did not arrive until around 10 December.

In the conception of at least one expert, the very emergence of writing may have been what signed the death-knell for the old Goddess-centered religions of our species. Leonard Shlain MD, Chief of labroscopic surgery at the U.C. San Francisco Medical Center reached a series of conclusions that set the academic world alight. In 1998 he published the book *The Alphabet Versus the Goddess*.[5] Shlain suggests that the use of writing forced our brains to undergo a necessary change, or at least to function in a different way.

The human brain is divided into two sections, or hemispheres. It is known from experimentation that the two hemispheres of our brains have slightly different responsibilities. When we speak and listen, both hemispheres are involved. The right hemisphere, for example, examines non-verbal clues, such as body language, whilst the left hemisphere processes the words we hear in a lineal sense. However, the use of written language forces the brain into a predominantly "left hemisphere mode." Shlain believes that many of the tasks, emotions, and values generally considered to be "female" are controlled in the main by the right hemisphere. Meanwhile, those facets of nature usually associated with a masculine drive or context are left brained.

A synthesis of Shlain's thesis is that right-brained responsibilities predominated in pre-literate cultures so that, for example, "images" are extremely important. It was, he suggests, under these circumstances that the more peaceful period coinciding with either Goddess worship, or at the very least greater Goddess awareness, is most evident. The arrival of writing changed the mental balance of individuals, and so therefore, inevitably the societies in which they lived.

Shlain has his critics and, in some ways, I number myself as one of them. The Indo-European races that at the very least "infiltrated" the old Neolithic cultures of Europe were not themselves literate, but this fact did not prevent them from being both patriarchal by inclination or violent in disposition. Leonard Shlain's explanation is surely only a part of a bigger picture, in which population explosion, dispossession of land, and necessary, warlike incursions into new territories all played a part.

Once writing did emerge, we find aspects of the Great Goddess in all the literate cultures, born of countless generations of oral tradition. In Ancient Greece, she had many names and faces. This is partly due to the fact that each area comprising the loose confederacy that formed Ancient Greece contributed in some way to its ultimate religious pantheon. Egypt too had a multitude of goddesses, but none personified the original Neolithic Earth goddess as well as the most important Egyptian female deity, Isis.

Isis, alternatively known as Ast, was amongst the oldest of the many gods and goddesses the Egyptians eventually came to worship. She is invariably portrayed in the form of a woman carrying a scepter of papyrus. She bears a crown that supports two horns, between which is a disc. Sometimes Isis has radiant wings. These she "fans," to bring to life the body of her murdered husband and brother, Osiris.

Her story is one of sorrow and ultimate rejoicing. This fact alone might be partly responsible for the popularity of her cult. Ultimately this spread far beyond the bounds of Egypt and out into the whole known world. Isis is often described by experts as having "evolved from a very early form of corn spirit." Her chief claim to fame in Egyptian history is the loyalty and love she showed for Osiris, with whom her own story is intimately connected.

Isis had many names and ruled over much of human endeavor. She was accepted across Egypt and beyond as being goddess of the harvest and of food generally. Her season is the Spring. This is the time when the sleeping seed of the earth begins to germinate. It is the commencement of the process that leads to the ultimate bounty of the Autumn.

Isis was married to Osiris, an equally ancient deity. His worship certainly predated any written records in Egypt. Since writing came very early to the civilization, it is almost certain that the migrants who first wandered into the fertile Nile Valley brought something of both Osiris and Isis with them. The essential point of the Osiris myth is that he died and was reborn in a cyclic manner. This parallels absolutely the young god and old god of Minoan origin. The Osiris story is, in this respect at least, almost identical with those of the Greek Adonis and Attis. In each case the death of the god is mourned by an adoring goddess, who strives to bring her consort back to life. The Egyptians believed that Osiris had shown humanity how to plant and harvest corn, so he shares the vegetation associations with Isis. He may have done so since the dawn of humanity's consideration of such matters. The position of Osiris, as the sacrificed corn god, reflects a theme we will be forced to examine time and again, even in a Christian context.

Osiris was the son of Nut, a great sky-goddess and of Ra, chief Egyptian deity. Osiris became a just and mighty god and ruled the land of Egypt well. He civilized the people of the two kingdoms and taught them the rudiments of creating a wonderful home for themselves in the Nile Valley.

Although Osiris was generally loved, he did have one enemy, namely the god Set. Set decided to kill Osiris and did so in a cunning way. Set had a beautiful sarcophagus made. Its dimensions would house the body of Osiris and no other. Inviting many deities to a wonderful feast, Set produced the coffin and persuaded the guests in turn, to try it for size. When the time came for Osiris to lay in the sarcophagus Set and his co-conspirators quickly slammed the lid. They then sealed up all the joints with molten lead. The coffin was set adrift on the Nile, coming ashore a great time later in Byblos where it lodged in the branches of a tamarisk bush. Eventually the bush grew into a tree and the coffin of Osiris remained inside the trunk. So beautiful was the tree that Melcanthus, King of Byblos, had it cut down. He used it as a pillar to support the roof of his palace, little knowing that the body of Osiris was within it.

Meanwhile Isis had heard about her husband's treacherous murder and hastened to Byblos. Disguised as a nurse she took charge of a royal infant and thereby gained admittance to the palace. Eventually she identified herself. The tree was cut open and the sarcophagus was exposed. Isis took it by sea back to Egypt before setting off to find her son Horus. While she was away Set came to the place where the body of Osiris lay and cut the body into fourteen pieces, which he scattered throughout the country.

Upon hearing what had happened Isis hurried back and began to search for the many parts of her husband's body. She found them all, except his phallus, which, some stories say, she fashioned instead from beeswax. Osiris was restored to life by the faithfulness of his sister and wife Isis. Their son, Horus, eventually grew to manhood and took his revenge on Set.

Other versions of the story relate that Osiris was never restored to life, but took his place as King of the dead. The battle between Horus and Set goes on forever. Only when Horus wins will Osiris once again be able to take his rightful place as King of Egypt. In the meantime, all Pharaohs of Ancient Egypt took on aspects of his personality and became "in some magical way" Osiris, during the period of their reigns. They were the reborn Osiris, legatees of the birth, death, and birth cycle.

It is quite possible to see in this story an enduring theme which is present in almost all civilizations. There is a traditional folk song from England, called "John Barleycorn," which has a similar tale at its heart. The song relates the trials and tribulations meted out to John Barleycorn. John is cut down, beaten violently, and then murdered in the initial verses of the song. The listener is not supposed to realize, until the last verse, that the words relate to barley, the cereal crop. The last line makes it plain that though abused, beaten, and killed John Barleycorn will always rise again.

The story of Isis and Osiris is a yearly one. In its original form, the dismemberment of the body of Osiris was synonymous with the cutting, threshing, and grinding of corn. In this context, Isis is the Mother Earth herself. She alone has the power to take the seed corn and make the crop grow again, so that Osiris, the golden corn, can live once more.

There are great similarities between this story and the tale of the Greek Dionysus. Dionysus is a composite deity, but he too has associations with vegetation. He also originally owed his existence to cereal worship. The tales surrounding him are many and varied, but there is an underlying theme similar to that of the Osiris myths.

Dionysus was sometimes the son of Persephone, who herself could be equated with her mother Demeter. Both these deities are Greek counterparts for the Egyptian Isis. In other versions of the tale, Dionysus was married to Persephone, or even to Demeter. But in all the stories Dionysus was set upon by his enemies and killed in a rather gruesome way. He was dismembered and his body was boiled, roasted, and eaten. Somehow his wife/mother/sister managed to gather all the parts together again, and the god was reconstructed. The only section of his anatomy to escape the indignity of his various other bodily parts was his penis.

The phallic allusion of the story led to a yearly ceremony in which Greek women would parade about with baskets on their heads. In each of the baskets was placed a representation of the

Penis of Dionysus, carved from the wood of a fig tree. There is a sexual pun at work here because the fruit of the fig bears a striking resemblance to the female vagina.

An enduring similarity of the stories of Osiris and Dionysus lies in the fact that the penis is specifically mentioned in them both. In some versions of the Egyptian tales, Isis finds the dismembered phallus of Osiris first. In the Dionysus version his phallus survives the attempt of the villains to destroy every part of the god.

There are even versions of the Isis story in which the goddess uses the dismembered penis of Isis to inseminate herself. Alternatively, she does so with the aid of the member that was of her own manufacture. The intended purpose of both these stories is essentially the same as that proposed by the song John Barleycorn. By giving up his life, the hero provides the means for its continuation. All these stories are, at base, explanations of the repetitive and certain cycles of nature. The hero dies, but the one enduring and sustaining influence is that of the goddess. She clearly represents the fertility of the Earth, which is directly responsible for the continuation of life.

Of particular interest with regard to the stories of Dionysus is the clear recognition that they came to Greece from Crete where they played a part in Minoan beliefs. The certainty of this lays in the fact that Dionysus was associated with the Mysteries of Demeter. These Mysteries were celebrated annually at Eleusis, not far from Athens. Prior to their celebration at Eleusis, the Demeter Mysteries had rightfully belonged at Knossos. This palace was the spiritual and temporal heart of Minoan Crete.

The worship of both goddesses, Isis in Egypt and Demeter in Greece continued. The cult of Isis went on until the fourth century AD in Egypt, and the Mysteries of Demeter were also celebrated well into the Christian era. Both have, at their heart, a sexual imperative, though they allude as much to the fecundity of nature as to humanity. It is my belief that they spring from the same source and are associated with one of the oldest and most enduring religious cycles known to our species. Similar stories exist almost everywhere and we know that the Demeter and Dionysus versions of these tales were being told in Minoan Crete. There is a proven relationship between Ancient Crete and the Megalithic peoples of western Europe. It is surely safe to presume that our Megalithic ancestors told stories that were broadly similar.

The Sumerians and the later Babylonians had goddesses with almost identical associations to those of Isis and Demeter. One of the most important deities to the Sumerians was "Nisaba," who was specifically venerated as the goddess of barley, but who was also responsible for writing and learning. Later, the Babylonians venerated "Ishtar." Ishtar had many faces and names but she stood alone to the Babylonians as the chief goddess of fertility, both in humans and in nature.

A particularly important deity, with similar attributes to Isis, Demeter, Nisaba, and Ishtar, was "Astarte," who was alternatively known as "Astoreth." She was, at various times, worshiped by the Philistines, the Phoenicians, the Egyptians, the Canaanites and a host of Semitic peoples. The significance of Ishtar cannot be understated. She was often referred to as "Queen of Heaven" and "Mother of the Gods." Particularly associated with her worship were the dove and the bull.

Amongst those peoples who had venerated Astarte from time out of mind was one specific Semitic confederation of tribes we know collectively as the Hebrews, or originally "Hibaru." Written evidence about the Hebrews comes to us most specifically through the pages of the Old Testament of the Bible. However, this has to be read with a degree of circumspection. Many of the genuine incidents mentioned in the Old Testament took place centuries before the period at which they were first written down. In the period between Solomon (mid tenth century BC) and the writing of much of the Old Testament, (around 500 BC), the religion we now know as Judaism had undergone a significant transformation.

Those who wrote the stories of Creation, the Flood, the Exodus, and the rest, were doing so in the light of "their own" beliefs, which colored all they penned. The writers cannot be considered to have been historians in the modern sense of the word. For example, to the dyed in the wool patriarchal monotheists the Hebrews had become by AD 500, all conception of goddess worship was an abomination. The once revered Astarte had become a somewhat evil demon "Astoreth" and though the great leader, Solomon, is glorified in the Old Testament for his kingship of the Hebrews, he is taken to task for his goddess-worshiping ways, which were probably universal amongst the Hebrews during his era.

Nevertheless, the Judaic scribes did us a favor because they left in the Old Testament a significant amount of information regarding Hebrew beliefs at the time of Solomon.

Like Isis, Astoreth had been, amongst her many other attributes, the goddess of the harvest. Those places where grain was threshed from its stalks after the harvest took on a significant religious significance. We know about the importance of threshing floors from a number of different cultures and they are alluded to frequently in the Old Testament of the Bible. One, in particular, gets a significant mention. It was located on Mount Moriah, somewhat to the west of the valley of the River Jordan. King David bought this sacred threshing floor from a group known as the Jebusites. In the fullness of time his successor, Solomon, would come to build the most significant temple ever created by the Hebrews on that very spot, once sacred to Astarte, the Mother goddess. To Solomon, and to us today, the place was called "Jerusalem."

CHAPTER 4

From Minoan Crete to Judaism and Christianity

Historical sources show that the Hebrews founded the city of Jerusalem around 1000 BC, during the reign of King David, who was superseded by the even more famous Solomon. However, there had been a settlement in or around the same location for a considerable period. People were living just to the southeast of the present Temple Mound as early as 3000 BC. The first suggested name for the settlement is "Urasalim," meaning "Foundation of God," though this is by no means certain. Ancient sources refer to the Canaanite king of Salem, Melchizedek meeting the Hebrew patriarch Abraham in the place where the Temple would eventually stand.

Even by the period of Solomon, Hebrew dominance in the region was by no means absolute. For some generations the Hebrews had been a "client tribe" living in Egypt. Some time during the thirteenth century BC, the Hebrews came north from Egypt and re-entered the lands their ancestors had formerly occupied. There they came face to face with the Canaanites, a Semitic people with a similar ancient ancestry to their own. Gradually, the Hebrews established dominance in the region, though not without encountering significant difficulty from another and in some ways more difficult enemy, the Philistines. Why the Philistines were in the region at this time, who they originally were and where they came from is an important part of our story.

At some time between 1650 BC and 1450 BC the peaceful and prosperous people of Minoan Crete awoke to see a blinding light coming from the northern horizon. This was followed, some moments later by an ear-piercing explosion. The sound must have raced up and down the mountain valleys of the island, throwing the populace into confusion and panic. It would have permanently deafened those who were not in a sheltered place. Anyone seeing the light directly would have been instantly blinded. But the Minoans did not have long to collect themselves. Very soon the sky darkened and a wall of water hundreds of feet high descended onto the beaches and inlets of northern Crete. The tidal waves crashed ashore with unbelievable ferocity. Whole townships were washed away in seconds and farmland across many kilometers was inundated by sea water. Meanwhile men, woman, cattle, sheep, and creatures of every kind were swept to their deaths in the boiling waters of a previously calm sea.

The sleeping crater of Thera, on the island of Santorini, north of Crete, had exploded with a ferocity rarely, if ever, experienced during the history of humanity. Over fifty cubic miles of rock were flung high into the air. The rock was immediately pulverized into tefra, a fine volcanic ash. This quickly spread over a huge area north and south of Santorini. The island of Santorini, also known as Thera, was the site of a prosperous Minoan settlement. Anyone there at the time would have died in seconds, though it is thought that most of the inhabitants had left in fear of the earthquakes that preceded the eruption.

No coastline in the vicinity was safe from the tidal waves. The fine dust rained down over a vast area for days. The explosion was so big it was certainly heard at the far end of the Mediterranean. So great was the amount of debris thrown into the atmosphere that it must have had a bearing on global weather patterns for years. No part of the Earth was totally immune from the devastation meted out in the death throws of Thera, but no place suffered as much as Santorini itself, together with the Island of Crete.

Santorini had originally been circular, with the main settlements being on the leeward side of the volcano. Here they received the winter sun every day. After the eruption the remnants of the Island looked like a Taurus-shaped three-quarter ring. Miraculously many artifacts of the flourishing Minoan community on Santorini survived under tons of ash. The main settlement is being gradually resurrected, though the community was large and the work will take generations to complete.

The survivors, those from the south of Crete or people sheltered by the high mountains, found their world altered forever. Land that had not been ruined by salt water lay under meters of hot, acrid volcanic ash. Such land would not bear crops again for a decade or probably much longer. The glory that had been the very first European super-civilization was gone for good. Probably within weeks or months, the invaders arrived. These were a more warlike people from the Greek mainland, with whom the Minoans had previously been trading. There may even have been existing dynastic relationships between the two peoples. The Mycenaeans, as we know them, manufactured a new Crete, modeled on their own language and customs.

The Minoan navy was scattered. Dispossessed and with only their excellent skills as sailors, many of the Minoans became the pirates they had sought so hard to eradicate from the area. They became the infamous "Sea People," mentioned in Egyptian documents and specifically associated with the "Coifi," the name the Egyptians had always had for Cretans. Prior to the disaster, the Minoans had patrolled the eastern Mediterranean. Their intention had been to keep shipping lanes safe for the extensive merchant navy that the island also possessed, since trading was the lifeblood of this vibrant civilization. Now the law keepers became expert law-breakers.

Leaving their blessed island, waves of Cretans sailed east, past

Cyprus and on to the shores of the Levant. There they came ashore and settled in the coastal fringes around Gaza. There must have already been Minoan colonies in the area, because burials of a Minoan nature, predating the Santorini eruption, have been found in the region. The newcomers would have consolidated such settlements. It wasn't long before the tough little men of Crete were forcing their way inland. Reaching the Jordan Valley they pushed north to the shores of Galilee, where they beat off the defense of the Canaanites and founded their own settlement at Be'et Shien. Later they moved into areas around the western shores of the Sea of Galilee. It was about the time of these settlements, some two to four hundred years or so after the Santorini disaster, that these people confronted the Hebrews, who around this period in history become known as the Israelites.

For some time a sort of confederacy existed between the Israelites and the Cretans, who by now we can call the Philistines. However, the legendary King David, who united Israel and who reigned from 1000 BC to 962 BC, had such resounding victories over the Philistines that they were never again a serious threat to Hebrew domination of the region. By this period, the two cultures, Hebrews and Philistines, had been in direct contact for several generations and, as the Bible concedes, a degree of cultural intermixing certainly took place.

It was David, a former tenacious guerrilla leader, who conquered Jerusalem, capturing it from the Jebusites, another Semitic tribe. Though he was freely offered the sacred threshing floor on Mount Moriah for the location of the eventual temple, palace, and administrative buildings, King David preferred to purchase the land from Arau'nah, the leader of the defeated Jebusites. The Bible tells us:[6]

22: Then Arau'nah said to David, "Let my lord the king take and offer up what seems good to him; here are the oxen for the burnt offering, and the threshing sledges and the yokes of the oxen for the wood. 23: All this, O king, Arau'nah gives to the king." And Arau'nah said to the king, "The Lord your God accept you."

24: But the king said to Arau'nah, "No, but I will buy it of you for a price; I will not offer burnt offerings to the Lord my God which cost me nothing." So David bought the threshing floor and the oxen for fifty shekels of silver.

25: And David built there an altar to the Lord, and offered burnt offerings and peace offerings...

The Israelite establishment of their own capital city in Jerusalem was far from the end of the difficulties for this location. Jerusalem could probably tell more stories of conquest and upheaval than any other place on the Earth. The Jewish race clung to the site tenaciously, considering it to be the most sacred place on Earth.

The Old Testament tells us that the great King Solomon, whose reign followed that of King David, consolidated his hold on Jerusalem and decided to make it his greatest city. On the large mound near the center of the city where the threshing floor had been, he built a fabulous complex of royal apartments and administrative buildings. The most important structure in this complex was the Temple. The Bible is very specific about the date of this construction. Using Jewish records it can be reliably dated to 971 BC. According to Bible chronology in the Book of Kings, this was exactly 480 years after the Israelites had left Egypt.

The Jerusalem of King Solomon would almost certainly surprise many orthodox Jews these days. Jews of Solomon's period differed radically from their modern counterparts. As we have seen, many of the oldest stories relating to the origins of the Jews were not written down until much later, sometime between AD 600 and 500. Immediately prior to this date, Jerusalem had been captured by the Babylonians. Many of the Hebrews from the region were living in exile, as prisoners and slaves of King Nebuchadnezzar. The Israelites were at this period, a conquered people. Leaders of the exiled Jews were desperate to retain a sense of their "uniqueness." As a result, Jewish scribes "massaged" ancient folk tales and extant historical accounts in order to portray the past they "wanted." This did not necessarily coincide with what had actually taken place.

Even though they may not be authentic historical documents, the Hebrew stories are very old. It is quite understandable that readers of the Bible assume that these must be genuine first hand accounts of actual happenings in Jewish history. In fact, this cannot be the case. Many of the Old Testament stories show a parallel with Babylonian legends. There is every indication that the writers were heavily influenced by the culture that had overthrown their own. Nevertheless, the writers of the stories, captives in Babylon, still believed the Jews to be "God's chosen people." This fact has been deliberately reflected in their handling of the Old Testament stories, which developed and grew during the Babylonian period.

By modern standards, the builder of the first Temple, King Solomon, would not be considered a good Jew. Not only did he have 700 wives and at least 300 concubines, he established an alliance with the old enemy Egypt. Indeed, one of his wives was an Egyptian princess. If the Bible stories are to be believed Solomon also had a liaison with the Queen of Sheba, who was most probably from the region we now know as Ethiopia and certainly was not of Jewish blood. Exotic influences appear to have been quite acceptable in Jerusalem under Israel's most famous kings. The Great Temple, primarily built to house the sacred Ark of the Covenant, was not even built by Jewish craftsmen. It was constructed by foreign hirelings from Tyre.

The almost fanatical monotheism of later Judaism was clearly not present during the time of Solomon, despite the fact that the later chroniclers try to suggest it was. The writers of the Old Testament retrospectively berate Solomon for his religious leanings but it is still made clear that Solomon did not only worship the all powerful "Yahweh" but that he was also devoted to the Goddess Astoreth.[7]

> 5: For Solomon went after Ash'toreth the goddess of
> the Sido'nians, and after Milcom the abomination of
> the Ammonites.

There is strong evidence that the God of the Hebrews had originally enjoyed a consort goddess. This character, sometimes called "Lilith," was demonized by the later writers of the Bible. Tradition asserted that the meeting place of God and goddess was within the sacred Ark of the Covenant, housed in the Holy of Holies in Solomon's Temple. With the destruction of the first Temple, in 586 BC, the divine coupling could no longer take place and the Israelites gradually lost all knowledge of their original religion.

So, by the period of Solomon, we find the Hebrews to be a Semitic people, not at all unlike their counterparts the Canaanites, and probably also significantly affected by dynastic and common contacts with the Philistines, themselves the survivors of the ravaged Minoan civilization. The whole concept of Jewish "uniqueness" and an almost fanatical adherence to the single God Yahweh lay some time in the future. As we have seen, there were significant Philistine/Minoan settlements in Gaza, and also strung out around the Sea of Galilee. One of the most important of these was at "Migdal," now el Mejdel, an ancient village that will prove to be of pivotal importance to our story.

Western fascination with the Levant, and especially with the Galilee area, quite understandably revolves around the story of Jesus and the origin of the offshoot of Judaism that Christianity is supposed to be. In order to fully comprehend how Goddess worship survived, partly in Judaism, but was then transmitted into Christianity, we must understand a little more about the area of Galilee, into which Joshua Ben Joseph, more commonly known to us as Jesus, was born.

If one follows the careful chronology of the Bible, generation by generation, it is possible to work out that Jesus, specifically a product of the house of David, was born exactly 40 generations after the great King Solomon, builder of the first Temple in Jerusalem. The number "40" is highly significant, both in terms of Megalithic geometry and with regard to the number of times it appears in the Bible. (See Appendix 1 and the description of the Phaistos Disc.) Examples are the 40 years the Israelites are supposed to have wandered in the wilderness during the Exodus and the 480 years between the Exodus and the building of the Temple (480 is 12 times 40). Another, earlier example is the story of Noah, in which it rained for 40 days and 40 nights. The number 40 is also important in the life and ministry of Jesus himself. The New Testament tells us that Jesus wandered in the wilderness for 40 days, prior to the beginning of his ministry. In this context, the 40 generations between Solomon and Jesus could be seen as particularly noteworthy. This fact was not lost on future generations, as we shall see.

Jesus may well have been considered by some to be a natural "Rabbi" or "teacher" but he came from a region in which orthodox Judaism was not necessarily the accepted norm.

The Bible asserts that Jesus lived in Nazareth, a village well south of Galilee. However, it has now been shown that this cannot be the case because Nazareth did not exist during the era of Jesus and wasn't founded until the third century AD. A far more likely candidate is "Gennesaret," on the western shores of the Sea of Galilee. This was close to Migdal, the Minoan/Philistine settlement mentioned above.

To the best of my knowledge no Philistine, and therefore ultimately Minoan remains, have been found at Gennesaret, though the same is not true of Migdal, where remnants of Minoan wall frescos and other artifacts were found in abundance.

Migdal has another claim to fame. It was well known in the time of Jesus for being the place where sacrificial doves were reared for the temples. "Migdal" can be taken to mean the place of the doves.[8] The dove is an enduring representation in Minoan art for the Goddess herself. It is quite conceivable that this connection between sacred doves and Migdal was no coincidence. It probably goes back to the time of the Philistine/Minoans, way back in the reign of King Solomon. We have seen that one of the sacred symbols of Astarte, the form of the Great Goddess favored by Solomon, was the dove. Representations of temples, the columns of which are surmounted by doves, have been excavated from Minoan layers in Crete. Also associated with Astarte was the bull, a distinctly Minoan characteristic, perhaps suggesting that Astarte herself was Minoan in origin.

The story of the ministry of Jesus is played out on a wide canvas, but there are many locations that figure time and again. Galilee is surely the most important of these. It is around the shores of the lake that so many of the Bible stories take place. In addition, we find Jesus active down a large part of the valley of the river Jordan. It was in the River Jordan that Jesus was baptized by his cousin John. The Bible relates that the Holy Spirit descended from heaven in the form of a dove. Meanwhile a voice from above, gender unspecified, proclaimed "This is my only begotten son, in whom I am well pleased." The inevitable end of the Jesus story takes place in Jerusalem, with all its attendant importance as an early center of Goddess worship and the site of the sacred threshing floor.

Our present knowledge of the life and teachings of Jesus comes to us via the New Testament of the Bible, which is accepted by the mainstream of Christianity. However, in Nag Hammadi, in Egypt, versions of the story of Jesus highly divergent with the established Gospels were discovered in 1945. These are generally known as the "Gnostic" Gospels. Outlawed in the very early days of Christianity, the Gnostic Gospels have only survived thanks to them being secreted away and rediscovered in very recent times. The finds at Nag Hammadi are fourth-century copies of second- and third-century documents and they tell a very different story about the life and ministry of Jesus.

If the Gnostic Gospels are to be believed, no disciple was

closer to Jesus or more important, than Mary Magdalene, who gained her name because she came from Migdal – the place of the doves. The orthodox Gospels of the Authorized Bible carry only fleeting references to Mary Magdalene. She is often confused with a prostitute whose life was saved by Jesus when she was about to be stoned to death, though any connection is assumed, since the prostitute in question is not mentioned by name.

Though sidelining her, in comparison with the Gnostic Gospels, the orthodox Gospels of the New Testament do give some indication as to Mary's obvious importance. It is she who anointed Jesus' feet with precious ointment and who was the first to see him in his risen state, after the crucifixion.

Galilee, the area where both Jesus and Mary Magdalene were born was, at the period of Jesus, peopled by individuals who were not really Jewish at all. Judaism, as its name implies, sprang from the beliefs of the tribe of Judah, and from Judea. Galilee had never owed allegiance to the Kings of Judea and in a religious sense remained a hotbed of alternative beliefs. The cults of Adonis, Attis, and Isis flourished there, together with a host of other religions. The expert and writer Morton Smith emphasizes that the main influences of Galilean religion around the time of Jesus were "native Palestinian, Semitic paganism, Greek, Persian, Phoenician, and Egyptian."[9] Galilee itself was actively referred to at the time as "the land of the Gentiles." If Jesus genuinely wanted to reform Judaism, Galilee would seem to be a strange place to embark on the attempt. In Galilee he was surrounded by people who were freethinking pagans.

The plain fact is that there is no absolute proof that Jesus himself was a Jew. This statement might seem odd, in the light of prevailing and accepted norms. Certainly, Jesus is portrayed in the Gospels as having heated discussions on matters of Jewish law with the eminent Pharisees of his day. However convincing these stories may appear, this is unlikely to have been the case. Pharisees did not rise to prominence until a later period, around 50 years after the supposed crucifixion of Jesus. In other words the stories of Jesus discussing Jewish law could be, and most probably are, a series of later insertions. Nevertheless, if it is to be accepted that Jesus was truly born of the house of David, his Judaism at some level is not really in doubt despite his heretical tendencies.

Even if Jesus considered himself to be a follower of Judaism, it has to be remembered that this faith by the first century AD was quite different to that of Solomon and David's time. It is quite possible that the beliefs of Jesus were more fully in step with older and less radical Jewish ideas. The Babylonian experiences of the Jews may have forced them down more pragmatic paths but this does not imply that all sections of the community were willing to accept the orthodox view of Judaism. Jesus was certainly such a person, for it was his fervent belief that the "spirit" of Jewish law was more important than its strict interpretation in a moment by moment sense.

Upsetting though it might be to some believers, it is quite valid, bearing in mind the available evidence, to paint a picture of Jesus and his ministry that is very much at odds with orthodoxy. This "alternative" view is extremely persuasive and is best approached via the Gnostic Gospels and the very different account they give of events we all thought we understood very well. No person has a greater part to play in the events described in the alternative Gospels than Mary Magdalene.

CHAPTER 5

Mary Magdalene and the True Story of Jesus

The word "Gnosis," as associated with the Gnostic Gospels, is Greek and means "knowledge." Broadly speaking, Gnostic Christians believed that the God of the Old Testament was inherently evil, as was the material world. They accepted that "true" spirituality was revealed by Jesus. Gnostics considered that the most important task for any mortal was to "free" the soul from the body by way of a hidden wisdom or truth, thus achieving salvation. Early Christian Gnosticism has been said to have much in common with both Taoism and Buddhism.

It should be remembered that in the decades after the death of Jesus, different groups of his followers took a number of alternative paths, drawing on specific elements of his ministry. The Gnostics were one such group and, for a considerable period, there were many of them. Why they did not survive to have a bearing on the orthodox Church as it appears today we shall see in due course but it is to this group of "alternative" Christians that we owe the cache of documents that were found buried in Nag Hammadi, Egypt in 1945.

These include a number of different Gospels, or parts of Gospels, which sometimes complement fragments that have come down to us from other sources. It is generally thought that the Nag Hammadi documents were written down in the fourth century AD, but from material already documented as early as the second century AD. This assumption is based upon the great similarity between the Nag Hammadi documents and parts of the same documents of a known age from elsewhere.

A striking fact about several of the Gnostic Gospels is that they show Mary Magdalene in a very different light to the way she is portrayed in the orthodox Gospels. Indeed, in the case of the Gnostic examples she has a complete Gospel named for her.

In this work, we find Mary at least on a par with Jesus' male disciples, and in many ways more important. It is clear from the Gnostic Gospels that Peter, Jesus' leading male disciple, had no love or respect for Mary. Nevertheless, it is also made obvious from the text that the disciples generally accepted that Mary Magdalene did hold a special place in Jesus' affections. Even Peter has to admit the fact. In the Gospel of Mary he says:

> Sister, we know that the Savior loved you more than other women. Tell us the words of the Savior which you have in mind since you know them; and we do not, nor have we heard of them.

Mary tells the disciples what Jesus has said to her directly, but Peter complains bitterly, suggesting that the Master would never impart more to Mary than to his male followers. One of the other disciples, Levi, says to Peter:

> But if the Savior made her worthy, who are you to reject her? Surely the Savior knew her very well. For this reason he loved her more than us.

There is the direct implication here of a special relationship between Jesus and Mary. The non-canonical Gospel of Philip specifically refers to Mary Magdalene as "The disciple Jesus kissed on the mouth." What is more, the same Gospel calls Mary Magdalene Jesus' "koinonos," which can be literally translated as "sexual partner."[10]

In *The Templar Revelation*, by Lynn Picknett and Clive Prince,[1] the authors also make a strong suggestion that the relationship between Jesus and Mary Magdalene was of an intimate nature. They cite a number of reasons for believing this to be the case.

As I will demonstrate, the path that the Christian Church took in the centuries after the death of Jesus, put paid to any suggestion of female participation in the ministry of the Church. Nevertheless, the authorities that took a red pen to those New Testament Gospels destined to become established Christian doctrine did a less than competent job in eradicating Mary's influence. What is more, they left important clues as to the path that Jesus' teaching took or what it was meant to imply.

It is specifically towards the end of Jesus' earthly life that we find strong hints as to his innermost religious leanings. On the evening before the crucifixion, Jesus met with his disciples for a last meal. This gathering is described in detail in the established Gospels, Jesus leaves no doubt as to his understanding of what lies before him. One extract, generally ignored by other writers on this subject is particularly revealing. In the Gospel of Mark 14:22 we find:

> While they were eating, Jesus took bread, gave thanks and broke it, and gave it to his disciples, saying, "Take it; this is my body."

Immediately after this, in Mark 14:23 and 24 we read:

> And he took a cup, and when he had given thanks he gave it to them, and they all drank of it. And he said to them, "This is my blood of the covenant, which is poured out for many."

Jesus could not possibly have failed to recognize the rich symbolic thread in the words that he had obviously chosen very carefully at such a pivotal moment in his ministry. This analogy, to bread and wine, makes it plain that he is equating himself with the dying corn gods that were absolutely prevalent in the belief patterns of so many people in his native Galilee.

Like Osiris or Dionysus, Jesus will rise again. Even by the period in which Jesus lived, this was a story as old as humanity itself. With absolutely no insult intended to Christian believers I would suggest that it is impossible to ignore the fact that Jesus, at this moment, was specifically allying himself with belief patterns that were deeply etched into the psyche of his Semitic, Galilean disciples.

Events after the crucifixion once again demonstrate quite clearly that there is an intended link between the story of Jesus and that of Isis and Osiris. At what stage this entered the Gospels, and why, must remain something of a mystery. But one example is so point specific that it could not possibly be ignored, even by the most fervent theologian.

The Gospels tell us that on the third day after the crucifixion, Mary the Virgin and Mary Magdalene went to the place where the body of Jesus had been laid. The stone at the entrance to the tomb had been rolled away. In the account offered by St. John's Gospel, Mary, seeing a man she takes to be a gardener, says to him:

> "They have taken my Lord and I know not where they have lain him."

Though she does not realize at the time Mary is actually

speaking to the risen Jesus.

Lynn Picknett and Clive Prince demonstrated in their book, *The Templar Revelation*, that these words from Mary Magdalene are virtually identical with those spoken by a priestess during the rites of "Isis," which were celebrated each year in Egypt but which would have also been well known in Galilee.

In her guise as Isis the priestess would say:

> "Evil men have killed my beloved, and where his body
> is I know not."

It is highly likely that Jesus and Mary Magdalene were deliberately playing out the role of Osiris and Isis. Even the form of Jesus' death becomes significant in this context, since the "cross" had been a revered symbol of Osiris for many centuries before New Testament times.

Mary Magdalene's part in the ministry and life of Jesus has quite clearly been sidelined by the established Gospels of the New Testament. As a result, it is difficult to learn anything specific about her true biography. Even the Gnostic Gospels offer little tangible evidence. However, there are certain facts that can be gleaned.

Christian orthodoxy definitely does suggest that Mary had been a common prostitute, though this is tradition, since the written evidence does not bear out such an assumption. What can be ascertained is that if Mary Magdalene was a prostitute, she was a rich and influential one. One particular story that has survived in the orthodox Gospels makes this clear. This is the story of a female disciple by the name of Mary, universally identified as Mary Magdalene, who washes the feet of Jesus, using precious ointment.

The Gospel of St. John, Chapter 12:3 says:

> Mary took a pound of costly ointment of pure nard
> and anointed the feet of Jesus and wiped his feet with
> her hair; and the house was filled with the fragrance
> of the ointment.

Mary is berated for this act by one of the male disciples, who suggests that the cost of the ointment had been three hundred denarii, a considerable sum of money and an amount that, at this period, could probably have fed a family for a year. Clearly, Mary was a woman of substance and no mere hooker.

There is also a very strong tradition that Mary Magdalene knew the wife of Pontius Pilate, the Roman Governor of Judea who washed his hands of Jesus' life prior to the crucifixion. It is highly unlikely that the wife of so important a man as Pilate would have any sort of contact with a Galiliean prostitute.

For reasons that have never been fully explained or understood, Mary Magdalene positively rocketed to fame during the medieval period but there are strong indications that the Gospel chroniclers knew only too well how important she was to the events during and shortly after the life of Jesus. In order to discover how this might be the case it would be useful to take a short look at a subject that might appear odd to modern readers but which was once extremely important. The subject is "Gematria."

Gematria is a system by which hidden truths and meanings within words can be stored in a document and then subsequently retrieved by a sufficiently knowledgeable individual. It works on the principle that every letter (or sometimes phonetic sound) has an equivalent number value. To the modern ear this sounds like superstitious nonsense but in a historical sense there is nothing fanciful about gematria. We know that the principle goes back at least to the eighth century BC, when the Babylonian King, Sargon II, built a wall around a place called Khorsabad. The wall was designed to be exactly 16,238 cubits long, because this represented the numerical value of his name.

In Jewish mysticism gematria goes back so far it is impossible to ascertain when it began. An example of gematria in a very early Christian context lies in the Greek word for "dove." In Greek, dove is "peristera." In gematrian terms, the numerical equivalent of this word is "801" which is the same as the numerical value of the Greek letters alpha and omega, which of course also represent "the beginning and the end."

The Gnostic Christians, whose Gospels surfaced at Nag Hammadi, were great believers in gematria and many modern researchers accept that there are deliberately hidden messages within the words of the Gnostic Gospels that only reveal themselves to the initiated.

Perhaps even more pertinent is the name of Mary Magdalene itself. In its Greek epithet it becomes "h Magdalhnh," which in Pythagorean gematrian terms equals the number 153. This fact has a profound significance. 153 is also the number that indicates a figure well known to mathematicians. This figure, which is almond shaped () is known as the "Vesica Piscis." In the ancient world, the Vesica Piscis was very important. For obvious pictographic reasons it represents the female vulva but its implications are more far reaching than a simple physiological description. The Vesica Piscis is directly associated with feminine regeneration and fertility in a religious as well as a purely practical sense. This is our first contact with "the sacred cauldron of new birth" that eventually came to be associated with the Holy Grail of medieval legend.

Representations of the Vesica Piscis are to be found in examples of cave art going back well before the Neolithic period. It is a symbol that seems to be almost as old as our species.

We can be certain that this particular connection between Mary Magdalene and the Great Goddess is no modern invention. The association between Mary, the number 153, and the Vesica Piscis, was well known to Christians within a very short time of Jesus' life.

In the orthodox Gospels no more is heard of Mary Magdalene after the events immediately relating to the Resurrection of Jesus and none of the later books of the New Testament make any reference to her. This is probably not surprising. The form of Christianity we accept today is directly attributable to the branch of the Christian Church established by St. Paul. Paul was a confirmed misogynist, as many of his writings demonstrate. What is more, the Church Fathers who "codified" Christianity, at the first Council of Nicea in AD 325, were totally opposed to women being associated with the ministry of the Church in any way.

One might assume that these facts would have put paid to the fame of Mary Magdalene once and for all but nothing could be further from the truth. Although there was a significant period during which the Magdalene barely figured in either Church history or tradition, by the early medieval period, she positively exploded in popularity across the Christian world, and particularly in western Europe.

Nobody quite knows where the legend arose, but from a very

early period, Mary Magdalene became associated with southern France. It was suggested that she had traveled there, after the crucifixion, to seek sanctuary. She is said to have arrived at a village in the region of the modern city of Marseilles.

Tradition relates that Mary's ship weighed anchor in a place now called Saintes-Maries-de-la-Mer. This is a short distance from Marseilles and well within the region that is today known as the Camargue. In this place the memory of Mary and her companions is kept alive. The Magdalene herself may well have become confused in popular memory with the characters supposedly with her at the time of her arrival. Even more likely is that they have become split from one single personality to form three Marys. There was Mary Magdalene herself, together with Mary Jacobi and Mary Salome. This sounds very much like a triad of Roman goddesses and was quite a common representation, especially in Romano/Celtic art.

The actual number of persons present on that day depends upon which version of the story is accepted as fact. Some of the tales also have Lazarus and Martha on board the ship. A further version sees Joseph of Arimathea dropping the Marys off in France, before traveling on to Britain himself.

The tale of what happened to the Magdalene after her arrival in France is also dependent on the story in question. There is plenty in Saintes-Maries-de-la-Mer to associate her with the town and more than one church there remembers her presence. There is also a black statue to be found in Saintes-Maries-de-la-Mer, similar to the Black Madonnas of other locations. In this instance, the statue is referred to as St. Sara the Egyptian. Sara is said to have been a servant to the Marys at the time of their arrival. The statue is deeply revered by people of gypsy blood who come from all over Europe to celebrations held in Sara's honor. Sara is known as "Star of the Sea," which is the title also associated with the name Mary itself and is an epithet specifically referred to by St. Bernard of Clairvaux, a character who will prove pivotal to our story. Every year the gypsies carry the black statue of Sara down to the ocean and dip it reverently into the water.

In all probability, Sara represents another distorted version of the Mary Magdalene story, or something even earlier. There was a temple to the goddess Diana in the town, on the steps of which Mary Magdalene is supposed to have preached. It is likely that Goddess worship, in one form or another, never did relinquish its hold on the rural Camargue. The multiple faces of the Magdalene in this place are no real surprise in this context.

East of Marseilles we find the settlement of Sainte-Baume. Here there is a cave that tradition says Mary occupied for years as a hermit. This story is almost certainly untrue. However, before Christianity came to these parts Sainte-Baume, like much of the region, was a known place of Goddess worship. Aspects of Goddess adoration certainly took place in and around this large cavern. Not so far away is Saint-Maximin-la-Sainte-Baum, where the Magdalene is supposed to have died. Festivals are held in her honor in the village at regular intervals. At such times her supposed skull, in a golden reliquary, is carried in procession around the streets.

As far as I can ascertain, nobody has ever carbon-dated the skull in question, to determine its true age. The trade in saintly relics was so ferocious and so unscrupulous in the medieval period that the chances of this actually being Mary Magdalene's skull are probably quite remote. The possession of Mary's bones would have been worth a fortune to the ecclesiastical authorities of the town. They would have been mad not to capitalize even more than they did on the stories of her presence there.

Nobody knows for sure where the Magdalene lies, and a search for her true resting-place has probably worn out more shoe leather than all the pilgrims to the region have ever managed to do.

Whether the French folk tales regarding the Magdalene are true or not, she is positively revered in the region, where many churches are dedicated to her. Her supposed presence in the region also caused a sensation in literature in 1982 when it became a central theme of the best selling book *The Holy Blood and the Holy Grail*, by Michael Baigent, Richard Leigh, and Henry Lincoln.[12] These authors claimed that at the time of her arrival in France, Mary Magdalene was carrying the child of Jesus. The child was a son and Baigent, Leigh, and Lincoln claim that he grew to manhood, marrying into a royal bloodline within the Frankish kings of the region.

The story of the Holy Blood and the Holy Grail is one of intrigue and conspiracy, featuring a particularly shadowy society calling itself the Priory de Sion. This society, the authors claimed, is still at large in France and beyond. The Priory de Sion is extremely powerful and has often pulled the strings of society on the way to its ultimate goal, which is to restore the rightful bloodline of Jesus to the now non-existent royal throne of France.

Anyone reading *The Holy Blood and the Holy Grail* in the more skeptical days of the early twenty-first century might be forgiven for finding it to be intriguing nonsense. After all, a great deal of effort, by way of several further books and more than one documentary television series, has been put into debunking the book's central themes. These investigations have shown some of the most recent representatives of the Priory de Sion to be nothing more than petty criminals and con men. Like most people of my age, I had read the book when it first appeared. I found it gripping and mysterious but its themes did not particularly stick in my mind. Only with my own much later researches did some of the things Baigent, Leigh, and Lincoln had to say come back to haunt me. As I hope to demonstrate, this seminal work continues to stimulate and to intrigue – even if it is for reasons that the authors themselves could never have guessed at.

I am forced to believe that there is at least a strong possibility that Mary Magdalene did travel to France and that the bloodline of Jesus was present in the early days of the Frankish royal family. There are questions arising from my own, independent, research that cannot be answered in any other way. However, the most important aspects of reverence for Mary Magdalene, and also the Virgin Mary, was not known to the authors of *The Holy Blood and the Holy Grail*. The core of their book rests on the assumption that the "great heresy" within the developing Church of western Europe lay in the fact that Jesus was the father of at least one child. In reality, the true great heresy is associated with a continuing group of people who have taken a very different view of religion altogether. To these individuals the life and ministry of Jesus represents only a "sub-plot" in a much more expansive and far older story.

At the time of my rediscovery of the salt line system of western Europe, thanks to Xaviar Guichard, I knew little about such matters. In the years that followed, I spent every spare moment at my disposal, traveling up and down the theoretical positions of the salt lines, where I knew they must fall within my own country. Britain is small but populous and an exploration of all the fascinating places that lie on the salt lines is far from over.

However, one of my earliest realizations regarding the salt lines, apart from a recognition of the number of Megalithic monuments they bisected, was how many churches, some truly ancient but others of post-Norman construction, lay fairly and squarely on the lines.

The distance between the salt lines of longitude varies as they run north towards the poles but generally speaking, across Britain, they are a good 20 miles apart. Meanwhile the distance between salt lines of latitude is a universal 60 miles or so. The chances of any significant site falling upon any of these lines, or within 1 minute of arc of them, is therefore not great. It was obvious to me from the beginning of my research that there are far more churches on the salt lines than should be there by chance. A further mystery lay in the fact that by far the most common church dedications on the salt lines were those to St. Mary the Virgin and St. Mary Magdalene.

Had someone in the early days of Christianity in Britain been aware of the existence of the salt lines and deliberately placed their churches upon them, using the feminine dedications of the Virgin and the Magdalene? Might it be the case that sites already significant for maybe thousands of years were simply replaced by these churches? It became obvious that to answer these questions, I would need to make myself something of an expert in the development of Christianity and that meant going back to the period just after the death of Jesus, to Jerusalem and to Rome.

CHAPTER 6

A Deliberate Perversion

One of the greatest miracles of Christianity is represented by its own survival. Put in context, Christianity was a fringe belief, thrust into a maelstrom of differing pagan religions, and at a pivotal and dangerous time in the history of the region where it appeared. It gained its initial momentum very slowly, and from two different directions.

Although Christianity quite quickly found its way to Rome, the center of the known world at the time, it also flourished in its own heartland, in and around Jerusalem. The Jerusalem Church, at first headed by a man called "James the Just" had several factions within its own ranks, some of which believed that it was not possible to be a follower of Christ and also a Gentile, in other words not born of the Jewish faith. However, there were ambiguities in the known teachings of Jesus that could be translated as an acceptance on his part that a Jewish background was not necessary in order to follow Christian doctrine, so Gentiles were accepted.

Despite the power and the undoubted legitimacy of the Jerusalem Church, modern Christianity primarily owes its existence to one man. Saul or Paul of Tarsus, later St. Paul, was born in Cilicia, only a few years after the death of Jesus. Paul was of Jewish blood but also had Roman citizenship, most probably because of good family connections.

Paul was a Rabbi and a Pharisee, whose training brought him to believe that the emerging Christians were a threat to Judaism. As a result, he became an avid persecutor of Christianity. Then, as legend has it, whilst on the road to Damascus, he received a vision of Jesus, an experience that turned his life around. Henceforth, he began to preach the words of Jesus, though often in a way that incensed the Fathers of the Jerusalem Church.

Ultimately, and after extensive journeys to embryonic Christian communities across a wide expanse, Paul was taken as a prisoner to Rome. There he was executed, sometime after AD 60. Christians in and around Rome were already under suspicion as far as the Roman authorities were concerned, and for a number of different reasons.

Although the Roman authorities were famously tolerant as to the religious beliefs of their client peoples and states, what they found difficult to swallow in this case was the Christian habit of accepting the validity of their own God and no other. This was particularly irksome during the reign of the Claudian Emperors, most of whom were worshiped as gods during their own lives. Christians suffered greatly under the last of the Claudians, the Emperor Nero (AD 54–68), but also heavily under a whole host of later Emperors. However, no matter how severe the persecution, the new faith gained significant ground, both in Rome and elsewhere.

The Jerusalem Church fared less well. In AD 66 there was a great Jewish uprising against Roman rule in Judea, which was dealt with by unparalleled brutality on the part of Rome. Jews had always been suspected by Rome of being disloyal to the Empire and, like the Christians, they refused to accept the divinity of Roman Emperors or their pagan deities. Jerusalem was effectively destroyed by the Roman legions and embryonic Christian communities there would have fared no better than Jewish ones. In fact, since they were also being vigorously persecuted in Rome, the Christians of Jerusalem may well have been singled out for special treatment.

From the very earliest days of the faith, Christianity suffered from numerous "schisms." Not every group saw Jesus' message in the same light. We have already seen how differently the Gnostic Christians interpreted the life and teaching of Jesus, though they were far from being the only schismatic group in existence. St. Paul spent considerable time and effort trying to make wayward Christian communities toe a party line that had not really been established in the first years after the death of Jesus.

It is therefore at least partly a matter of luck that Christianity of the St. Paul variety flourished and grew across the three centuries following Jesus' life. Of course, Christians of any persuasion were not being universally slaughtered across these three hundred years. Some Emperors were more tolerant than others, whilst at the same time large communities of Christians lived either beyond the direct sway or immediate notice of the ruling Roman authorities.

In the end, it was not Christianity that managed to change the heart or religious beliefs of Rome, but rather the needs of an Empire that saw a way forward by using and manipulating this thriving new faith. The truth is that by around AD 300 Rome was in deep trouble. She was being attacked on many of her borders and subjected to numerous revolts and civil wars within her territory. One particularly smart Emperor, Constantine, reasoned that a common religious faith within the Roman Empire might represent the very glue that would hold it together.

Constantine was born in the late 280s, the son of Flavius Valarius Constantius, a man who would also come to be Emperor of Rome. Constantine was proclaimed Emperor at the death of his father in York, England in AD 306 and although a struggle for supremacy followed, Constantine proved equal to the task. As to his Christianity, there are many stories, but few of them are likely to be much more than fables. Constantine had been a devotee and friend of the earlier Emperor Diocletian (AD 284–305), who was an avid anti-Christian and who had instigated a terrible slaughter of Christians beginning in the year AD 303. If Constantine had been a Christian at that time, or had even been particularly tolerant of the faith, it is unlikely he would have stayed high in Diocletian's estimation for very long.

Constantine had to fight a frightening series of civil wars in order to prove himself as Emperor, and by this time he was already showing an apparent acceptance of the God of Christianity. Prior to this, he is known to have been a fervent worshiper of a deity called "Sol Invictus." Constantine's apparent conversion to Christianity, as the *Encyclopaedia Britannica* puts it was "closely associated with his rise to power," and may have been entirely fuelled by the needs of his office and what he saw as being the good of Rome.

Soon after consolidating his position as Emperor, Constantine ordered any persecution of Christians to stop and even returned a considerable amount of confiscated property to those of the Christian persuasion.

By the year 313 the Emperor was showing how important he considered a "single faith" for the Empire to be. He wrote letters at this time indicating that there must be only "one" Christian Church and showing his intolerance for schisms of any kind. Once again, it would be fair to suggest that his thinking was motivated as much by the needs of politics as the requirements of faith.

In the summer of AD 325, Constantine convened the first Council of Nicea (present Iznik, Turkey). The purpose of this Council was to establish once and for all that Christianity was to be the major faith of Empire and to make certain that everyone knew what sort of Christianity this was going to be. Problems had arisen with a heretical Christian sect knows as "Arians." Arians believed that Jesus was not divine, and was therefore a "creation" of the one, supreme God. Roman Christians stuck to the doctrine that Jesus was "as one" with the Godhead, and indistinguishable from it. Ultimately, the Council of Nicea decided against the Arian view, which henceforth became a heresy. It wasn't long before Christians were being persecuted again, but this time by other Christians.

The Council of Nicea paved the way to the established Roman Church. This Council and its successors decided what Christians "had" to believe, and in which Gospels these "truths" were to be found. In addition, Constantine's Church officials were not beyond tampering with existing Gospels if they didn't quite match up to the Emperor's expectations.

Gnosticism, as all other schisms, were outlawed, which is why the Nag Hammadi Gospels came to be hidden in the first place, laying untouched until 1947. All Gnostic books and Gospels that could be seized were destroyed, together with those of other heretical Christian sects.

Any surviving aspects of feminine influence or importance within Christianity that may still have existed before Nicea ceased and one very important definition made during the reign of Constantine ensured that Christianity became a "male only" preserve. The Emperor Constantine was not very good at Greek, but he would have known enough to understand the meaning of the Greek word "Sophia." It was the word the Christian Greeks used to denote what we now refer to as the "Holy Spirit." St. Paul and his followers had ensured that by the fourth century, this word, and what it implied, was probably the only tangible remaining link with the Osiris/Isis nature of the teachings and ministry of Jesus and the way his immediate followers had understood it.

It is not by chance that the name "Sophia" is now universally given to girls. Even two thousand years ago Sophia was a word replete with feminine overtones. Those who attached this name to the third part of the Christian Trinity had done so in full knowledge of the feminine overtones of the word. Literally, Sophia means "wisdom." That the Ancient Greeks should have equated wisdom with females in any shape or form is strange in itself, since the Greeks were not kind to women, who had little or no part to play in the way society was run.

Many pre-Nicea Christians had depicted Sophia as a dove, a practice that remains in the case of the Holy Spirit. When Jesus had been baptized in the waters of the River Jordan, by John the Baptist, New Testament accounts indicate the Holy Spirit entering the Messiah in the form of a dove (Matthew 3:16):

> And when Jesus was baptized, he went up immediately
> from the water, and behold, the heavens were opened
> and he saw the Spirit of God descending like a dove,
> and alighting on him;

As Latin overtook Greek as the language of Christianity, so the Holy Spirit, described as Sophia, began to disappear, to be replaced by a more nebulous and still little understood concept, the Holy Spirit, that even modern theologians struggle to explain.

The Empire was large, so Constantine's persecution of heretical sects did little to prevent their survival and many centuries after the Council of Nicea the established Church was still fighting a constant and bloody war to retain its hold over a sometimes unwilling population. Various new forms of Gnosticism emerged, some probably related to the original Christian Gnosticism. The chief amongst these was Manichaeism, often considered to be a heretical Christian sect but probably rightfully representing a religion in its own right. Late proponents of Christian Gnosticism were the Bogomils and the Cathar.

A quite early expression of Christianity and one that will play an important part in later stages of our story, was monasticism. It has been suggested that the monastic ideal of asceticism, celibacy, and solitude were strictly Christian inventions. In fact, even Judaism had monasticism of a sort. It has long been suggested that Jesus, and most certainly John the Baptist, were influenced greatly by a Judaic sect known as the Essene.

As far as is known the Essene sect began around the fourth century BC, in Palestine. Followers of the sect, mostly but probably not exclusively men, were strict adherents of the law of Moses and in some ways were better Jews than their city dwelling counterparts. However, there were significant differences, though these were not fully understood until comparatively recently.

The Essene lived in isolated communities, mostly strung up and down the Jordan Valley. Undoubtedly, the most famous of these was Qumran, where a series of chance discoveries in 1947 altered history's perspectives on the previously little understood Essene.

In the years leading up to the great Jewish Revolt of AD 66 the Essene brotherhood, guessing what was to come, had secreted copies of their holiest books in a series of caves, close to Qumran. When these were discovered, from 1947 on, they threw new light on a sect that had so much in common with what Christianity itself would throw up, over a thousand years later. The documents found at Qumran are collectively known as "The Dead Sea Scrolls."

The Essene believed in ritual bathing, they always wore white and survived not as a result of alms received from others but through their own unremitting hard labor. Unlike the Jews as a whole they lived by a solar rather than a lunar calendar and, in a practical as well as a spiritual sense, they looked towards the creation of a "New Jerusalem." To this end Essene teachers had written specific books, detailing every aspect of the creation of the New Jerusalem and the coming war that would be fought against the Devil and his host. It has often been claimed that by "the Devil and his host," the Essene were specifically thinking of the Romans, who ruled their region at this time, though it is clear from documents such as "The War Scrolls" and "The Jubilee Scrolls" that this was not exclusively the case. It has been thought that the Essene and all they believed were destroyed by the Romans in the years after AD 66. Early Christian monasticism may or may not have owed much to the Essene, though it will become clear later that their lives and ideals were far from forgotten.

Evidence I collected that related to a period a good thousand years after the death of Jesus and the disappearance of the Essene gradually led me to realize that not all the schismatic Christians specifically condemned by the Council of Nicea had been eradicated at that time. I knew of course that Arian tendencies and their counterparts had remained to plague the developing Church but the group of people I found lurking below the margins in the pages of history were of a very different sort. They would emerge around the tenth century in France and through a series of brilliant actions and maneuvers would come very close to changing for good the beliefs of an established Church of which they were clearly not a part. Their actions would lead to democracy, industrialization, and to the world we know today. However, for the sake of a clear chronology it was necessary to demonstrate just how the Christian Church in the period between the fourth and the tenth centuries had singularly failed to eradicate one vitally important aspect of religion that was as old as humanity. Try as they may, the Church Fathers could not kill the Goddess.

CHAPTER 7

The Rise of the Virgin and the Origin of the Nativity

The Roman Empire was extremely large and was populated by literally hundreds of races and ethnic groups, all with their own particular backgrounds and beliefs. It might have been Constantine's dream to turn all of these people into obedient Christians overnight, but it was never going to happen.

Somewhat later than Constantine's time, edicts were being made by Church leaders regarding the best methods of coercing reluctant peoples falling under the sway of the Empire to accept Christianity. Specific instructions were given, particularly by the great Church leader St. Augustine. Missionaries were told to build churches on the sites of existing places of worship, right across the Empire, so that the local populace would eventually adopt the new faith as a matter of course. There are significant examples of this deliberate policy in Britain. Not far from my home, in a village called Rudstone, the local parish church shares its site with what may be the largest standing stone in Britain. This stone was hacked from the living rock and dragged maybe 20 miles to its present spot, probably five thousand years ago. So impressive is the standing stone at Rudstone, it is quite clear that it represented a place of great religious significance to our ancient ancestors.

The church is a baby in comparison, only dating back to about AD 1000 but it exists as a potent example of a policy that was deliberately followed by the Church for many centuries. Rudstone and hundreds of other pagan sites that now sport churches demonstrate just how successful the strategy was, though the Church also learned to "bend with the wind" in other ways, and in ways that left the Great Goddess virtually intact in the comprehension of people all over the Roman Empire.

From time out of mind, the Roman Empire had taken a specific attitude towards the gods and goddesses of its client peoples. The Romans themselves had many deities and it wasn't hard to equate a local god or goddess in another country with a member of the Roman pantheon. An example of this was the city in England now called Bath. Here the Romans found natural hot springs, already dedicated to a goddess who was called "Sulis" by the locals. The Romans built great bathhouses on the site, but they did not attempt to eradicate the memory of Sulis from the minds of the locals. To the Romans, Bath was known as "Aqua Sulis." They equated Sulis with their own goddess, Minerva, and everyone lived happily with an easy compromise.

The developing Church, though Judaic in origin, was Roman in concept and so the methods used to bring people to the new faith were not so different than those used in the pre-Christian era. However, Roman Christianity was basically patriarchal in nature and so the concept of a goddess was anathema. This fact might have proved difficult except for two strategies on the part of the Church Fathers that they presumably hoped would ease the transition between paganism and Christianity.

Firstly, the Church could always rely on the presence of the Virgin Mary. Extremely early in Christian doctrine Mary began to adopt a unique position. She was referred to as "The Mother of God" and also as "Queen of Heaven." This created a slightly uneasy situation that, in some ways, has continued until the modern era. Arianism had no real problem with Mary, since it proposed that Jesus was as much a "creation" of God as any other human being. However, the Council of Nicea had declared that Jesus literally "was" God, which made Mary's position somewhat ambiguous.

If Jesus was God, and Mary was the mother of Jesus, then clearly she was also the Mother of God. Since the deity himself was also God, it followed that the Virgin Mary must be, at some level, the wife of God. This last is a title she has never been granted and the established Church has always fought shy of taking the logical step of elevating Mary to the rank of divinity. Nevertheless, there are sects within the Catholic Church even today that seek this honor for what amounts to the "Goddess of Christianity."

With the rise of Christianity, disgruntled locals, when faced with Christian missionaries who it seemed were intent on making them relinquish belief in a goddess who had been dear to them since time out of mind, would be offered the solace of the Virgin Mary. It is still Catholic policy for believers to pray to Mary to seek her intercession with God. Even this may not be an entirely Christian concept. The old Sky God was a fearful character: dark, brooding, and malevolent. This aspect of the nature of God can be seen time and again in the pages of the Old Testament of the Bible. The Goddess, on the other hand, was ever-present, comfortable, and even domestic. People may not have been able to appeal to the great, thundering Sky God personally, but they might prevail on the Goddess to do so on their behalf.

The second weapon in the armory of missionary Christianity was the canon of saints available to it. It is not supposition but hard fact that a distinct number of still existent Catholic saints began their careers as deities in their own right. I have already mentioned St. Bridget, who was originally Brig or Brigga, one of the most important goddesses of the Celts. She is far from being alone and there was a time when virtually all communities could still pray to their own local deities, now transformed into Christian saints.

The cult of the Virgin Mary started very early in the Christian story. She was especially revered in Ephesus, formerly a city dedicated to the goddess Artemis, yet another manifestation of the original Great Goddess. The Temple of Artemis in Ephesus was one of the seven wonders of the ancient world. Some Christian legends assert that the Virgin Mary traveled to Ephesus, after the crucifixion and that she remained there for the rest of her life. Tradition has it that the "Hail Mary," one of the oldest and most popular prayers known to Christianity, was first spoken in Ephesus, in the year 431. The Ephesus Church declared the Virgin Mary to be "The God Bearer" at this very early period. An edict confirming this title was published to counteract a heretical group of local Christians who referred to Mary as merely "The Mother of Christ." Since this seemed to infer that Jesus was separate from God, it was necessary to elevate Mary. Although the Roman Church took some time to latch onto this reasoning, it gradually accepted the position of Ephesus.

Some local deities readily lent themselves to being converted into the Virgin Mary. One such example was "Rosemerth," a goddess of the Franks, whose worship in parts of northern France and in particular in Lorraine, extended well into the Christian era. In addition, the worship of the Greek goddess Demeter and the Egyptian deity, Isis, continued in many places, alongside Christianity. So popular were these two goddesses that the developing Church had to find a suitable response. Early Christianity was also up against another belief pattern that had been gaining ground within the Roman Empire for centuries. It was extremely popular with soldiers and their families and was known as "Mithraism."

Mithraism, literally the worship of the god Mithra, was Persian and of very ancient origin. However, its Roman form appeared around the same time as Christianity began to gain ground and long after worship of Mithra had ceased in Persia. There was a strong Gnostic element to the belief, probably because it had been much influenced by Platonic philosophy. Adherents of the faith in its Roman form believed that the "soul" had come to inhabit human flesh by a series of unfortunate events. Like the Gnostics, they accepted that only through a realization of the illusionary nature of matter could the soul ever escape from its human captivity.

What sets Mithraism apart from other Roman pagan beliefs is its rapid rise to popularity and the way it was directly associated with reverence for the Emperor. It quickly became a favored belief pattern of soldiers, slaves, and freedmen, together with people who specifically wanted to rise quickly to positions of authority within the State. This was especially the case during the reign of the Roman Emperors Comodius (AD 180–192), Septimus Severus (AD 193–211) and Caracalla (AD 211–217). However, Mithra was still extremely popular by the reign of Diocletian (AD 284–305), the Emperor who reigned immediately before the civil unrest that led to the reign of Constantine. The Emperor Constantine himself is said to have originally worshiped "Sol Invicta," which was merely another name for Mithra.

Mithraism fell from popularity as a state sponsored religion at almost exactly the same time that Constantine turned towards Christianity, probably for a host of reasons that are not difficult to ascertain or understand.

The parallels between the Roman deity Mithras and the story of Jesus as it has come down to us today are so great, that few experts would deny a direct connection. This is particularly true in terms of the earliest part of Jesus' story, as related by the

Gospels of St. Matthew and St. Luke. These Gospels are thought by a significant number of modern experts to have been written later than either that of St. Mark or St. John, both of which commence their stories when Jesus is already an adult. The actual order in which the canonical Gospels were written is fairly immaterial, though it is plain that the two relating the story of the Nativity drew heavily on religious and mythical sources outside of Jesus' life and teaching. When one sees what the followers of Mithras believed about him, it is easy to understand why.

Early Persian stories about Mithra, predating Christianity by many centuries, say that Mithra was born in a cave, the son of the Sun and of a virgin mother, who is referred to in the Persian texts as "The Mother of God." Mithra was considered by his followers to be the savior of humankind and, in the stories, he refers to himself as "the light of the world." If this all sounds familiar, we should also bear in mind that Mithra was born on 25 December, whereas the Jesus of the Nativity cannot have been born at this time of year, for several obvious reasons.

(The New Testament relates that Jesus was born whilst Joseph and Mary were traveling to take part in a census. Such procedures did not take place in the winter. In addition, the story of the Nativity says quite specifically that there were shepherds in the fields tending their flocks. The region is extremely cold in winter and shepherds would not be out in the open with their sheep at this time of year.)

Followers of Mithra, despite its somewhat Gnostic overtones, believed in a celestial heaven and in hell. They accepted that, after death, they could achieve life everlasting, at the will of God, though this would not come before "Judgment Day" at which time the faithful would be resurrected and taken into heaven.

If all of this fails to convince, those worshiping Mithra believed he was put to death on a cross and buried in a cave. Subsequently, he rose from the dead and took part in a meal with twelve disciples, the number "twelve" in this case relating to the twelve signs of the zodiac.

Since the tales regarding Mithra predate Christianity by such a long period of time, only one of two reasons for the commonality of the stories are possible, with a third that is so ridiculous as to not warrant serious consideration:

> Early Christians borrowed heavily from an extremely powerful religious sect that was "officially" extinguished during the reign of the Emperor Constantine.
> The events of Jesus' life actually did parallel those of the Mithra story cycles, either by chance or by deliberate intention.
> The ridiculous third explanation is one dreamed up by Christians at some unknown date. They suggested that the parallels between the life of Mithra and that of Jesus were created by the Devil and placed back in history at a time before the birth of Jesus, in order to deceive and confuse Christians.

In my comprehension, only the first possibility is rational or likely. It is also quite understandable for a number of reasons.

Constantine made a deliberate decision to adopt Christianity as the official religion of the Roman Empire. Having done, so it would have been difficult to leave the worship of Mithra in place, particularly in the higher echelons of either the civil administration or the army. Despite what Church history says to the contrary, there are strong reasons for believing that Constantine continued to worship Mithra, as Sol Invictus, until very close to the end of his life.

But Constantine was nobody's fool. He knew that if to become a Christian (and therefore to retain one's favor with the Emperor) merely meant changing the name of one's deity, it would be a sensible course of action to take.

In Roman terms, it was a close-run thing between Mithraism and Christianity as to which belief pattern would become the required model for the Empire. Constantine made it possible for believers of both faiths to get something from the compromise.

However, there was another gain, and one that would come near to satisfying believers of other persuasions. Mithra could be seen as a form of the "sacrificed corn god" of the pagan religions. His mother, the Virgin, granted the title of "Mother of God," was clearly a form of the Great Goddess, who bore striking similarities to Isis, the worship of whom was still extremely popular by the reign of Constantine. It should be remembered that in the Isis stories, she inseminated herself with a phallus made from beeswax, and as a result gave birth to her son Horus. This was, therefore, a virgin birth.

Constantine, in his constant interference with Christianity around the time of the Council of Nicea, found a way forward for the Empire that all but the most die-hard zealots of other religions would find acceptable. The new Christian faith was not especially demanding. Mass was celebrated in the vernacular – the Latin mass did not appear until much later, around the time of Charlemagne. As we have seen, the cult of the Virgin developed very quickly, as a direct response to the Goddess worshipers. When they prayed to the Virgin, they knew they were praying to the same deity their ancestors had revered since time out of mind. By the year 431, less that a hundred years after the death of Constantine, Mary the Virgin had recovered practically all the respect, reverence, and importance that had once been due to the Goddess herself. What is more she was, at least by this time and very probably before, referred to as "The God Bearer."

Despite the best intentions of Constantine, and later Emperors, the writing was on the wall for the Empire. By the second quarter of the fifth century, the legions were being withdrawn from the outlying states and Gaul fell to the Franks during the following decades. Strangely enough, the difficulties experienced by Rome in the southern part of Gaul (present day France) led them to call upon the assistance of a race of people who carried the old Megalithic blood. These people, from the Baltic, had been Goddess worshipers since time immemorial and they would have a tremendous part to play in its survival, right up to the present day.

CHAPTER 8

Through Changing Times

Two groups of people feature predominantly in our story between the end of Roman rule in what is now France, up to the eleventh century. Both are intriguing in their own way and they came to be so intermixed that it is difficult, by around the ninth century, to differentiate between them. These people were the Merovingian Franks and the Burgundians.

Orthodox history relates that the Merovingian Franks were simply part of a wider Frankish group of Germanic peoples who exploited the collapse of Roman rule to extend their sphere of influence. Folklore and tradition has a different tale to tell and it is one that proves particularly fascinating in the light of what followed.

The Merovingians were a branch of the Sicimbrians, a group of people who entered the region we now call France around the third or fourth century. Exactly where they came from originally has always been open to conjecture. They were a strange people, with some fairly unusual customs. Merovee, father of the dynasty, was said to have been fathered partly by a man, and partly by a sort of half-man and half sea-creature hybrid.

Although able enough on the field of battle the Merovingians were essentially farmers. They were very much more civilized than many of the peoples of western Europe during their era and seem to have marched into France more or less unopposed. The Merovingians came to control vast areas but it was in the region of the Ardennes that the Merovingians first carved out a kingdom for themselves. It was based around the modern town of Stenay.

Merovingian society was civilized and quite learned. The culture produced great goldsmiths and amassed significant wealth. Many of the gold objects found by archeologists in the area came from the Merovingian treasury and mint in the latitudinal salt line town now called Sion. This city stands high in the Swiss Alps. Merovingian craftsmanship was superb, and can be viewed today in the British Museum. Much of the treasure found in the Sutton Hoo boat burial of East Anglia, England was Merovingian in origin.

In the manner of their rule Merovingian kings were very much akin to a modern constitutional monarchy. These rulers believed themselves to stand above the day-to-day decisions necessary to rule a nation. Such tasks were passed to a lower class, the representatives of which eventually came to be known as "Mayors of the Palace." The Merovingian monarch represented the soul of his people. The kings often had many wives and like the Old Testament hero Samson, Merovingian kings rarely if ever cut their hair.

The chroniclers of the Merovingians claimed that the Sicimbrians, of which they were part, had originally come from Troy, in what is now Turkey. A fanciful notion perhaps, but the Merovingians also claimed that they were of Arcadian descent. Arcadia is a region of mainland Greece and lies in the west of the Peloponnese. In fact, neither of these claims is necessarily at odds with the wider truth. It is quite conceivable that the Sicimbrians had found their way up the Danube from Greece, mixing with Germanic peoples on the way and had eventually come to the Ardennes.

The stories of Merovee and his peculiar parentage may carry certain associations held in common with Arcadia. There, statues of half-human, half aquatic creatures have been found in significant numbers. Arcadia was also a hotbed of Goddess worship. It was in this region that the adoration of Demeter, the

Greek goddess originally of Minoan origin, reached its zenith. As far as the Troy connection is concerned, it is interesting that the capital of Champagne, annexed by Clovis after 496, still bears the name of Troyes.

One of the most sacred symbols to the Merovingians was the bee. Depictions of this creature cast in gold have been discovered in Merovingian tombs. The bee was also an enduring symbol to the Jews. In addition, the bee was held in great reverence by the people of Minoan Crete. An excellent example of a gold bee was found in the ruins of the palace of Malia and can be seen in the Heraklion museum in Crete. The Minoans were great keepers of bees and exported honey in great quantity when their civilization was at its height.

Surely any connection between the Merovingians of the fifth century AD and the Minoans, whose civilization came to an end in 1500 BC is most unlikely? In fact probably not. The connection is via the Jewish race that stood at the root of the Merovingian family tree.

The Hebrews came to the Promised Land well before the reigns of the great kings, such as Saul, David, and Solomon. The Bible tells us that their leader, Aaron, divided the land amongst the twelve tribes of Israel. Amongst the share enjoyed by the tribe of Benjamin, was that land around the city of Jebus. Jebus would later be known as Jerusalem. Benjamin was probably one of the larger tribes in what was sometimes a very fragile confederacy. There were quite often struggles between the tribes but probably none as serious as the rift that split Benjamin from the greater mass of the Israelite people. This split came some decades before the reign of King Saul, and still very early in Israelite history.

The causes of this rift were probably many and varied. The Bible paraphrases them into a single event. This is itemized in the Book of Judges, chapter 21. The story deals with a Levite, who was traveling with his concubine and a young manservant through Benjamite territory. Contrary to the rules of hospitality already in place amongst the people of Israel, he was accosted one night in a Benjamite township. His concubine was multiply raped and ultimately died from her injuries. The Levite appealed to the twelve tribes at a great council and orders were given for the Benjamites to hand over the culprits. According to the story they refused to do so and a series of battles ensued. These resulted in the Benjamites being seriously depleted in numbers. All the other tribes of Israel made a solemn vow that they would never allow their daughters to marry a Benjamite henceforth.

Undoubtedly there is some great truth underpinning this tale. Such was the ferocity of the fighting against the Benjamites that a percentage of the tribe fled Palestine. Contemporary accounts bear this out. Robert Graves in *The White Goddess*[13] relates that there was an exodus from Palestine to Arcadia. The leader of these exiles was named "Daanus," the son of "King Baal." This name is likely to allude to "Baal," the masculine counterpart of Belial. Both these deities were held sacred to a sub-group of the Benjamites, known as the "Bela." The very name of the sub-tribe betrays their religious preference. Baal was a cure-all name given by the Hebrews to the god worshiped by their neighbors.

It may have been these refugees that supplied the momentum to the Demeter worship in the area of Arcadia. The account suggests that they became blood tied to the rulers of the location. It is far more likely, however, that what the Benjamites had to offer merely supplemented local Arcadian beliefs. It will be recalled that the Merovingians never cut their hair. This is not at all a Greek practice, but it was common amongst certain groups of the Hebrews. This practice may well have been prevalent amongst the Benjamites. It was passed down through the Arcadian connections, also to be practiced by the Sicimbrians.

Certainly the Merovingians believed that this was their ancestry and race memories are often extremely reliable. Developing cycles of the Grail legends had a distinctly "Arcadian" feel to them, as we shall observe. There is also an instinctive tendency of later writers and artists to look to the "Elysian Fields" of Arcadia for their inspiration. This may well be related to genuine memories of a prehistoric episode in the ancestry of western Europeans.

Laurence Gardner claims there was a direct lineal descent from Jesus into the line of the Merovingians.[14] This assertion might be taken as being at best "speculative," were it not for the fact that it is also perhaps the most important central theme in *The Holy Blood and the Holy Grail*, by Baigent, Leigh, and Lincoln.[15] This connection is likely to have come through an intermixing of Merovingian blood with that of the Burgundians, the second group of people important to this part of our story. Whether this tradition is true or not, it is certain that by the eleventh century, descendants of the Merovingian Franks "believed" it to be the case. And what it is almost certain is that the Sicimbrians, and therefore the Merovingians, were at least partly of Jewish blood.

It is with a description of both the Merovingian Franks and the Burgundians that Xaviar Guichard's salt lines and my own research into Megalithic geometry begin to take on a specific importance to our story. The first Merovingian stronghold in the Ardennes was Stenay, which at 49 degrees 29 minutes north stands at a latitude exactly 17 Megalithic degrees north of Jerusalem. The Benjamites, ancestors of the Merovingians, had controlled Jerusalem and the area around it before it became Solomon's capital city and long before the Temple was built there. The geographical relationship between it and Stenay is almost certainly no coincidence. The knowledge necessary to "place" their capital so accurately was part of the Philistine legacy and ultimately Cretan in origin.

The best known of the Merovingians in a modern sense was Clovis, who came to power in 481. The reason that history pays special attention to this ruler is that he brought Christianity to the wider mass of his people. He accepted the faith for himself and also as his state's religion. The story goes that the wife of Clovis, Clotilda, herself from the region of Burgundy, was already a Christian. Eventually she managed to persuade Clovis to accept the faith. He was baptized on Christmas Day 496 in the longitudinal salt line city of Reims. This city occupies a place in what was to become the Champagne region of France. Champagne shows itself time and again to be of supreme importance to our story.

Clovis ruled well, or at any rate successfully. He gained a hold on new territories and extended the kingdom of the Merovingians well beyond its former borders in the Ardennes. By his death, Clovis had acquired the cities of Troyes and Amiens. (Troyes would become the most important salt line and Grail city of them all.) These were added to Reims, which by 496 had already fallen to Clovis and his army. In return for his support, the Roman Catholic Church made a pact with Clovis. The Church stated that his successors would forever be considered Holy Roman rulers. The extent or depth of Clovis' own devotions is a matter for conjecture. He founded many abbeys and other religious institutions, though it is generally accepted that his pact with the Church, as with the earlier Constantine, was probably essentially a political move.

The reign and life of Clovis ended in 511 and his lands were split amongst his sons. The line that interests us devolves from Clotaire I, who inherited the Kingdom of Soissons. It is from this Clotaire that we eventually come to Dagobert II, a character who is crucial to all that followed.

By the time Dagobert was due to take control of his birthright, the Merovingian kings were much weakened by ministers who sought to gain control of the various thrones for themselves. Dagobert's father, Sigisbert III died in 656, probably murdered. The young Dagobert was taken prisoner by the Mayor of the Palace, and so was unable to ascend the throne of Austrasia. He eventually escaped and fled to Ireland and then Britain.

After some years, it was possible for Dagobert to claim his rightful inheritance. In 674 he was recognized as being the King of Austrasia. Dagobert was a good ruler. He had gained much influence in the south of France, thanks to a judicious second marriage with Giselle de Razes, an important princess of Visiogoth blood. Although a capable king, Dagobert was not an especially good Christian monarch in the eyes of the Church and did little to curb the excesses of heretical sects such as the Arianists. It is equally likely that he held some rather errant religious views of his own. By this time, he had close ties with the far south of France and its Visigoth inhabitants. The Visigoths were not good Roman Catholics either and their heretical tendencies may have rubbed off on Dagobert, who was also partly of Burgundian blood.

So it was that Dagobert gained many enemies, both in the Church and within his own ruling faction. Things came to a head on 23 December 679. Dagobert was out hunting in the Forest of Wouvres, immediately adjacent to his capital at Stenay. As he lay down to rest, he was treacherously stabbed through the eye by one of his servants. The crown was seized by his first minister, Pepin the Fat.

Dagobert and his wife Giselle had a son called Sigisbert. There is no record of him having been killed at the time his father was assassinated, or subsequently. The most likely explanation is that he escaped with his mother to the family holdings in the south of France and there lived out his life. The reason that we don't see him again in the historical record is probably due to the fact that Pepin's family very quickly consolidated their hold on Austrasia. Later rulers of the region did believe that Sigisbert had survived. They were adamant that Sigisbert's ancestral line had passed into the Bouillon and Lorraine families. The murdered Dagobert came 20 generations after Jesus, with Godfroi de Bouillon, a man who figures prominently in the great heresy that was to follow, coming exactly nineteen generations later.

The Orthodox Church behaved in a very strange way with regard to the murdered Dagobert. Against all odds, considering Rome's dislike for him, he was canonized. There is absolutely no doubt that he held the position of saint, though books on Catholic saints produced today find his canonization difficult to substantiate. The Vatican has always kept quiet about the matter. Stenay, his capital and the place of his burial, became a shrine to St. Dagobert. Successive rulers, especially Godfroi de Bouillon, took special care of both the town and the church where the relics lay.

It was not until the time of the French Revolution that the bones of Dagobert were removed from Stenay. Did the Church feel guilty that it had betrayed its sacred pact with the Merovingian line? We will never know, but the feast day of St. Dagobert is still celebrated on 23 December, at least it is in some Catholic churches in the Ardennes.

The second group of people who played a pivotal role in what I came to call the great heresy, the Burgundians, had radically different origins from the Merovingian Franks. However, by the time of Dagobert, the bloodline of the two peoples was so intermingled they can be considered to be virtually synonymous.

The Burgundians were always quite certain of their own history, which orthodox historians readily accept. They came from a region well to the north of their eventual homelands where they had been an important group of tribes living along the edge of the Baltic Sea, and in particular on an island which is today known as Bornholm. In the Middle Ages Bornholm was still known as "Burgundarholm," a testimony to the point of origin of a people who would become pivotal to the history of France and to the world as a whole.

Bornholm is a fascinating island, replete with the same Megalithic legacy found across Britain and parts of France. Historical excavations in the area prove conclusively that the people living in Bornholm in late Stone Age and Bronze Age times were directly related to the Megalithic cultures further south and to the west. The island would be singled out for special attention during the explosion in church building that took place from the eleventh century on. It contains many examples of "round towered" churches, many of which can be shown to be occupying sites of religious significance that were clearly ancient when Christianity came, quite late, to the region. Significant interest was shown in the island by a strange group of fighting monks, known as the Knights Templar, an institution that will also prove pivotal to our story.

By the first century AD, the Burgundians were moving into the Valley of the River Vistula. There they encountered another people, known as the Gepidae, against whom they were unable to defend themselves. As a result, they moved westward, until they came to the borders of the Roman Empire. Over a period of time the Burgundians became auxiliaries, or "foederati" of the legions and as a result they gradually began to carve out a kingdom for themselves, which by the fifth century AD included part of the Rhine Valley and which eventually became centered on Savoy, near Lake Geneva.

The gradual decline of Roman influence in the region allowed the ever-willing Burgundians to annex even more territory, eventually extending into the Rhone and Saone river valleys. By around AD 500, the Burgundians were becoming one of the most important peoples in the region, contemporary with the Merovingian Franks further north, and ably ruled by the famous law-giver "Gundobad," who reigned from 474 to 516.

It was a niece of Gundobad, Clotilda, who married Clovis, the first Christian ruler of the Merovingian Franks, forming a blood tie between the two peoples. Clotilda was already a Roman Christian at the time of her marriage in 493, though most of the Burgundian leaders, such as Gundobad, were of uncertain Christian pedigree, probably favoring Arianism.

In the year 534, Burgundy was annexed by the descendants of Clovis, though the blood ties between the Merovingians and the Burgundians were, by this time, extremely strong. What is most important about Burgundy, which by 561 had grown even larger, extending well up into central France, was its fierce sense of autonomy. It became the center of opposition to the later Carolingian rule of France, under a king called Boso, a man whose bloodline was relatively untainted by the Carolingians. Although Boso had to relinquish large areas of what had been the "Greater Burgundy," he retained a sizeable kingdom, which held out against Carolingian domination until about 933. In my opinion, this pivotal period of several hundred years, between the founding of Burgundy until the tenth century, sowed the seeds of the great heresy that took place between the eleventh century and the fourteenth century. This, in turn, would have a profound and lasting part to play in the development of the western world henceforth.

The form of Christianity that was predominant in both the Frankish kingdom of the Merovingians and in large parts of Burgundy was of a very particular sort, and markedly different from that which would follow with the arrival of the Carolingian rulers, of which Charlemagne would be the greatest example. When Clovis was baptized, in 496, there was a distinct lack of potential Roman Christian missionaries whom he could call upon to spread the new faith amongst his people. He, and successive Merovingian rulers, therefore turned his gaze westward, toward Britain and Ireland. Good relations existed between the Christians of the Merovingian lands and those of the far west. For example, Dagobert, the king who would eventually be murdered near Stenay in the year 679, had spent a considerable period during his years in exile with monks in both Ireland and England. His time in these islands coincided with an important event, the Synod of Whitby, which took place in 663 and 664.

The modern Catholic Church would have us believe that the

Synod of Whitby was pivotal in the development of the Church in Britain and Ireland. Prior to this time, there were significant differences between what has come to be known as "Celtic Christianity" and the Roman Christianity further east. The Celtic British and Irish tradition owed its existence to a group known as the "Culdees," a word which can literally be translated as "The strangers amongst us."

Tradition relates that a group of Christians had come to the shores of Britain as early as AD 37, anxious to escape the early persecutions that were taking place in their native lands. They were welcomed by the local king of the West Britons, "Avaragus." These people were lodged in the college of the druids, and Avaragus later granted them twelve hides of land, on which the first church in Britain was built. The location of this church was Glastonbury, a significant Megalithic salt line location and one that we will return to before long. There is strong historical evidence for the validity of this story. In the Doomsday Book of 1088 we find:

> The Domus Dei in the great monastery at Glastingbury.
> This Glastingbury church possesses in its own villa XII
> hides of land for which have never paid tax.16

This embryonic group of people, who were certainly in place long before Roman Christianity came to Britain around the time of Constantine, continued to exert a gentle influence over Britain and Ireland. What seems extremely likely, bearing in mind the dress, bearing, and some of the apparent beliefs of the Culdees, is that they were heavily influenced by the Druids, a priestly class amongst the Celts. The Druids were still extremely important to

British society when the first Culdees arrived in Britain.

A book of incantations, spells, and prayers, the *Carmina Gadelica*[17] has examples that come from a very early date and contains early Culdee Christian prayers. Most of these retain a strong "nature" content and are very reminiscent of what we know of druidic beliefs. Not too much is known about the Druids themselves, but their places of worship were always out of doors. Druid is said to mean "Oak Man" and the Roman historians accepted that the Druids, whom they sought so hard to destroy, predominantly met in oak groves. What nobody denies is that at very the heart of Celtic pagan worship, personified by the priestly Druids, lay the worship of the Great Goddess.

However, the Druids were far from being simply itinerant holy men. They were the people to whom the incessantly warring Celtic tribes turned to for arbitration. Every Druid underwent years of rigorous training and they were the oral repositories of the history and tradition of their people.

There is no doubt whatsoever that Culdean Christianity owed at least something to its partly Druidic roots, a fact that became apparent as time went by and which eventually led to the Synod of Whitby in 663–4. Ostensibly, the synod was meant to deal with differences in dress, hairstyle, and religious dates that existed between the Culdees and their Roman counterparts. Matters had come to a head because the Anglo-Saxon king of the north of England, Oswiu, was a Celtic or Culdean Christian, whereas his southern English wife, Eanfled, was of the Roman persuasion.

For at least two centuries, Culdean monks had carried the Christian story as they saw it, across the Channel to the lands of the Franks. Roman Christian influence in the region, especially in northern France, had been limited but a jealous and increasingly more aggressive Roman Church wished to stress its own greater relevance, in Britain, Ireland, and France. The Synod of Whitby provided the opportunity.

This great meeting, high on the cliff above the fishing port of Whitby, on the northeast coast of England, was probably far less important than the modern Church would have us believe. True, the Roman faction won the day, particularly regarding the date upon which Easter should be celebrated, and with regard to the correct hairstyle and clothing for monks. Culdees, like their Druid forebears and the Essene of the Jordan Valley, always wore white, and also shaved their heads in a druidic fashion. However, not only did a significant number of the Culdees leave the Synod refusing to accept the new edicts, in reality very little altered in terms of Culdee ideas and forms of worship. It wasn't really until after the Norman Conquest of England in 1066 that the full force of Roman Christianity was put in place across much of Britain.

In my estimation, the people of northern and central France never quite forgot their own Culdean Christian roots. The most important monastic Order we will look at in detail in due course was that of the Cistercians, who strongly reflected Culdean sentiments.

Despite the Synod of Whitby, local Masses in Britain and France continued to be celebrated in the language of the people and also reflected much of what had always been important in terms of indigenous belief. Only with the end of Merovingian rule in France did an irrevocable change begin the take place there, both in terms of religion and government. Along with the Culdean forms of worship existed a tenacious belief in the right to personal freedom, demonstrated by the Celtic races of Britain and those of Roman Gaul since Iron Age times. The actions of the Carolingian kings of France, both politically and in a religious sense, bred a deep resentment and fuelled the determination of a shadowy yet quite obvious group of influential people who began to take decisive actions of their own to recreate what had gone before. Like the Essene of pre-Christian and post-Christian times what these people sought was nothing less than the creation of a "New Jerusalem." More than anything else they wished to shake off the yoke of an ever more stifling feudal rule and to be allowed to practice a religion they saw as being their birthright. The center of operations for this influential group of people was Troyes, in Champagne, though they clearly represented yet another strand of the age-old Golden Thread.

CHAPTER 9

The Carolingian Split

T he killing of Dagobert II in the Forest of Stenay in 679 was pivotal in terms of the history of the region we know today as France, but it also led to fundamental changes across much of western Europe. Although the Frankish kingdoms continued to be nominally ruled for some time by kings of the Merovingian bloodline, in reality they held no power. For some generations, the administration of the Frankish kingdoms had been in the hands of a powerful group of civil servants known as "Mayors of the Palace." The person who is generally accused of ordering the death of Dagobert II was such an individual and his name was Pepin. He gave rise to a dynasty of his own, known as the Pepinids, which would eventually supply the Carolingian kings of France.

For decades the Mayors of the Palace had been carefully increasing their own influence and land holdings. The withdrawal of Rome had left a power vacuum across all of Gaul that was invariably filled by local rulers, or "dukes." Family squabbles, together with avaricious newcomers, led to local boundaries being constantly redrawn, so that, by the end of the seventh century the powerful and competing aristocratic claims had effectively put paid to all but nominal rule for many of the Merovingian monarchs. This was a state of affairs the suited the Pepinids who found ways and means of exploiting the potentially chaotic situation that was developing, and which they had helped to create. However, they refrained from taking the crown for themselves for some generations, ruling behind a series of "puppet kings" of the Merovingian blood, though from a "cadet" branch of the family and not directly related to Dagobert II, or ultimately Clovis.

A later and even more pivotal member of the Pepinids was the illegitimate son of another Pepin, Pepin of Herstal, the Mayor of the Palace of Austrasia. His name was Charles Martel and not only did he manage to reunite virtually all the old Frankish world but he sowed the seeds for a form of government that united State and Church in a brutal and repressive system known as feudalism.

There is little doubt that Charles Martel was a capable ruler and it is almost certainly thanks to him that at least parts of France did not find themselves under Muslim rule. What is more, despite a power and influence that saw him eventually ruling not only the old Merovingian kingdoms, but also Burgundy, he continued to nominally recognize the kingship of the Merovingians. Charles ruled ably though ruthlessly until 741 but was only able to do so on account of a political policy that would ensnare much of western Europe for centuries to come.

Charles Martel relied partly on conquest, but also on consensus, at least in terms of the rulers and virtual warlords whom he came to control. It would have been impossible for him to have achieved any of his objectives had it not been for many hundreds of local landowners who saw supporting his cause as being in their own best interest. Those who showed loyalty were rewarded with grants of land seized from local rulers who had proved treacherous, or who had backed the wrong horse. This was the hallmark of feudalism, a system of government that also suited the aims and intentions of the Roman Church. Martel was always keen to have the Church on his side and slowly began a process that drew Church and State ever closer. It wasn't always an easy alliance, especially in later times, but the iron grip of feudalism came to be as obvious in ecclesiastical matters as it was in civil ones.

On his death in 741, the land Charles Martel controlled was

divided between his two legitimate sons, yet another Pepin and Carloman. Carloman entered a monastery in 747, leaving Pepin as sole ruler. Throwing off the pretence of serving under a Merovingian king, Pepin was the first of the Carolingians to seek a crown for himself, which he achieved in 751 with the full backing of Pope Zacharias.

It must have been at this time that a significant number of people associated with the old Merovingian bloodline became convinced that the Carolingians were guilty of treason. To these same people it would have become abundantly clear that the promise made by the Church to Clovis, back in 496, had been broken. At the time of Clovis' acceptance of Christianity, the Church had promised faithfully that the Merovingians would retain a special religious status. This solemn oath on the part of the Church was shown to be worthless on the day Pepin III was crowned. Modern commentators, such as Baigent, Leigh, and Lincoln, claim that there was a rich and ultimately powerful skein within Frankish and Burgundian society that never forgave the Church for this treachery. They also suggest that the usurpation of the throne by Pepin III removed the bloodline of Jesus himself from the throne of France, something that a significant number of aristocrats of Merovingian blood found difficult to accept.

After Pepin III came his son Charlemagne, the most famous of all the Carolingians and a man who has passed into history as being something of a paragon amongst Christian princes. This may be the view from our position in time but to literally millions of people Charlemagne's rule must have seemed repressive, cruel, and contrary to the spirit of the old Germanic laws that had pertained in the past. Feudalism was the hallmark of Carolingian rule and was a system that built a sort of "pyramid hierarchy" into society. At the top was the king, who relied heavily on ever more powerful landowners, all of whom could command their own armies in times of war. Below these "dukes" came the middle aristocracy, who often had significant holdings of their own. These men owed loyalty to a specific duke, and through him to the King. At the bottom of the aristocratic pile, and close to the base of the pyramid, were men who perhaps controlled only one manor, though such a person would hold this "of" or with the permission of a greater lord.

Finally came the farmers and free men, below whom were the serfs, who were little better than slaves. All sections of feudalism relied on the adage "might is right" and a good deal of vying for position and battling for the acquisition of more land was inimical to the system.

Charlemagne was crowned as Charles I, King of the Franks in 768. Like others before him, he ruthlessly overthrew his relatives in order to secure his own absolute power and it wasn't long before he invaded northern Italy. By 774, in addition to his other titles, he was King of the Lombards. Although his invasion of Italy came as a result of a plea for assistance from the Pope, from that moment forward Charlemagne effectively "owned" the Church, which he and his successors began to mould into an institution that admirably suited their own political intentions and ideas of kingship.

Back in the days of Clovis the pact with the Church essentially said that popes held the right to make or depose kings, but the coronation of Charlegmagne's father, Pepin III, demonstrated that "the man who has the power deserves to be king." So much influence did Charlemagne have over the Church that in the year 800, he was declared "Holy Roman Emperor." This was the final nail in the coffin lid of the Church's treachery. Back in 496, it had pledged itself, forever, to the Merovingian cause and bloodline. Now it absolutely, and in a very public fashion, simply broke its sacred promise.

There is no doubt that both the Church, and the new kings concerned, were acutely aware of the implications of these actions. Why else would both Pepin III and Charlemagne have taken Merovingian brides immediately after their coronation? Few were fooled by what was taking place, either in terms of the treachery of the Church, or with regard to the change in governmental principles that took away so many of the rights that individuals had formerly enjoyed, and which feudalism destroyed.

Herein lies the mystery within our story that is simply impossible to explain. It would seem that probably around the time of Charlemagne, a relatively powerful group of people living in Burgundy, and in particular Champagne, took it upon themselves to oppose the developing repression from both State and Church. We cannot give names to the individuals concerned because by the time their actions become apparent, it is clear that the people concerned were working to plans that must have been laid down decades or even centuries before their own period.

This group of people was first recognized by my co-writer Stephen Dafoe and myself and mentioned in our book *The Templar Continuum*.[18] Because their power base came to be predominantly the city of Troyes, capital of Champagne, we named these people the "Troyes Fraternity." However, it is clear that their agenda was already very old and that the Troyes Fraternity merely represented an element of the Golden Thread.

What we definitely do know about the Troyes Fraternity is that its members made a number of conscious decisions, the effects of which would be played out across several centuries. It is clear therefore that the people concerned were very patient. Exactly when the series of pivotal decisions were made is impossible to say, but certain facts about the beliefs and conclusions of the Troyes Fraternity are beyond doubt. It sought to:

1 Destroy the power-base of the Roman ruled Church

2 Replace it with a Church based in Jerusalem

3 Institute organizations that were specifically intended to destroy feudalism and to restore the rights of individuals

4 Elevate the "feminine" within established beliefs to such an extent that Christianity effectively changed its nature altogether.

5 Effectively destroy national boundaries and create a form of "internationalism" that would restrict the power of individual rulers.

At no time did the Troyes Fraternity (or whatever it really called itself) admit its own existence and nor did it openly seek to make its desired changes by way of force. Unfolding events show that it was composed of people who came predominantly from manorial holdings or from towns and cities that were bisected by longitudinal or latitudinal salt lines. I will demonstrate that those concerned clearly knew where the salt lines ran and in fact an exercise I undertook regarding the results of the Norman Conquest of Britain positively proves that, to some people at least, the salt lines were well understood.

History records in great detail a list of the lords, knights, and churchmen who supported William, Duke of Normandy, when he chose to invade England in 1066. The result of this invasion was the death of the Anglo-Saxon king of England, Harold Godwinson, and his replacement with William, who became William I of England but who is generally known to history as William the Conqueror.

I studied this list very carefully and, wherever possible, I ascertained where the Norman and French manorial holdings of those who fought for William at Hastings in 1066 had been. I then made two further lists, one detailing William's allies who had come from salt line holdings across the Channel and those who had not. The next step was to spend weeks seeking what land William's supporters had been granted in England, as a reward for their loyalty. The results were staggering. Those lords and knights who had enjoyed salt line holdings in Normandy and France, were also far more likely to receive salt line holdings in England.

It is important to stress once again that the salt lines of both longitude and latitude are about 59 minutes of arc apart. (See the maps detailing the French and British salt lines, figures 1 and 2.) If a tolerance of 1 minute of arc is allowed, there is only a 1 in 30 chance of any given location being on a salt line. So clear was the tendency of salt line supporters of William to also occupy salt lines in England that over two thirds of the present British aristocracy, most of whom ultimately owe their origin to the Norman conquest, still have holdings that straddle salt lines.

Very few supporters of William who had not enjoyed salt line holdings in Normandy or France received them in England. This means, no matter how unlikely it may appear, that knowledge of the salt lines definitely did exist at the time of the Norman Conquest, a date that is pivotal to events happening in France at the same period. How such knowledge had been retained, almost certainly across at least 3,000 years and probably more, I simply cannot explain. Nor am I able to say "who" had the knowledge. Common sense would suggest that it was a person or people yielding great power, and since England was effectively carved up and redistributed by William of Normandy himself, it is not beyond reason that he was in on the secret.

It was my initial rediscovery of the salt lines of Britain and France that had allowed me to identify the origins of what I referred to as the "great heresy." This began soon after the Norman Conquest of Britain and I will show the chief protagonists in the story that is to follow to have come, almost exclusively, from salt line locations.

Whether or not the interested reader wishes to accept these extraordinary salt line discoveries is, to a great extent, irrelevant. The events that unfolded from the tenth century on are a matter of fact, not conjecture. The existence of Xavier Guichard's salt lines may have led me to a recognition of events that history has failed to connect but of the reality of the events themselves there is no doubt. However, it should be remembered that both the Merovingians and the Burgundians had long and complex histories, both ultimately originating in the Neolithic period of western Europe. The Burgundians in particular were of the old Megalithic blood, in other words from the culture that, according to Guichard, had planned and marked the salt lines in the first place.

There is another fact that is of great importance and which may also indicate that a knowledge of the salt lines and their positions had never been lost. In the days before modern France existed as a single nation state, the area was split into a number of different kingdoms and regions.

Longitudinal salt lines, as they pass through France, are roughly 70 to 80 kilometers apart, growing closer together as they run north towards the pole. The latitudinal salt lines are always 111 kilometers apart. Despite this, the capital cities of French Flanders, Normandy, Burgundy, Champagne, and Brittany were all salt line locations. To put this in perspective, we are dealing with an area of land from the Belgium border in the north, to southern Burgundy in the south. In width the area extended from the North Sea coast, right across to Lorraine in the east. Only the area around Paris, under the direct control of the French crown, is excluded from this salt line ruled pattern.

Of course, none of these great cities, Lille, Rouen, Troyes, Dijon, or Rennes, as regional capitals, was founded in the medieval period. This is also true of other great salt line cities of France, such as Caen, Reims, Sens, and Besancon. All of these cities had already existed for centuries, most since at least Roman times and it is more than likely that even the Romans were using locations that already had a civil or religious significance.

Louis Charpentier in his book *Mysteries of Chartres Cathedral*,[19] makes a very pertinent suggestion regarding the name of some of these cities. He proposes, for example, that the original name for Troyes was actually Troy-Is. Similarly Rennes would have been Renn-Is and Reims something like Ream-Is. All these locations are known to have been the sites of temples dedicated to the goddess Isis in Roman times. Bearing in mind the Romans' habit of equating local gods and goddesses with those within their own pantheon, the cities concerned could well have been centers of Goddess worship since time out of mind, hence the "Is" suffix to their names. This may explain why they had been deliberately placed on the salt lines, where they would have survived as places of reverence and worship at least since Bronze Age times.

The more one looks at the development of Roman Catholicism across many centuries, even before some pivotal decisions were made in Troyes around the time of Charlemagne's reforms of Church and state, the greater is the feeling that "alternative agencies" were at work. What Stephen Dafoe and I chose to call the Troyes Fraternity we also came to know as "the Golden Thread through the tapestry of time."

With their knowledge of the salt line system of Europe, which also infers an understanding of Megalithic geometry, we would expect such people to be masters of mathematics, proto-science, and astronomy. This is exactly what we discover them to have been. If we lift our eyes from the pages of orthodox history books, we can see the Golden Thread gleaming brightly amidst the murk of history long before the Carolingians came to the throne. What I have come to realize we are looking at is nothing less than a surviving, often hereditary priesthood, tracing its roots so far down into the earth of our common history, it is impossible to fathom how deep they reach.

These amazing people have left a plethora of clues for those who know where to look, and exactly what to look for. One such example is the historically loaded symbol of the "rose," the regular appearance of which is a certain sign that Goddess worship has flourished, unmolested and without interruption, for countless generations.

CHAPTER 10

By their Signs you shall Know them

No icon from history proves more pointedly the survival of a Megalithic priesthood well into the modern era than that of the rose. This flower is directly related to the Goddess and, latterly, to her Christian counterpart, the Virgin Mary. However, like so much else associated with this gripping story, what looks like an innocent enough symbol turns out to have very complex connections. Unfortunately, without the "cipher key" that a knowledge of Megalithic geometry and astronomy offers, almost everything that is truly important about the symbolism of the rose remains known only to the initiate. This state of affairs is about to change.

Many carved grave slabs of Crusader knights from a period after the eleventh century, discovered in the Holy Land, carry a representation of the sword of the knight who lay beneath. In the case of grave covers relating to one particular sort of Crusader, men belonging to the monastic Order known as the Knights Templar, the stone carver has often depicted roses entwined around the blade of the sword. A casual observer might suggest that this was merely Christian iconography, since the rose is a flower often associated with the Virgin Mary. And Mary was, after all, the patron of the Templar Order.

In fact, the roses on Templar graves are much more likely to relate to a pre-Christian deity whose origins lie deep within the history of northeastern France, and in particular, in Lorraine. It was veneration for this deity, whose name was Rosemerth, that inspired agencies from Troyes, and particularly the massively important St. Bernard of Clairvaux, to seek the elevation of the Virgin to the rank of "Queen of Heaven." The motivation for his desire to do so had originated in a place called Sion Vaudemont. This location is a hilltop church and village overlooking the longitudinal salt line that slightly bypasses the city of Metz in Lorraine.

It was in this location, in the year 1070 that the ruling lord of Sion Vaudemont had proclaimed himself to be the vassal of "The Queen of Heaven." This was a title unknown for the Virgin Mary in the West at that time. He was undoubtedly referring, not to Mary, but to Rosemerth, that female deity of the Franks who was a direct counterpart of the Great Goddess of ancient Europe. She had been worshiped in Sion Vaudemont for hundreds of generations. A statue of Rosemerth had been found in the location and was venerated as if it represented the Virgin herself. Even at this late stage in history, religious beliefs tended to be very confused in rural backwaters. It is doubtful if ordinary worshipers at the time would have fully understood the difference between a tutelary goddess and the Virgin Mary of Christian belief.

The present meaning of the rose cross has changed somewhat. This is a distinction that is of the greatest importance. Even in its altered form, the Rosecroix is very close to the Grail legends. A subsequent chapter will deal with this subject specifically. But it is clear that although "rose" in the context of the Rosecroix is now taken to mean the color of the cross, in its original form this was not the case. The Templar graves show that the first rose cross was the image formed by the flowers of the rose entwined around the cruciform shape of a Templar sword.

The use of the rose anywhere in Christian symbolism is apt to throw up a suspicion of Goddess worship. The rose is not merely representative of the Virgin Mary herself. It cannot be so because the Lorraine deity Rosemerth predated Christianity by centuries. And here lies the disparity. The Templar knight buried beneath the rose cross might have had little or no idea of the pagan symbolism of the flower. However, his Grand Master may have understood very well. Both would have observed the same image and each took from it the meaning that he considered to be relevant.

The association of the rose and feminine-orientated religion has never been forgotten. Many of those experiencing visions of the Virgin Mary have described rose petals falling from the sky during the visitation. Numerous female saints whose lives have been dedicated to the Virgin are pictured carrying roses or are named for them, such as St. Theresa of the Roses. But like so much else associated with Goddess knowledge, the use of the word "rose" is double speak and has a multitude of meanings to the enlightened.

One manifestation of the rose is that Gothic invention, the "rose" window. Most of the great Gothic cathedrals possess a rose window. These are large and circular, and always at the western end of the church, and therefore pointing to the west, the region of the dead. Some of the finest medieval glass went into the construction of rose windows. Many of these still remain a blaze of light all day long, even though the bright light of the day does not reach the western side of cathedrals until late in the afternoon. Rose windows contain many elements, usually radiating out from a central medal. Some of them are colossal in size and all of them are said to be dedicated to the Virgin Mary.

It could be from the rose window that "compass rose navigation" first derived its name. Prior to latitudinal and longitudinal navigation, people found their way about with this more primitive form of navigation. Using this principle a particular location, Bristol for example, was considered to be the center of a circle.

From this "node" lines, similar to the spokes of a bicycle wheel, radiated out in all directions. Other locations could be the hub of alternative compass rose systems and the lines from these often crossed each other. By this means it was possible to establish some sort of navigation pattern and to keep track of position and heading. Xaviar Guichard, who discovered the salt lines of longitude and latitude, believed that, originally, compass rose lines had represented the basis of a dry land navigation system. He thought that these were used to transport salt from areas where it was abundant, to places where it did not naturally occur. He was adamant that the original salt lines had been of the compass rose variety. Using the "al" type place names as markers, Guichard had plotted many compass rose systems across western Europe. These, he believed, had been laid down in early Bronze Age times. The later development of these systems had been the longitudinal and latitudinal salt lines.

But compass rose systems have an inherent flaw. It is a fact that the further one travels from the hub of the rose, the greater is the distance between one radiating line and the next. It is for this reason that latitudinal and longitudinal navigation is superior, since in such a system the lines remain parallel.

Moving closer to our own time the face of a compass is often called "the compass rose." Once again, this may be attributable to the old rose windows, or it may owe something to the compass rose navigation system. The compass as we know it today is not thought to be an ancient invention. It is very likely that Vikings used pieces of "loadstone," suspended on strings, to ascertain the direction of north and south. Loadstone is a naturally occurring magnetic rock. A piece of it cut with a point on either end, when allowed to rotate freely, will always attempt to point to magnetic north and south.

Roses once represented a valuable commodity in Europe, and never more so than during that period immediately after the First Crusade, which took place in 1099. Roses, especially Damascus roses, were fragrant, and a multitude of products could be made from them. The production of rose related items relied on different means of extracting and utilizing the potent essential oil. This was useful in counteracting the worst excesses of a society that must have been universally smelly. Nowhere was better placed to make money from this interest in roses from the Middle East than the Champagne city of Provins. Most of the larger French cities of the medieval period became essentially famed for one specific product and in the case of Provins it was roses. Provins was the site of one of the great Champagne fairs, held annually in northern France.

So lucrative was the trade of Provins that the place was jealously guarded by its overlords. Few people realize the fact but Provins, although far from the shores of Britain, is the true origin of the emblem of England, which is a double rose of red and white.

The family group that was eventually to become known as the Lancastrians were Dukes of Provins. This had come about because of the old Norman blood ties that stitched together large areas of England and France. So important was Provins to the economy of this power base that they took for their personal emblem the red rose. Meanwhile another branch of the family, who would eventually attract to themselves the title of Yorkists, also laid claim to the Duchy of Provins. Not to be outdone by the Lancastrians, they adopted the white rose as their badge. A bitter war broke out between the two factions. This was eventually nothing less than an English Civil War, which, on and off, spanned many decades. This series of battles has gone down in history as the Wars of the Roses. It was an amalgamation of the two roses that eventually became the emblem of England.

The real secret of the symbolism of the rose is quite illuminating. It is based on a fact that would have had a particular significance to members of the surviving Megalithic priesthood. It lies partly in the sexual habits of the plant and also in the sexual allusions that have become attached to it.

The stylized rose of Medieval and modern heraldry is the dog rose (*Rosa Canina*). This five-petal variety is common throughout much of Europe and is a wild flower of the hedgerows. The blooms, though pretty enough, are fairly unprepossessing. In due course they die back and are replaced by the rosehip, which is the fruit of the plant. But there is something quite special about the dog rose, and it is a quality that is shared by only a handful of species to be found in our meadows and hedgerows. The dog rose does not have to be cross-fertilized from another plant in order to produce fruit. The various sexual parts of a single bloom of the dog rose do not mature at the same time. If fertilization does take place, it is likely to be from another flower, or possibly from a different bush altogether. But if the flower is not pollinated at all, it will still yield a rosehip in the autumn. This means, essentially, that the dog rose is capable of "virgin birth."

It is hard to see how this particular quality of the dog rose could fail to play an important part in the association of the flower with the Virgin Mary, but it may not have commenced with her. Virgin birth, as a concept, was certainly adopted by the Christian Church, but, as we have already seen, it is not unique to the institution.

One of the later offshoots of the great heresy, which commenced in the tenth century, is the developing interest in the study of alchemy. Alchemy, although a subject of great interest during the Middle Ages, is now almost totally misunderstood. Most people assume that the prime intention of the alchemist was to turn base metal into gold, the mysterious "transmutation." This indeed may have been one of the aims of alchemy but it should be seen as a byproduct of a very complex subject. The study of "internal alchemy," has far more to do with the spiritual transmutation of the individual than any connection with transmutation of metals. Within the world of alchemy, the rose has an important and quite surprising part to play.

It is the belief of those who practiced internal alchemy that one way to achieve spiritual enlightenment was through a detailed study and practice of the sexual act. There is absolutely nothing sordid or disreputable about the concepts involved, which are also embraced by the study of tantric yoga. Tantric yoga is an Indian technique and remains a subject of deep and serious discipline to the present day.

The male initiate to internal alchemy, wishing to achieve spiritual enlightenment, requires the help, guidance, and sexual services of a woman who has herself been trained in the mysteries of the discipline. Her role in this process was seen as deeply sacred. It was present in the workings of numerous mystery religions, some of which extend as far back into human history as it is possible to view. The "Holy Whore," who provided the guidance, wisdom, and ultimate sexual union that freed the spirit of the initiate lies at the very heart of our search for the truth of the Grail. We shall see time and again just how important she is to every aspect of the old religion and the attempts that were made to inculcate it into medieval Christianity. But the part the rose played in these matters is also of supreme importance, and proves to be yet another allegorical spur to the initiate. There is important symbolism at work here.

In the early stages or life the rose bloom is tightly coiled into a bud, and it is the symbol of the rosebud that was seen, in alchemy, as representing the female clitoris. The female human clitoris, although still not generally considered to be a subject for polite conversation in many circles, is unique amongst human organs. It has no male counterpart. It is the only human organ that has evolved specifically to give pleasure and for no other reason. This fact annoys Darwinian evolutionists no end since the clitoris seems to be something of a puzzle in evolutionary terms. Evolutionists might suggest that only an organ capable of offering such pleasure could induce women to contemplate an act that must ultimately lead to the pain, danger, and responsibility of childbirth. However, this argument is not entirely valid since sexual intercourse does not need to take place in order for the clitoris to be stimulated. The relationship of the rosebud to the clitoris represents potent alchemical symbolism. As we shall see, it is directly related to the sexual imperatives present in the Grail legends.

It has long been suggested that the "ogive," the specific curved and pointed arch peculiar to Gothic architecture, represented, in the minds of the first Gothic builders, the female vagina. To walk in through the magnificently carved ogive door of a Gothic cathedral can therefore be seen as passing through the vagina of the Goddess and into her sacred womb. These great doorways are "ribbed" and it isn't hard to see how they could be likened to the female vagina. There are many such doorways, not only in cathedrals but also in more humble Gothic churches, where the point of the ogive contains a carving of a rosebud. The intention is obvious and in these instances we see not merely the symbol of the holy vagina but of the clitoris too.

It is my contention that much of what the surviving Megalithic priesthood saw as being truly important in their religious beliefs was transformed into visual allegory of this sort. Symbolism of this kind would mean nothing to those who were not party to the full scope of the spiritual beliefs in question. However, the initiated were informed at every step of the spiritual journey that it was to the most adored and sacred part of the anatomy of the Goddess that they were being directed. The spiritual ecstasy offered was equated with the ecstasy of sexual union, and this could not be complete without the clitoris.

However, the Megalithic message is not merely a religious one; it encompasses scientific factors too. The dog rose can be used as a powerful aid to understanding the movements of a very specific member of the solar system. This is Venus, the very planet that had maintained an unbroken link with femininity and the Great Goddess herself.

Megalithic peoples were great Venus watchers. They knew that the cycles of the planet, when seen from the Earth, could be linked to the passing of the Earth year. A transit of Venus, in which the body of the planet can be observed to pass across or behind the face of the sun, happens five times during every eight Earth years. Eight Earth years and five Venus periods represent the same period of time to within a day or so.

What makes this period even more important is the fact that in the eighth Earth year, the zodiac position of the happening will be virtually the same as it was at the start of the eight-year period. When seen from the Earth, Venus, after passing across the face of the Sun, (the inferior conjunction or transit) becomes a morning star, which rises immediately ahead of the Sun and precedes it across the sky. So bright is Venus that she can be seen during the lightest part of the day.

Over a period of days, Venus moves away from the Sun, and then, as a peculiarity of our own position in space relative to Venus and the Sun, the planet appears to fall back in towards the Sun again. This time Venus passes behind the disc of the Sun (the superior conjunction). Venus emerges, several days later, as an evening star, following the Sun across the heavens each day and setting after it. The evening star phase continues, with the planet eventually reaching its maximum distance before once again falling back towards the Sun for its passage across the Sun's face (the inferior conjunction). This is a pattern repeated time and again, until the fifth inferior conjunction. By this time eight Earth years will have passed. In terms of astronomical observation

Figure 3

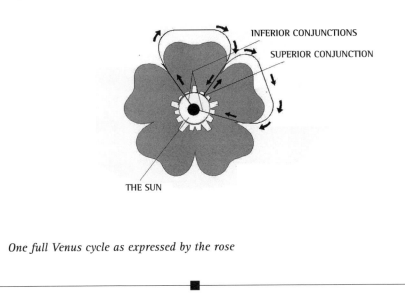

INFERIOR CONJUNCTIONS

SUPERIOR CONJUNCTION

THE SUN

One full Venus cycle as expressed by the rose

this is an important span of time, because it can be used as a method for tracking the notoriously complex patterns of the Earth's Moon. These coincide, both in terms of phase and zodiac position, with the Venus cycles and the eight Earth year period. The Moon has also always enjoyed strong Goddess connections.

The petals of the dog rose map out these happenings perfectly because if the center of the flower is seen as being the Sun, the path of Venus away from the Sun and ultimately back towards it again can be traced along the edge of the petals. This may be easier for readers with little or no astronomical understanding to follow if they take a look at figure 3.

An alternative method of viewing the face of the dog rose as being representative of the planet Venus can be seen in conjunction with a device that carries the name of the rose to this day: the Christian rosary.

The rosary is a string of prayer beads. Its origins are not known, though its name also certainly associates it with the Virgin Mary. To most Christians who use it the rosary represents a method of keeping track of a specific number of prayers. Although other religions use strings of prayer beads, which is what the rosary represents, the number of beads on the rosary is unique to the Christian version. The circular section of the rosary contains 50 beads, which are separated into units of ten by the inclusion of an extra bead between the groups, often of a different or larger sort. Extending from the circular section is a further string containing three beads, usually marked at either end by another large bead. Finally, the end of the further string invariably carries a crucifix.

The rosary is known to have been in use at the time of the First Crusade, and this is when the device is first referred to specifically. Prior to this, Christian prayer strings often carried 150 beads. At some stage between the years 1100 and 1200, the present arrangement seems to have been adopted. Christian tradition relates that it was in the year 1208 that the Virgin Mary appeared to St. Dominic, giving him a rosary and instructing him in its use. Since it is known that the present arrangement of beads predates the time of St. Dominic, this story cannot offer a particularly reliable date. However, there is no doubt that the use of the present rosary is contemporary with the Gothic period of architecture and the period of the great heresy.

It was common for the user of the rosary to travel round the beads with a finger and thumb, saying the prayer known as the Ave Maria once for each bead. As we have seen, the Ave Maria is said to date from the year 431 in the Church based in Ephesus, now Turkey.

A picture of a rosary, laid out flat, can be seen in figure 4. It

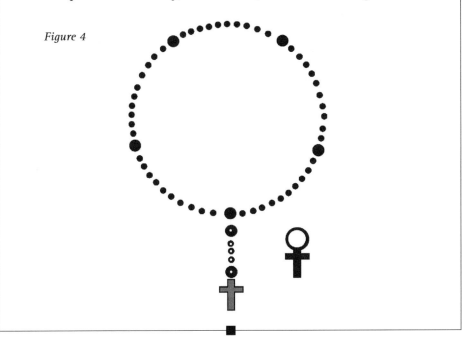

Figure 4

is a great wonder to me that I have not read anywhere of the true significance of the rosary in astronomical terms, or with regard to its symbolism. The design of the rosary, with its crucifix in place, conforms exactly to the recognized symbol, not only for the planet Venus in astronomy and astrology, but also to "woman." If the circle is slightly manipulated so that it becomes more oval, the "Ank" is produced. The Ank is of Egyptian origin and was a potent symbol that had both royal and feminine overtones.

Both the face of the rose and the beads of the rosary can be seen in two different ways.

Figure 5 shows what happens when the dog rose is placed within the rosary. In this example, the center of the rose is seen as being the Sun. Each successive passing of Venus away from the Sun, and then finally back again, corresponds to one petal of the flower and also to one section of the rosary. The full period of Venus, when viewed from the Earth, takes 584 days to complete. To anyone truly understanding the rosary, each ten beads would conform to a period of 292 days, since this is the period from inferior to superior conjunction. In this case, each bead represents about 29.2 days. This period conforms quite closely to the time that elapses between new Moon cycles (29.53 days). Even more importantly, it is inextricably linked with the menstrual cycles of women. The menstrual cycle differs from individual to individual, and it is often assumed to be of about 28 days. In reality, it is more likely to follow the synodic lunar cycle of 29.5 days. It is therefore not at all unusual for women to menstruate around the same phase of the Moon each month.

Traditionally the Earth's Moon has also been associated with the female cycle, and it is easy to see why. It is even possible

Figure 5

that the Moon's passage across the sky somehow regulates the menstrual cycle. In the "magical" eight-year period Venus completes its five cycles. During this time, the Moon will have passed from new to full and back to new again 99 times. In the same period, it will have returned to the same degree and sign of the zodiac 107 times. The two phenomena, plus the five synodic cycles of Venus all coincide to within a day or so.

To map the patterns of the Moon and Venus absolutely accurately with the beads of the rosary would be impossible because of the necessary splitting of days. All the same there does seem to be a deliberate intention to reconcile the astronomical movements most closely associated with the feminine principle and physical processes involved.

Later we shall investigate how these matters relate to the "Pentangle," the mysterious five-pointed star that lies at the heart of all Venus observation and Goddess worship. The pentacle is shown in place across the face of the rose in figure 5.

The rosary is significant to the conception of a female Godhead in two ways. Firstly, it is a method of remembering cycles of prayers specifically dedicated to the Virgin Mary. However, it has also been carefully created to give those possessing the key a good insight into the behavior of the heavenly bodies most closely equated with feminine Godhead. Venus and the Moon have been considered "feminine" in western religion since time out of mind.

A final point concerning the relationship of the shape of the dog rose to the observed behavior of Venus lies in the shape of the edge of the petals. These curve in towards their centers, forming, as it were, a valley between their two extremities. Such is the nature of the solar system, when viewed from the Earth, that there are periods in the cycles of all planets when they appear to move backwards within the zodiac. This phenomenon is called retrograde motion. It is purely a line-of-sight happening. It occurs because the Earth is also traveling around the Sun. The existence of retrograde motion in the case of Venus seems to be "written in" to the observed shape of dog rose petals. The petals describe the fact that Venus sometimes appears to move backwards in zodiac terms, even though its essential journey is forwards.

All of these aspects of the rose would have been well known to a shadowy group of people who probably met regularly in the palace of the Dukes of Champagne, in Troyes, in the years following the reign of Charlemagne (768–814). They, and their sons and daughters, observed a gradual tightening of the noose of feudalism, bringing war, death, and misery to their lands as well as watching a Church that became yearly more authoritarian and rigid. Forms of worship threatened to sideline the position of the Virgin, and therefore that of the Goddess.

These people considered themselves to be the true political and religious guardians of the regions they had inhabited for centuries and, as the situation deteriorated, there came a recognition that something had to be done. The "great heresy" that followed was the only possible response and it would eventually destroy the power of feudalism and the Catholic Church for good.

CHAPTER 11

The Plans are Laid

The first tangible evidence of the plans being carefully laid by the Troyes Fraternity was the election of Pope Urban II, in 1088. Those ordering events in Champagne had most certainly been planning for some decades before this, though the election to the papal see of Urban II was the launch platform for a host of other actions.

Some light is thrown on this matter when it is realized that Urban II's original name was Odo of Lagery and that he was born near Troyes, in the heart of Champagne, of noble parents closely allied to the Court of the Counts of the region. Plan number one on the agenda of the Troyes Fraternity was to maneuver the crowned heads of Europe into co-operating with a bold venture. The objective was to create the right circumstances under which the combined forces of Christendom would co-operate to attack the Holy Land.

Not only had Odo been born in Champagne, he had also been an archdeacon in Reims, one of the most important cities in the region, and he eventually became Prior Superior of Cluny, the most famous center of reformed monasticism in Europe. Cluny, as we shall see, was a place where the Troyes Fraternity wielded significant influence. Cluny was situated near Macon, in Burgundy, immediately south of Champagne and was a jewel of a monastery that was particularly dear to the hearts of the Burgundian rulers, who, it is clear, formed part of the Troyes Fraternity. Odo himself was blood tied to a number of the characters who played an important part in what was to follow and during his reign as Pope he always looked favorably on his native lands and its people.

In my estimation, Odo became Urban II solely "because" of the power and influence of the rulers of Champagne and

Burgundy. Throughout his entire time in the Vatican he fought tenaciously against an antipope, Clement III, who had been placed on the throne of the Vatican in 1080 by Henry IV, the Holy Roman Emperor. Through its whole period of influence the Troyes Fraternity never lost an opportunity to plague, annoy, and even attack successive Holy Roman Emperors. Undoubtedly it did so as a sign of its own contempt for the office and specifically for Charlemagne, its first recipient, the man, who with his father, Pepin III, had stolen the sacred birthright of the Merovingian kings.

Odo of Lagery, as Pope Urban II, went on to achieve a great deal as pope, but history shows that nothing was more important to him than the task he had been set by the Troyes Fraternity. This was quite simple. Urban was to call for a crusade that would ultimately leave the Holy Land and especially Jerusalem in supposedly Christian hands. He would probably have needed little encouragement for a whole host of reasons, even had he not been dancing to the tune of the Troyes Fraternity. Number one on his list would have been the proliferation of dangerous and unpredictable armed men who were storming all over western Christendom, with little else to do but cause problems, particularly for the Church.

One of the byproducts of feudalism was a plethora of "younger sons" of noble families, all trained from childhood to kill people in the most barbaric manner imaginable. The adage "might is right" was entirely appropriate for such violent times. The world had discovered the age of the mounted knight, a formidable fighting machine that might be equated with the armored tank of a later age. William of Normandy had shown how successful well-trained and equipped horse warriors could be when he defeated the English in 1066 and the message had not been lost on other parts of Europe and beyond.

A population explosion amongst the landed classes meant that there were literally thousands of hot-headed young men, rampaging about the countryside, spoiling for a fight with just about anyone. This was not a prospect that the Church relished, particularly since its own officers and property were so often vulnerable to the squabbles that broke out regularly amongst the minor aristocracy. In addition, Muslims were biting off large chunks of once Christian-ruled territory, not only in the East, but extending up into the soft underbelly of western Europe. Christianity was on the defensive and anything that could reverse such a depressing trend would have looked attractive to popes of the period.

However, there is some surprise, even amongst scholars today, as to why the Pope should have considered the Holy Land as a place to be singled out for such treatment on the part of the European states. Spain and southern France would have been a more logical region to fight a crusade against Islam. The Encyclopaedia Britannica says:

> Why this energy was channelled into a holy war against Muslims in a distant land is uncertain ...

The general excuse is that Christian pilgrims bound for the sites singled out as important during the life and mission of Jesus were being harassed by Muslims and were encountering difficulties going about their business. In truth, there is little or no evidence that this was the case. True, the forces of Islam were on the march and were threatening Byzantium, but relations with the agencies ruling Jerusalem, which was generally an open and very cosmopolitan place, had not been deteriorating.

A dozen other possibilities for Urban's call to arms have been suggested but none of them hold as much water as the simple explanation that "someone" wanted to control not only Jerusalem, but also a string of trading contacts that ran through the Levant. I hope the evidence will demonstrate that the organization I call the Troyes Fraternity, as part of the Golden Thread, had more to gain than anyone.

So it was that Urban II, at a great gathering just outside Clermont Ferrand in the Auvergne, France, made his first plea for a crusade in 1095. He followed this with a tour through numerous cities and states, all the time encouraging, harassing, and even bullying the divergent forces of feudalism to join together in this great and glorious quest. So it was that on Friday 15 July, 1099 the Crusaders breached the walls of Jerusalem and poured through to claim the city as a Christian acquisition.

What is of extreme importance is the identity of the man who led the forces that were first through the breach. He was none other than Godfroi de Bouillon, Duke of Lorraine and a person who knew himself to be of Merovingian descent. Godfroi was also related to many of the other characters who will emerge as our story unfolds and his presence in Jerusalem on that fateful day was no coincidence. Close on his heels was his kinsman, Ettiene-Henri, the ruler of Champagne at the time, who if not the prime mover in the Troyes Fraternity, certainly played a crucial part in its running. Ettiene-Henri's brother, Hugh, would become the first Count of Champagne.

Godfroi de Bouillon was a man with a mission. Much of his childhood was spent at or close to the important stronghold of

Sion de Vaudemont, once the most important administrative and religious center in Lorraine and a place mentioned earlier in connection with the cult of Rosemerth that had developed there. In addition to Sion de Vaudemont itself, both Godfroi's titles, Lorraine and Bouillon, center on longitudinal salt lines and he had strong dynastic ties with the family ruling Champagne at the time of the First Crusade.

Godfroi was directly related to the martyred Merovingian, Dagobert II, who had been treacherously murdered, almost certainly with the consent of the Church, in 679. Godfroi appeared nineteen generations after Dagobert on his father's side. A history of his life shows that he had never desired anything other than to be a crusader and to play a part in capturing Jerusalem. It is a fact that Godfroi sold practically everything he owned to raise sufficient funds to take what amounted to a private army to the Holy Land and strenuous efforts were made back in Champagne and Burgundy to ensure that he and his own private forces would be first into the city.

As a reward for his efforts, Godfroi de Bouillon was offered the chance to become the first Christian king of Jerusalem yet, with a singular and sudden burst of modesty, he point blank refused this specific honor. Within a few short months, he was dead. With virtually his last breath he confirmed his own suspicions that he had been poisoned. Godfroi's brother, Boudoin was present in the city at the time. Although at first only willing to accept the same title that Godfroi had created for himself, "defender of the Holy Sepulcher," Boudoin of Boulogne was eventually prevailed upon to take the crown and, almost certainly with great reluctance, became Boudoin I of Jerusalem in December of the year 1100. There were very good reasons why both Godfroi and his brother Boudoin were reticent to take the Jerusalem crown and they form part of the encoded story cycles surrounding the Holy Grail, which will be dealt with in a subsequent chapter.

Historians have singularly failed to recognize either the Troyes Fraternity, or the actions it took regarding the capture of Jerusalem. Part of the reason for this ignorance lies in the fact that those ordering events in Champagne were working on several fronts simultaneously. It was only the recognition of the salt line connections of the people concerned, together with a careful piecing together of events that followed, that alerted me to either their existence or their ultimate intentions. With patience and great skill, the Troyes Fraternity, as a strand of the Golden Thread, was organizing the pieces of a giant chess game that covered most of western Europe and also the Near and Middle East. The second stage of the plan, run concurrently with "creating" a Champagne Pope, had been the formation of a new and very special monastic Order.

Another very influential member of the Troyes Fraternity immediately ahead of the First Crusade was a man who had been born in that very city. He would become known as Robert of Molesme and he came from the same noble, ruling elite that would characterize all the major movers and shakers in this fantastic story.

Like Godroi de Bouillon, Robert was coached from childhood to fulfill the part he was to play in the ingenious strategy that was put into place at the end of the eleventh century and appears to be much more than simply "the right man in the right place." As a youth he had entered the Benedictine monastery of Moutier-la-Celle and soon became Prior there. Moutier-la-Celle lay only a few kilometers from Troyes and was much patronized by the rulers of Champagne. No doubt encouraged by them, Robert left Moutier in 1075 and built a new and even more austere abbey in Molesme, also in Champagne. This was the second of his attempts to hijack the Benedictine Order and to create from it an offshoot that would suit his own purposes. The first had been somewhat earlier, at St-Michael-de-Tonnere, yet again in Champagne.

With significant backing from Troyes, Molesme prospered, and was under the strong influence of the great Burgundian monastery of Cluny, where the reforming zeal within monasticism had first been inspired. However, Molesme did not quite suit Robert's purpose, or that of the Troyes Fraternity. With the First Crusade already underway, in 1098, and with a small group of handpicked recruits, Robert was granted land by the Counts of Champagne and the rulers of Burgundy. The area chosen was south of Dijon, capital of Burgundy, and close enough to the center of power for regular communication to take place. The new monastic Order took its name from the region it now inhabited, which was called Citeaux. Henceforth it would be known as the Cistercian Order. Citeaux stands on the same longitudinal salt line that passes through Dijon. (See figure 1.)

Robert did not stay long in Citeaux before returning to Molesme. His purpose was merely to "found" the new Order, the day-to-day running of which was first of all nominally left to one of his deputies, Alberic, but very soon the infant Order was being carefully managed by a man who had been specifically trained by Robert. The man in question was Stephen Harding, one of the few characters in the early stages of the plans laid down by the Troyes Fraternity who was not of Champagne or Burgundian birth. Stephen was English, though he had been carefully rehearsed in the previous years as to what would be expected of both him and the new monastic Order. He suited the position well because he was Anglo-Saxon by birth and heavily influenced by the old Culdean form of Christianity mentioned earlier.

Stephen Harding carefully began to structure the infant Order, writing its various rules and, in careful co-operation with those ruling these events, he laid the foundations for the greatest monastic Order Christianity would ever know. Stephen was not the greatest of the Cistercians, a singular honor that fell to another and even more influential character, Bernard of Clairvaux, but he was a capable administrator and saw the Cistercians through their first, crucial years.

The Cistercian way of life was deliberately hard and unremitting and it was structured like no other Christian monastic Order that had gone before. Nominally, it called itself "reformed Benedictine" but it differed markedly from its supposed parent.

There are two distinctly different ways of looking at the Cistercian Order. From the perspective of the "man in the street" at the beginning of the twelfth century, it represented the acme of the monastic ideal. It espoused extreme poverty, hard work, and prayer. This is how it would come to be viewed and is the reason why it flourished so well – virtually exploding across the landscape of Europe and beyond. But there is another Cistercian Order and one that was meticulously planned to serve a very specific purpose within the remit the Troyes Fraternity had set itself. It is also clear that the Cistercian Order had aspects that, if not considered un-Christian, could certainly be traced to pre-Christian times.

Cistercianism, in a day-to-day sense, was a two-tier system. It was composed of choir monks, who were broadly similar to

Benedictine monks in at least some respects, but it also had a lay brotherhood, which differed from any of its predecessors on the monastic scene. The primary objective of the Cistercian Order was to "grow" and it did so rapidly because of a series of strategies that carried a stroke of genius.

The Cistercians were, from the word go, sheep breeders. The choice of this humble animal for the foundation of what turned out to be a virtual empire had historic parallels. It went way back into the period of the Megalithic priesthood, of which the Troyes Fraternity was the latest manifestation. Sheep breeding and wool production had been practiced on a massive scale in Minoan Crete, with up to 50,000 sheep being owned by the Palace of Knossos alone. It was the absolute mainstay of Minoan civilization. There is strong evidence that the Essene communities of the Jordan Valley had also earned their living by rearing and shearing sheep. There is absolutely no doubt that sheep rearing was a tried and tested strategy and a hallmark of the Golden Thread for over six thousand years. It had built the most powerful and vibrant civilization ever to prosper in Megalithic Europe and it had also fostered a pre-Christian monastic Order with which the Cistercians had much in common. In line with their long and illustrious predecessors, the Cistercians took sheep rearing and made it into an art form. On the way, they sowed the seeds of the modern world and of capitalism.

The Cistercian method of survival and growth was essentially quite simple. The infant Order would search out a piece of marginal land, which it would occupy. Because of its piety and ostensible Christian zeal, the Cistercians would never be refused rights to the areas it occupied by those who held the land. Donations of more land, and of money, were never refused.

However, the phenomenal growth of Cistercianism is not a response to charitable donations as much as to a series of strategies that any modern business corporation would embrace enthusiastically.

Every Cistercian house was a virtual "company" in its own right. It was composed of choir monks and lay brothers. Both choir monks and lay brothers were expected to spend a significant period of each day doing physical work, in addition to the many calls for prayer. Nobody was excused the unremitting toil that epitomized Cistercianism. Each morning the choir monks would meet in the chapter house, and discuss the running of the abbey and its finances. Each choir monk had an equal vote on matters of importance and the prior of each house, as well as the other officers, were democratically chosen in chapter.

Unlike other monastic Orders, the lay brothers were allowed to live in "granges," which were farms, sometimes far from the walls of the abbey. Lay brothers, though not as educated as choir monks, and not ordained priests, could and did become choir monks on occasion.

Each Cistercian abbey was an island of democracy within a great sea of dictatorial feudalism. Within its walls grew the embryo of everything that was to follow and which is still held dear in the hearts of democratic peoples the world over – the right to a share in the determination of one's own life and prosperity. In the case of Cistercianism, this right was willingly deferred on the part of the individual in favor of the Order as a whole – but the right remained immutable nevertheless.

Nor did the sheer genius of Cistercianism remain within single abbeys. When a particular House had achieved a degree of prosperity, usually through clearing sufficient land and raising enough sheep to produce valuable wool that could be sold on the open market, it sought to "clone" itself elsewhere. (Some Cistercian abbeys specialized in other commodities. For example, Morino in Scotland made carts, which served other Cistercian houses and which were also sold on the open market.) At such times a group of monks, usually twelve in number, would leave the "mother house" and found a new abbey somewhere else. This "daughter house" continued to owe a duty to its founding abbey but was run independently on a daily basis.

In a few short decades there were dozens of Cistercian abbeys, stretching from the Holy Land in the east, to Ireland in the west and from the Baltic down to the shores of the Mediterranean. Every one owed an allegiance to its mother house and all owed a responsibility to Citeaux, where the experiment had begun. Priors from each monastery would regularly travel to the appropriate mother house and all priors would be expected to go once each year to Citeaux. The Prior General of Citeaux, and therefore the whole Cistercian family of abbeys, was elected by a conclave of all the other priors and could be removed by them if necessary. Similarly, an individual prior could be replaced if the chapter thought their conduct ill advised or unbecoming.

Just how historians have failed to recognize in Cistercianism the seeds of the political and economic mechanisms that built the modern world is probably the greatest mystery of my many years of research. Cistercianism, and its companion Order, Templarism, were deliberately and knowingly created to destroy feudalism and its lap-dog, the established Roman Church. It is absolutely no coincidence that the dedication of each and every Cistercian monastery was to St. Mary.

CHAPTER 12

The Man who Changed the World

In terms of wealth, the Cistercian Order would eclipse every monastic Order that had preceded it and probably stands as the most successful of all time. This fact is mostly due to the forethought that went into planning the institution and the way it managed so successfully to hijack the selective piety of landowners and to exploit a rapidly increasing population. The achievements of Cistercianism would have been phenomenal in themselves and yet they represented only one facet of the Troy Fraternity's overall strategy.

The ultimately huge network of abbeys, granges, and other holdings that the Cistercians built and acquired saw the landscape of many countries dotted with pockets of self-sufficient democratic communities. By papal decree and by its own Order the Cistercian movement gave nothing away to any other institution; it was freed from paying taxes in every country it inhabited and it possessed a willing and skilful labor force. Both choir monks and lay brothers were fed and had shelter, in an age where neither could be taken for granted. When Cistercians grew sick or old, they were cared for in custom-built infirmaries and, above all, they were safe from what certainly was a cruel and violent world beyond the gates of the abbeys.

Cistercian monks wore white habits of sheep's wool, a departure from the Benedictine Order of which they were supposed to be a part. They also washed regularly, something that shocked other monastic institutions, since washing was considered both unhealthy and an unnecessary and vain indulgence. This was something the Cistercians shared in common with the Essene and it has been suggested that the name "Cistercian' referred specifically to the "cisterns" in which water for communal washing was stored. In the ruins of Qumran and at other Essene centers in the Jordan Valley, evidence has been found of shallow baths, which are taken to be places of ritual immersion. Also like the Essene, the Cistercians looked towards a "New Jerusalem."

In our book *The Templar Continuum*, Stephen Dafoe and I showed that the parallels between the Cistercians and the Essene were so great it is virtually certain that St. Stephen Harding, and those planning the Cistercian movement, possessed copies of Essene books. These would not otherwise be known to the world until the discoveries at Qumran during the middle of the twentieth century.

The plans for the Cistercian Order, laid down by St. Stephen Harding and the Troyes Fraternity, were meticulous. However, its greatest leading light and certainly one of the most important men ever to be born in western Europe did not become a Cistercian until some years after its creation. His name was St. Bernard of Clairvaux.

St. Bernard of Clairvaux was the son of Tescelin Sorrel and Aleth, the daughter of the Lord of Montbard. He was born on the family estates of Fontaines de Dijon, Burgundy, in the year 1090. The place of his birth still exists and a check with a satellite navigation plotter shows the building itself to be as plumb on the longitudinal salt line that runs at 5 degrees 1 minute East of Greenwich. Fontaines de Dijon is extremely close to the mysterious little village of "Is," a location that carries the name of the ancient Goddess to this day and which was an important center of Goddess worship during Roman times and probably before.

Bernard was closely blood tied to a number of Champagne families, including the Montbards on his mother's side. Tescelin, his father, was a cousin to the Counts of Champagne. Only a deep understanding of this man, his motivation, ideas, and actions is likely to open the door to a better understanding of the Troyes Fraternity and its imperatives as part of the Golden Thread.

Throughout all of his life, Bernard left messages, the meaning of which were quite evident to the elect, though the majority of them would have meant nothing to the uninformed. Most importantly, Bernard was not simply "in" the Church, he "was" the Church of his day. He came to be far more powerful than any pope and almost certainly declined that office himself. It is inconceivable that the Vatican would have been denied him had he desired it. Nevertheless, he "owned" the papacy during his adult life and deliberately steered the Roman Catholic Church in a direction that would have been unthinkable before his day. Historically speaking the story of his life is a fascinating one but the full significance of his impact on western Europe is only really possible to understand in light of his true beliefs and intentions.

Little is known of Bernard's very early life. In true medieval style, some versions of his biography suggest that he lived a dissolute and wasted existence until he decided to take holy orders. Later tales tell of a deeply religious child, already the subject of "visions" by his third year. He exploded into history in the year 1112, when, at the age of 22 he suddenly appeared at the gates of Citeaux, at that time still a tiny monastery. Legend has it that Bernard arrived at the head of no fewer than 31 relatives and friends. Approaching the abbot, Bernard declared himself, and them, determined to join the new Cistercian Order so recently established at Citeaux. In all probability, he was expected.

From the date of his arrival, Bernard's rise was nothing short of meteoric. Only three years after arriving at Citeaux, and still at the relatively tender age of 25, Bernard left Citeaux. He was destined to found a new abbey at Clairvaux near Troyes, in other words as close to the seat of power in Champagne as possible. Here, on land specifically granted by Hugh, Count of Champagne, he was installed as abbot and began, immediately, to have a profound effect on Church affairs. This continued, not only within the Cistercian Order, but also far from the cloistered fastness of Clairvaux and to the very throne of the Vatican.

Bernard's own abbey of Clairvaux became the mother house of some 68 further Cistercian houses, though this was just a tiny fraction of all the Cistercian abbeys that would eventually exist worldwide. From the very start of his career, Bernard gained the reputation of being a strict disciplinarian. This seems to have done nothing to curb his popularity, with Church leaders and secular rulers alike.

By 1130, still only 40 years of age, Bernard was already in a position to virtually guarantee the Holy See of Rome to Pope Innocent II against the political intrigue and strong support of the antipope, Anacletus II. This action assured Bernard of a position of authority and influence within the Catholic Church of his day. Eventually one of Bernard's own novices from Clairvaux, Eugene III, was elected Pope. Beyond this point Bernard became, for the remainder of his life, the most powerful voice in Christendom.

Bernard was, at heart, a mystic. It was an event early in his personal career that is said to have had the most profound bearing on his later actions and beliefs. He was holding Mass before a Black Madonna, for which he had the most profound reverence. During the service, he claimed that the figure had lifted her hand to her breast, whereupon drops of milk from the Madonna had fallen into his open mouth. According to Bernard's own testimony, his life was henceforth changed forever. He rapidly became an enthusiastic champion of Mary the Virgin. Thanks to the position he held in the eyes of the Vatican, he was able to convince the western Catholic hierarchy to proclaim the Virgin Mary "Queen of Heaven." This was a position she already held in the eastern Churches but not in the West. Of course, this story must be taken with a pinch of salt because it is obvious that Bernard had been trained from childhood to occupy the position that became his. Undoubtedly, he was the most gifted and able of all his siblings because even his older brothers dutifully followed him into the Cistercian Order.

My research suggests that there was a very real attempt to "hijack" the established Catholic Church during the twelfth century, through a series of actions I have called "the great heresy." The special worship of Mary, as the latest representative of the Great Goddess, formed part of the daring plan. St. Bernard of Clairvaux was a prime mover in what can be seen as a very definite and deliberate perversion of established Church teaching, even though he is still deeply revered within the Church for his piety and humility.

To accuse St. Bernard of Clairvaux, one of the most famous doctors of the Church, of being party to such a plot, if not one of its prime movers, must seem like the most colossal heresy to fervent Catholics. But when all the evidence is reviewed, it becomes apparent that Bernard of Clairvaux was no Christian in the medieval orthodox sense of the word. He was, in truth, an advocate of a feminine principle within western religion and a lineal descendent of the Golden Thread. Bernard may well have believed in the life and ministry of Jesus, but if he did so, it was merely as one part of a continuum that was infinitely older. The fact that St. Bernard claimed Jesus as his personal savior has little to do with the matter in hand. There are innumerable examples of people from around the same period and later who behaved in exactly the same way as Bernard. Ultimately their actions prove that their apparent behavior was deliberately at odds with their true beliefs. These are radical statements, but I hope to show that they are well founded.

What mattered to Bernard of Clairvaux was the survival of a religion that was already ancient when the first pyramids were being built in Egypt. In his comprehension, it must be allowed to survive and flourish. Any price to be paid in the apparent loss of personal integrity was of little consequence. In terms of attitude to faith it seems that Bernard practiced the same principles as a group of people known as the Mandeans. The Mandeans are very much alive today and inhabit parts of Iraq. These people have beliefs that are singularly at odds with established Christian doctrine, but they have vowed to survive as a people with a unique culture. The Christian world eventually hedged them in on all sides. Their chief means of retaining the uniqueness that sets them apart is expressed as follows:

> When Jesus oppresses you, then say: "We belong to you." But do not confess him in your hearts ...

The well-defined group of which Bernard was a part understood very well the message he was really imparting. They were holders of an age-old truth. Knowledge of this fact imbues the words and actions of Bernard with a profound relevance. What those aware of the Golden Thread in Bernard's own time heard from their leader was definitely not the message that came across to orthodox Catholics. There was a deliberate duplicity of word and action that can be seen surfacing time and again throughout St. Bernard's remarkable career.

Of course, I do not expect those reading this book to simply accept this massive assertion on trust. Much of the remainder of this book is dedicated to showing why St. Bernard of Clairvaux acted in the way he did. In this respect, he was far from being alone. A better understanding of Bernard and his real motivations is possible when we take a close look at the main fascinations of his life. The evidence that follows, together with these imperatives, helps to demonstrate where his true allegiances lay.

1. Bernard showed a reverence for the feminine, expressed in his adoration of the Virgin Mary. This was quite at odds with the doctrine and dogma of the Roman Catholic Church prior to his day.

2. Bernard had a particular reverence for sacred architecture, of a type that suddenly appeared in France during his lifetime. He considered that church buildings should be free from any ornamentation that was not strictly necessary. He seems to have been responsible for the founding of many of the great Gothic cathedrals of northern and central France and took a personal hand in their design. There is certainly no doubt that he understood the principles that underpinned Gothic architecture.

3. Bernard believed that music was extremely important to worship. Under his guidance, music sung in abbeys took on a new beauty and a fresh meaning. He constantly stated that, in

worship, the ears were more important than the eyes. This falls in line very much with his reverence for the particular form of architecture he championed.

4. Bernard showed a particular fascination for anything associated with the life of the Jewish King Solomon. He had a great interest in Solomon's Jerusalem Temple, as described in the Old Testament. As we shall see, he was a prime mover in the formation of the Knights Templar, who were named for Solomon's Temple. Bernard also displayed what amounted to a virtual obsession with a strange piece of literature from the Old Testament, which is attributed to Solomon and which is known as "The Song of Songs."

5. On more than one occasion Bernard referred to God as being "Height and breadth and depth and width." This declaration underpins a fascination for numbers and for geometry. As we shall see, both lie at the heart of a true knowledge of the Golden Thread.

6. At a time when Jews in France and the surrounding regions were not especially popular, Bernard showed them great respect. On several occasions he traveled significant distances to protect a people who were not of his own faith. He personally stopped or prevented several pogroms. And all this came from a man who was apparently committed to a dogma that expressly blamed the Jews for the trial and crucifixion of Jesus.

7. Bernard was particularly interested in those locations where "Black Madonnas" were to be found. Many of these strange

dark statues are not Christian in origin, a fact that Bernard must have known. A high percentage of the great Gothic cathedrals originally planned or sanctioned by Bernard were on sites that housed Black Madonnas.

Little of this may seem particularly surprising, until the reasons for these specific interests and beliefs are understood. Once they are, Bernard becomes a man whose real motives are radically different from the ones that have been ascribed to him by orthodox sources.

The abbey that Bernard built, at Clairvaux, close to Troyes in Champagne, occupied a very important geographical setting and one that makes it obvious that its builder fully understood Megalithic geometry and that he was truly a priest of the Golden Thread. The site of Clairvaux is now a prison and only fragments of the original abbey survive but when this location is checked carefully on a detailed map, several factors make themselves known.

Clairvaux occupies a position on the latitudinal salt line to be found at latitude 48 degrees 11 minutes North and is in such a position that the circumference of the Earth at the latitude it occupies is "exactly" two thirds that of the equatorial circumference of the planet. There are very important reasons why this latitude would be significant in Megalithic terms. The distance across one Megalithic degree of the circumference of the Earth (East–West) is 60 Megalithic minutes of arc at the equator. At Clairvaux it is exactly two thirds of this, which can be seen as equivalent to 40 equatorial Megalithic minutes of arc. The number 40 is the most potent and important number of all to Megalithic mathematics. In addition, and perhaps most surprising of all, the position of Clairvaux was chosen with such meticulous care that the abbey can be shown to stand precisely 31 Megalithic degrees West of Solomon's Temple in Jerusalem. St. Bernard's own knowledge of these matters is aptly demonstrated by a specific event in his life.

Bernard was a great traveler, continually moving around on his diplomatic quests. Whilst he was on his extensive journeys to champion the cause of a new pope, Innocent II, around 1130, Bernard's underlings found themselves in a dilemma. Such was the popularity of Clairvaux that people were seeking to become monks there in great numbers. This meant new accommodation had to be built as the community grew ever larger and St. Bernard's lieutenants took it upon themselves to move the abbey of Clairvaux a kilometer or so further down the valley, to where more land was available. Work was already underway on this project when Bernard returned. For reasons that have never been fully understood before, Bernard was absolutely furious about the relocation of Clairvaux, and insisted that it be reinstated on its original site. Clearly, St. Bernard of Clairvaux knew the real importance of the "absolute" positioning of his abbey, attested to by his anger on this occasion.

The name of St. Bernard of Clairvaux will surface again many times in the pages that follow. He is an integral part of the story of Goddess survival in the modern world and of the Holy Grail. At a personal level, he was a remarkable man. He could be irascible, argumentative, and yet deeply likeable. So great is his historical influence that he was canonized within 20 years of his death. He was also formerly declared a Doctor of the Church as recently as 1830. St. Bernard is generally considered to have been the last of the Fathers of the Church. His saint day is celebrated on 20 August, which is the anniversary of his death at Clairvaux in 1153. By his own admission St. Bernard was a mystic, a fact that, despite his apparent pragmatism in matters of conduct, he never sought to deny during his life. The depth of that mysticism and the secrets it protected has never been revealed from the twelfth century up to the present day.

Late in the nineteenth century, the skull of this little man from Dijon was reverentially placed into a magnificent golden reliquary. The creation of this solid gold casket predated Bernard's own life by several centuries and how St. Bernard's only surviving remains came to be placed in it represents a story that is worthy of a book in its own right. The reliquary was then put in the Treasury of Troyes Cathedral, where it resides to this day on public display. It will be obvious to readers already that Troyes is clearly the most fitting place for this most revered relic and it was most certainly placed there by people who already knew most if not all the fantastic story that follows in this book. Those responsible were legatees of the Troyes Fraternity and were priests of the Golden Thread, which I hope to demonstrate is as alive today as it was when St. Bernard of Clairvaux walked the streets of Troyes himself.

Amongst so many remarkable achievements in the life of St. Bernard of Clairvaux, there is one accomplishment that stands out as being more important than any other. This was his championing and indeed virtual creation of a companion Order to the Cistercians. Instead of monks, who lived isolated and peaceful lives in or near to their abbeys, the new brothers would be ferocious warriors who would travel across the known world and beyond. This Order was properly known as "The Poor Knights of Christ and the Temple of Solomon" but it is best known today as the Knights Templar.

CHAPTER 13

The White Knights

Around the year 1118, a small group of minor French nobles arrived at the palace of King Baudoin II of Jerusalem. Baudoin I, brother of Godfroi de Bouillon, had died only months before and since he had no children, he had been succeeded by his nephew, Baudoin of Bourg. Baudoin II lived in a palace on the Temple Mount, close to the Mosque of Omar that still stands on the site. The French knights begged assistance and accommodation from the king. He graciously gave them the stables of the old Temple as their headquarters. Nine years later these same nobles returned to France. There, with the aid of St. Bernard, they were formerly declared to be a religious Order in their own right, with all the privileges that this inferred.

But why had this strange little group gone to Jerusalem in the first place and what did they do there for nine long years, prior to the official foundation of the Knights Templar? The general explanation for their presence was that it was their sworn desire to guard the roads from the coast to Jerusalem, in order to keep pilgrims safe on their journey to the Holy City. Clearly, this is nonsense. Firstly, there is no evidence whatsoever that the pilgrims in question were in any real danger and in any case nine knights, no matter how diligent, could not have had much of a bearing on the situation.

During the whole period of their initial stay the embryonic Templars never sought or admitted a single recruit to their cause, except for one, Hugh, Count of Champagne. We shall come to see that why he was a very special and noteworthy exception.

The truth of what the knights were really doing in Jerusalem has been a source of speculation for decades. The various possibilities have been discussed by so many authors that the total weight of the books produced would probably exceed that of Solomon's Temple itself. It is now often suggested that the original Templars spent the intervening period digging beneath the ancient stables, intent on discovering Jewish relics. These, it is said, may have represented actual treasure, or something of more intrinsic worth.

Some of the supposed early Templar actions have passed to modern Freemasonry, where a section of Freemasonic ritual was created at some time in the past that offers a graphic account of their exploits as "human moles." However, even this garbled account does little to indicate what the true finds might have been. Some light may be thrown on the mystery if we could discover more about the men concerned, the relationships they enjoyed with each other and the source of their shared enthusiasm for the project. Knowledge of the existence of the Troyes Fraternity can provide us with evidence that has never surfaced previously.

The first Templar knights were led by a minor aristocrat called Hugh de Payen. This man held a fief in northwest Troyes, at precisely that point through which the longitudinal salt line passes, (48 degrees 19 minutes North, 4 degrees 2 minutes East.). Hugh de Payen was a vassal and cousin of his important namesake Hugh, Count of Champagne and was without doubt a leading light in the Troyes Fraternity.

The original Templar band also included Andre de Montbard, who was none other than the uncle of St. Bernard of Clairvaux. In fact, many of the members of the first Templar brotherhood seems to have formed a tight little family group and, where it is possible to identify the points of origin of the original Templar knights, they were, to a man, of salt line ancestry.

Hugh de Payen may have been blood tied to the Montbards, who were St. Bernard's family on his mother's side. Meanwhile, the Montbard and Champagne families were also related to Baudoin II, which partly explains how the original nine knights came to be welcomed into Jerusalem in the first place.

The original story of the knights turning up at the gates of the palace in Jerusalem, dusty from their journey and with no visible means of support is clearly ludicrous. In reality, in twelfth-century France friends could not come much higher than the Counts of Champagne, who ruled a rich and powerful region. The influence of this family would have been enough to ensure the small band of a welcome at the court of Baudoin II. Hugh of Champagne himself seems to have been content to allow the first Templars to commence their expedition without him, though we can be reasonably sure that he was kept well in touch with the proceedings. It wasn't long before he joined them in Jerusalem and became a Templar himself.

Whatever the brotherhood forming the Templars had in common, apart from their salt line heritage, it was to make them unbelievably rich. For some unknown reason, historians have often played down the importance of the Templars in European affairs. Speculative writers have chosen the opposite direction, at times elevating the Templars to the rank of "supermen." Both points of view are equally at odds with the truth. What is certain is that the Templars took the world by storm. In a couple of decades, their place in European history was assured. It would be incredible to suggest that it all happened by chance. In reality, a great deal of planning, probably for generations, lay behind the Templar enterprise and their initial trip to Jerusalem.

No single group of people is more important in our search for continued Goddess worship than the Knights Templar. It was a combination of the knowledge they already possessed, plus the further insights from their nine-year stay in Jerusalem that allowed them to become the most influential institution in medieval western Europe. They are primarily responsible for the foundations of the world we know today.

Of course, the salt line connections of the first Templar knights might be nothing more than a coincidence. Even the family ties could be seen as being quite reasonable in an age where vested interest usually contained a dynastic element. In reality, the unraveling evidence shows that there was no coincidence and that the blood connections were of the utmost importance. Generation by generation, these families had passed on information which could only be fully exploited when something of tremendous importance was discovered in Jerusalem. But what could that "something" have been, and what was the existent knowledge that it confirmed?

Many authors have speculated that the prize might have been the Holy Grail itself. This has now generally come to mean the precious cup from which Jesus drank at the Last Supper. Miraculously it is suggested that this object had survived for over a thousand years. It was, asserted some writers, to be found secreted deep beneath the ruins of Solomon's Temple. However, no mention of the Grail being in any way associated with Christianity appeared until well after the first Grail story of Chretien de Troyes around 1180. Chretien did mention the Grail – but not in a Christian context. As we shall see, Chretien de Troyes was a prime mover in the Troyes Fraternity. Had he known that the Grail had such profound Christian connections he is unlikely to have omitted to mention the fact in his writings.

If the Templars had truly found the cup of Jesus, it is hard to see how or why they would have chosen to keep the fact a secret. The survival of the object would have been of the most tremendous importance to the Christianity of the day. Holy Communion lay at the very heart of Christian mysticism. To possess the cup once used by Jesus in the first Communion would have bestowed upon its possessors incredible status. It is hard to contemplate such a secret being maintained or even to understand why it should be.

Not all Grail stories, even the later ones, consider the Grail to be a cup at all. In some versions of the legend, the Grail is a stone. It has been frequently suggested that what the Knights Templar actually found in Jerusalem was the Ark of the Covenant. Essentially the Ark was a wooden box, covered in sheet gold and provided with long poles for handles. It was used to carry the sacred laws of the Hebrew people, carved onto two stones, as they had been passed down to Moses on Mount Sinai. The Hebrews believed that God himself lived in the Ark. The Ark was created whilst the Jews were wandering in the wilderness, immediately after the flight from Egypt. It remained with them through the 40 years of their stay in the desert until they eventually arrived in, and conquered, Palestine.

Once Jerusalem was secured, a permanent home was created for both the Ark and its contents. King Solomon, around the year 900 BC, constructed a magnificent temple on what had been the sacred Jebusite threshing floor. Within this building there was a room specifically created to house the Ark.

All of these facts are mentioned in the Old Testament of the Bible, but beyond the life of Solomon, no record of the survival of the Ark exists. It is as if the object simply disappeared from history. The very mystery of the disappearance of such a holy object has funded the many stories relating to the survival of the Ark. Some authors think that it was discovered by the Knights Templar, hidden in the cellars of Solomon's Temple. Later, it is suggested, the Ark was brought to Europe.

Once again, the question must be asked. If the Templars discovered the Ark of the Covenant, why did they choose the keep the find a secret? There is nothing regarding this assertion that stands up to any kind of scrutiny. A whole kingdom could have been bought for the sale of the true cup of Jesus or the genuine Ark of the Covenant. If the Templars had a genuine relic of this importance, the fact was never mentioned during the two centuries of their official existence. Neither has it surfaced since.

A few months after returning from Jerusalem in 1127, most of the original Templar knights found themselves involved in an elaborate ceremony. This was held, appropriately, in Troyes. In January of 1128 a council was convened during which the Templar Order was officially recognized by the Church. Its rules were accepted, having been drawn up by St. Bernard of Clairvaux to match those of the Cistercian Order. Hugh de Payen was granted the title of first Grand Master. Henceforth, the Templars would wear white mantles like those of the Cistercians but unlike their brother monks they would not shave. In a short time, Templars became quite distinctive with their long beards and ultimately, they sported the famous red cross that was to become their emblem. Their Order made it plain that they were to fight for Christianity wherever this was necessary, but especially in the Holy Land and particularly against the Muslims there.

The Templars functioned in a very similar way to the Cistercians, except for the fact that their predominant reason for existing was to fight. Like the Cistercians they were monks, who had taken solemn and binding vows. Although the Templars showed tremendous and even fanatical bravery in the face of their enemies, as the Order grew, only a very small percentage of Templar brothers would ever come to meet an enemy in battle. On the contrary, the vast majority of Templars existed to support and administer a growing empire of farms, churches, castles, ships, and other economic institutions. Like the Cistercians, the Templars were farmers *par excellence*, also specializing in sheep rearing. The advantage they had over the Cistercian Order is that they could travel and indulge in commerce with the secular world.

In 1139, Pope Innocent II, who was every bit St. Bernard's man, issued a papal Bull. In this Bull, Pope Innocent declared that, henceforth, the Templars would be responsible to no religious or secular authority but the Pope himself. There are clear reasons why this should have been a prudent move as far as the Holy See was concerned. The Templars were already becoming extremely powerful, particularly in military terms. The existence of such an army, which responded only to the wishes of the Pope, would have added tremendous weight to papal authority. It might even sway the judgment of otherwise wayward monarchs throughout Europe. In reality, the Templar Order became so powerful it behaved more or less as it wished.

But even before the papal Bull, Hugh de Payen had traveled extensively, gaining favor wherever he went. Almost as soon as the Templar Order was established, in 1128, he visited England. Throughout the whole realm, he was received with the greatest enthusiasm. However, in all his travels Hugh never mentioned one word about any Jerusalem discovery.

Everywhere the Grand Master went the younger sons of nobles

flocked to join the Order. Only two years later Hugh returned to Palestine, taking with him a personal entourage of 300 fully armed knights. Behind him, he left an already wealthy institution in Europe. Money was amassed from every conceivable direction, and most of it was put to good use making more money. None of it appears to have resulted from anything found in Jerusalem. During the two centuries of Templar existence, the same silence prevailed, though perhaps this is not so surprising, bearing in mind the nature of the Order.

Secrecy attended the real intentions of the Templars from the word go. Only on those occasions when financial transactions affected the exchequers of kings do we ever find any real reference to Templar wealth. This pattern went on for nearly two hundred years.

A knowledge of the Troyes Fraternity and its overall strategy demonstrates that the Templar Order had been an intended part of its *raison d'etre* from the word go. Under the pretence of traveling to fight for Christianity, the Templars spread their influence far and wide. They became the world's first bankers and they effectively created both credit and the check book.

Any person wishing to travel, for example from Paris to London with a large amount of money, could use the Templar network to ensure their safe arrival. Money would be lodged at the Templar headquarters in Paris and the client would receive a cipher note. Upon arriving in London, the merchant would go to the Templar headquarters there, where the cipher note would be redeemed for local currency. This was an extremely useful service at a time when roads and byways were plagued by outlaws. Of course, this service was not free. At the time, to charge interest was against Christian law, but who could argue with an institution that was under the direct authority of the Pope himself?

The Templars quickly assembled a large fleet of ships, both fighting craft and merchantmen. With great skill and overwhelming force, they patrolled the shipping lanes in the North Sea and the Mediterranean, creating safe passage for their own ships. Under the pretence of keeping their forces in the Holy Land supplied with horses and fighting men, the Templars created trading networks that were specifically geared to plans being laid within Champagne itself. Their command center was, and remained, Troyes.

Wool from England, much of which was produced by the Cistercian monasteries, was transshipped by the Templars to Flanders. There it was woven into fine cloth. Other Templars secured the roads of western Europe, building tolls and keeping thieves at bay. Finished woolen cloth from Flanders was taken to Champagne, where great fairs were established. Each of the cities of the region held fairs at specific times during each year. Merchants came to the Champagne fairs from all over Europe and far beyond creating a network of international trade that made the region famous for three centuries.

In an incredibly short period of time, the Poor Knights of Christ and the Temple of Solomon had created what amounted to a monopoly of trade throughout Europe and across the Mediterranean. In one way or another they made money from almost any transaction that took place, and all in the name of their support for Christianity. Meanwhile, the inner workings of their own institution remained shrouded in mystery. True, the rules of the Order were laid down for anyone to see, but what actually took place behind the secret walls of the Templar establishments was barred to all but the select few.

Amazingly, when the Order was outlawed and abolished in 1307, no trace of any great treasury was ever found. All that remained for the crowned heads of Europe to appropriate were the lands owned by the Templars. Even the vast Templar fleet, usually tied up at La Rochelle, disappeared from history without trace. Every Templar establishment in France and far beyond was ransacked. If anything of worth had been brought out of Jerusalem at the commencement of the Order – it was never rediscovered after 1307.

In my estimation, consideration of what the Templars might have actually discovered beneath the Temple Mound in Jerusalem is of secondary importance, as is the mystery of the years they spent there before becoming a fully fledged monastic Order in their own right. A close look at the popes who were in office between the nine knights arriving at the palace of Baudoin II and their return to France in 1127 shows that they were of predominantly Italian extract and were therefore not predisposed to support Champagne interests. In addition, the ecclesiastical mouthpiece of the Troyes Fraternity, St. Bernard of Clairvaux, needed years to build his influence to such an extent that he could come to persuade the Pope that an Order of fighting monks was either religiously legal or politically expedient. In other words it was important for the Templars to stake their claim in Jerusalem as quickly as possible but they probably knew that they must remain there years before recognition by the Church would be forthcoming.

Nevertheless, the question of the lost Templar years remains, as does the fact that they were billeted in the stables adjoining the royal palace, almost certainly right over the ruins of the first and second Jewish Temples. It should be remembered that there was not one, but two very definite Jerusalem connections associated with the Golden Thread and its European offshoot, the Troyes Fraternity. The movers and shakers in Troyes were of Merovingian descent, which meant they were also ultimately of Benjamite Jewish blood. In addition, the bloodline of Jesus, via Mary Magdalene, had passed into that of the Merovingians at an early date. It is quite possible that information regarding items safeguarded in the anterooms of the Jerusalem Temples had been passed down the generations. It seems therefore extremely likely that what the Templars had been dispatched to discover was likely to have been "knowledge" rather than any tangible artifact, which the Romans would almost certainly have removed in any case after the Jewish uprising of AD 66. Bearing in mind the great similarities between the Cistercians and the Essene of the Jordan Valley, ancient books were certainly already held by the Troyes Fraternity. It is quite possible that what they sought was further corroboration of their own past and heritage. Events that took place in Europe, both during Templar times and afterwards, substantiate this belief.

In a sense, so much has been written dealing with what the Templars may or may not have discovered in Jerusalem that this has merely served to obscure what was really happening during the twelfth century. A short recap might be helpful. A group of nobles springing from the Merovingian bloodline, and of ultimately Megalithic origin, began to find their ancient religious beliefs threatened by the strangle-hold of feudalism and an ever more repressive Christian Church. Elaborate plans were laid to alter both state and Church, in order to allow religious practices held sacred for thousands of years to continue. A multi-pronged strategy was formulated. This involved ensuring that

Jerusalem would be captured and that a representative of the Troyes Fraternity would be placed on the throne there.

Meanwhile, a new and revolutionary monastic Order was created, which would gradually subvert the very basis of the feudal economy. It was designed to grow rapidly and in order to ensure that it followed the appointed course, a young man born of a significant Troyes Fraternity family, Bernard of Clairvaux, was put in charge of it.

With Jerusalem secure and in sympathetic hands, the Troyes Fraternity then embarked upon the next stage of its plans – to build the largest and most powerful standing army the West had ever known. But this institution would be much more and the reality of its fighting acumen merely masked its economic intentions. Champagne was made the economic heart of Europe, and at the center of Champagne was Troyes, also the home base of the Templars. None of these situations can be divorced from each other and it is impossible to see these events as being coincidence. At the back of them all stands the form of the ancient Goddess and the sacred salt lines that had been laid down as early as 3000 BC. The form of the Goddess remains central to all that was taking place. In her new persona, as the Virgin Mary, every Cistercian abbey was named for her and hers was the name the Templars cried as they went into battle.

The greatest wonder of all is that every one of these plans and strategies was put into place with the absolute approval of the established Roman Catholic Church, which was outmaneuvered at every turn, for over two centuries. The same is true of the dictatorial monarchs of the region, whose power base was gradually eroded as international trade broke local monopolies and encouraged free enterprise.

However, not every churchman or king was stupid and there came a time when the great heresy was recognized for what it truly was. The destruction of the Templars and the gradual demise of the Cistercian Order could have put paid to the influence of the Golden Thread forever. It is fortunate for the freedoms most of us still hold dear today that over three thousand years of experience and knowledge were not so easily swept aside.

CHAPTER 14

The Grail Appears

If anyone doubts that the Holy Grail was an invention of the priesthood of the Golden Thread and its medieval manifestation, the Troyes Fraternity, they merely have to monitor its first appearance in western literature. Across several centuries, ideas about what the Grail might actually be and the adventures of those who sought it, captivated people throughout the whole of Europe and beyond. As we shall see, the Grail has a truly ancient pedigree. However, its medieval connection with the Goddess began in Champagne and during the pivotal period during which the Cistercians and the Templars were at their most powerful.

The Holy Grail was first mentioned in the Champagne city of Troyes, which has already figured heavily in the pages of this book. Later stories relating to the Grail originated in many different parts of western Europe but the Troyes story was most certainly the original. It was written around 1188, by a man about whom we know very little. His name was Chretien de Troyes.

Chretien's story is entitled *Le Roman de Perceval* and it is the tale of a hero, a young man by the name of Perceval. Perceval sets off on a mysterious journey, leaving behind his widowed mother. The young man wishes to gain his knighthood and the narrative deals with all kinds of adventures that he encounters on the way. During his travels, Perceval comes across an old man. This is the famous "Fisher King" of all later Grail stories. The Fisher King owns a castle, to which the young hero is invited. It is during a banquet at the castle that the Grail first appears. Very few details are offered regarding the Grail. We are told that it is created from gold and that it is studded with precious jewels. It is also made clear that whenever the Grail appears, it is carried by a beautiful young virgin. Beyond these few facts, Chretien remains silent regarding the Grail.

Chretien makes it clear in his narrative that Perceval is ignorant of the fact that he is supposed to ask a question relating to the Grail. This is a rather ambiguous question, and the closest approximation to Chretien's version in modern English would be: "Whom does one serve with it?" Much of what follows in this book will be aimed at answering this strange question of the Grail and also in explaining what the question means.

In Chretien's story Perceval fails to ask the question, and wakes the next day to discover that the Fisher King and everyone in the castle has mysteriously disappeared. He staggers from the castle to find that a terrible blight has come upon the land. Later he learns that the Fisher King is his own uncle. At the point where the story breaks off, Perceval undergoes a sort of religious crisis regarding the events in the Grail castle and this has a bearing on his subsequent belief in God.

If Chretien de Troyes did complete the tale of Perceval, the finished draft has not survived. This might be because a great fire ravaged the city of Troyes at about the time the story was under construction. It is equally possible that Chretien only half understood the truth of the Grail story himself

The origins of the Grail extend far back into prehistory. Although the Grail is sometimes referred to as a stone, or even a plate, most commonly it came to be thought of as a cup of some sort. Specifically it has become directly associated with the chalice used by Jesus at the Last Supper. In this regard, the symbol was far from new with the advent of Christianity. Its lineage goes back into the recesses of our most distant religious beliefs. There has never been any doubt in my mind that the basic allusion here is to the "sacred womb" of the Goddess, which had been transformed into magic vessels in the story cycles of many peoples. To the Celts, the direct legatees of the Megalithic West, the Grail had begun its life as "magical cauldrons," such as that possessed by an important hero and semi-divine character known as Bran.

These magic cauldrons were a form of "cornucopia" or horns of plenty and even in Celtic mythology, they are sometimes called horns. In fact, the association with the horn is very early, and quite symbolic. The horn is yet another representation of the womb and it was also a drinking vessel. The reverse aspect of the horn, i.e. its external features, was closely associated with the phallus. As a result, both male and female organs could be represented by the same object. The horns and magic cauldrons could supply food in times of famine, but some of them even had the ability to bring slain warriors back to life.

In Greek terms the horn, and therefore the sacred vessel of the womb, became the Krater, which also means cup. There is a constellation of stars known as the Krater. In modern parlance this is "Crater" and is a group of six stars to the south of Virgo, the Virgin. It is best seen from northern latitudes low in the sky in the spring. As the summer advances, so the Sun appears to move along the zodiac. As it does so, it gets closer and closer to Virgo. At this time the tilt of the Earth seems greater, so the Crater disappears from view. Crater is below and to the right of Virgo, the constellation that is so closely associated with the fertility goddess.

The Sun occupies the constellation of Virgo at harvest time. When the Sun "warms the virgin" the earth is fruitful. To the Greeks, Crater was sacred to "Krataiis," "the strong one," an alternative and oft-used name for Hekate. In turn, Hekate was identical to Persephone, one of the most evocative expressions of the Great Goddess. Women often wore amulets depicting Hekate. She was the goddess who helped at the time of childbirth. If Crater is a "womb," then it is undoubtedly the womb of the figure that is now known as Virgo, the Virgin. As the constellation of Crater dips to meet the horizon, so the bounty from the womb of Virgo spills out onto the land, bringing fruit and grain to the northern hemisphere.

Despite the fact that something akin to the Grail goes far back into the recesses of mythology, the work of Chretien de Troyes is the obvious starting point in terms of Grail stories in medieval times, since nothing before it carrying the actual word "Grail" exists. So truncated and obtuse is Chretien's contribution to the Grail that it seems to offer little that could have led the world into the frenzy that was to become the search for the Holy Grail since. But perhaps a better understanding of the world of which Chretien de Troyes was part may throw some light on the importance of this first little tale and what happened after.

Although little is known about Chretien himself, the city of Troyes during his period is not such a mystery. We do know about Chretien's patrons around the time he was composing the Perceval tale. Much of Chretien's previous work had been of a very different nature. Most of it was lyric poetry and had been dedicated to Marie de Champagne, the wife of the Count of Champagne, one of the most powerful regional rulers of the period and undoubtedly the latest representative of the Troyes Fraternity. But the Perceval tale was not created for Marie. This work was dedicated to Philippe d'Alcace, Count of Flanders, whose own domains lay predominantly further north, with his capital in the present day city of Lille. Nevertheless Philippe is known to have spent much of his time in Troyes, and we can take it that he too was a priest of the Golden Thread and a member of the Troyes Fraternity. Lille is one of the capital cities of old France that is sited on a longitudinal salt line.

Around the time that Chretien de Troyes was creating his Perceval story, western Europe was in ferment. Despite the best efforts of the Knights Templar, Jerusalem had recently been lost to the forces of Islam. This almost unthinkable event came after a century of dominance by kings allied to the Troyes Fraternity who occupied the throne of the Holy City. Everyone was blaming his neighbor for this terrible state of affairs. One fact was certain; there were not the resources, the will, or perhaps both, to reverse the disaster. Successive new Christian crusades had done little or nothing to throw back the hordes of Muslims. The Saracens, under the command of Saladin, finally captured Jerusalem in 1187 and Muslim forces would eventually use this gain as a springboard to oust the Christians from the Holy Land altogether.

All of this represented a monumental disaster for western and eastern Christianity alike but it was of even more significance to the Troyes Fraternity. It had been the pretence of access to the holy sites of Jerusalem that had allowed the economic power-base of Troyes to be built and nobody suffered more from the loss of the Holy Land than the Knights Templar.

St. Bernard of Clairvaux had been dead for 25 years when Chretien de Troyes was writing his first Grail story. It is quite conceivable that Chretien would have known Bernard, who spent much time in Troyes. The loss of this most pivotal character had clearly also been a blow to the aspirations of those ruling events in Champagne.

The Troyes of Chretien's period was a rich city, with a reputation for learning. It was certainly considered to be one of the most "civilized" places in the whole of Europe. People from all over the known world gathered in Troyes. So powerful had they become in the previous decades, the Counts of Champagne were now as good as kings in their own lands and though paying lip service to monarchs within the French domains themselves, they were, to all intents and purposes, autonomous.

At the center of all medieval cities lay the church. From humble parish churches to the great cathedrals, they were around every corner. Their presence demonstrated the absolute power of the Catholic Church as an institution. Troyes was no different in this regard to any other city. Successive Counts of Champagne were anxious to acknowledge the part Christianity played in welding together the fabric of their society, even if there was a degree of "pretence" involved. Such a course of action was extremely prudent. Despite the continued economic success and the power base the Troyes Fraternity enjoyed, the Roman Catholic hierarchy of Chretien de Troyes' time was massive, unyielding, and stifling, to prince and peasant alike.

Walking through the streets of Troyes in his own period, Chretien would have encountered a number of wonderful churches, many of which remain. He would also have seen a great and glorious cathedral. Though now crowded in by narrow, picturesque streets with numerous cafes and white-gabled houses, it is still one of the glories of France. This is the Cathedral where the skull of St. Bernard of Clairvaux is now housed in its magnificent reliquary.

Probably even during Chretien's life, there had been a huge revolution in church architecture. The massive, fortress-like, Romanesque churches of an earlier time were being replaced by the soaring masterpieces of the Gothic era. New techniques in building, supposedly discovered in the Middle East, were being employed. Instead of architectural forces pushing down hard on massive foundations that had to be gargantuan to take the weight, new techniques were employed. Flying buttresses and the use of the "ogive," a pointed arch that lies at the very heart of what became known as "Gothic" design, was allowing stresses to be distributed more evenly. In turn, this made it possible to give these very beautiful buildings much thinner walls. It also permitted vast window spaces.

New methods in glass making, the techniques of which are now lost to us, meant that the huge windows could become a blaze of colored light. This new glass did not depend on the quality of the light shining through it, but offered the same steady, radiant glow through even the most gray of winter days.

The best makers of glass at this time were Flemish, and therefore the subjects of Philippe d'Alcace, Count of Flanders. This was the man for whom Chretien de Troyes seems to have been working when he wrote the Perceval story. In the preface to his story of Perceval, Chretien states that the idea for the tale actually came from Philippe. Chretien would certainly have been very familiar with the Knights Templar. By the end of the twelfth century the Templars represented an institution that was rather less than a century old. They already constituted the single most important economic group in the whole of Europe. Troyes retained central command over the whole Templar Empire.

It is likely that the Templars had assisted in the design and building of many of Troyes' new churches. Templars were accomplished architects and masons. Their ideas and acumen had fully inspired the Gothic style of architecture that was rapidly gaining in popularity.

The Templars had gone from strength to strength and by the period at which Chretien was writing his tale of Percival, they virtually controlled entire economies. Hardly a decision was made by any monarch of the period that did not involve discussions with the Templars. Financially speaking they held the crowned heads of Europe in the palms of their collective hands. Nevertheless, by Chretien's era the Knights Templar were the subject of sustained criticism in certain sections of society. The gradual loss of the Holy Land was being blamed, in part, on their unwillingness to fight against Muslim forces with whom they were said to be too quick to form alliances. Such accusations were strenuously denied. Even an institution as large as that which the Templars represented could never have secured the entire Levant without significant assistance. Chronicles from the period demonstrate that the necessary commitment was definitely lacking, especially from the kings of Europe. Under these circumstances, the indignation voiced by the Templars is probably justified.

It is difficult to say exactly what medieval society as a whole really thought about the Templar Order. Those who inherited powerful positions within society certainly feared the Templars, and with good reason. This was a period during which no monarch could have afforded to support a large standing army of his own. The Knights Templar, on the other hand, now had thousands of men at arms, kept in a constant state of readiness. Such was their fighting skill that virtually no force, even if equal in terms of numbers, would have stood any chance of beating them in open combat. The Templar vow was that they would never leave a battle, or seek surrender, unless they were outnumbered by at least three to one. In practical terms, they never seem to have deviated from this undertaking.

Templar strength had not really been a problem to the crowned heads of Europe while the majority of the Templar knights were garrisoned far from Europe, in the Holy Land. However, with the fall of Jerusalem many of the brother Knights were back in the lands of their birth and no area had given birth to more of them than France itself. Monarchs had other reasons to feel rather uneasy about the Templar institution. For most kings, great or small alike, money was hard to come by. Wars were frequent and costly. Those waging wars would use any means at their disposal to get their hands on sufficient wealth to form and feed an army large enough to meet their needs. Often this money came from Templar funds. There are examples, from both France and England, of situations that necessitated the total exchequers of kings being deposited in Templar establishments. These were held in lieu of the vast amounts owed to them by the sovereigns in question.

The Templars often arbitrated in disputes between rulers and their vassals. Their impartiality seems to have been trusted implicitly during the eleventh century. By the middle of the twelfth century, things were probably different. The sheer economic and military strength of the Templars would have made it inadvisable for the most autocratic rulers to turn away their offers of arbitration, even if these were not so welcome.

The more time that passed, the greater did the wealth of the Templars become. Nobles who had fought in the Holy Land, and who may have been impressed by the Templar ideals, would often leave vast tracts of land to the Templars at their deaths. It has been suggested that coercion took place to bring about these ends. Most likely, these assertions represent part of the slur campaign that that would lead to the destruction of the Templar Order in the fourteenth century.

As we have seen, the Templars became the first bankers of Europe. Templar money was constantly being used and increased. Much of what we now accept as capitalism was forged from the feudal way of life endemic to Europe in the medieval period by the efforts, ideas, and sheer business sense of the Knights Templar. It was the Templar way of doing business that would eventually put paid to feudalism in the West. Ultimately, the principles to which the Order held and the services it offered were copied by the wealthy families that inspired the Renaissance. This came a couple of centuries after the Templars had been outlawed, but the methods used were exclusively theirs. As we shall see, in many respects the Templars, or at least their legatees, were still involved.

Chretien de Troyes did not directly mention the Templars in his Perceval story, probably for the sake of political expediency. However, later writers on the Grail theme certainly did. Almost from the very start, Templarism seems to be connected with the search for the Holy Grail. There are very specific reasons for this and the main one relates to "chivalry."

The knight as a military convention had already come into his own a century and a half before the time of Perceval. One of the reasons popes had been willing to create the Templars and to go on supporting the Order, lay in their fear of heavily armed warriors, against whom the ill-trained and equipped infantry of the period had no chance.

Over the years, the Church had suffered as much as anyone, partly because it was a tremendously wealthy institution that was vulnerable to aristocratic infighting. Before the advent of the

Templars, and other military monastic Orders such as the Knights Hospitaller, the Church had relied on the goodwill of its subjects to protect its own interests. If only "might" was right, then the Church itself was vulnerable to the mounted warrior knights. It was therefore fairly inevitable that Catholicism would ultimately come to adopt its own fighting forces, which, ostensibly, was exactly what the Knights Templar represented.

The evolution of the idea of "chivalry," demonstrated by warriors who were also monks, became popular, even with secular knights. The "quest," undertaken by Chretien de Troyes' Perceval, may not have been intended to represent a Christian ideal at all and it certainly was not one that involved a search for the chalice of Jesus. However, it was the sort of story that the Church was quick to recognize, and to adopt. In terms of the Grail, as it came to be understood, the chances of anyone actually finding the cup from which Jesus drank at the Last Supper must have seemed incredibly remote. But this was an age of incredulity by modern standards and successive Church leaders clearly saw in the developing Grail legends a way of focusing attention on the deepest mysteries of Christianity.

If the Grail, as an image of Jesus' suffering and sacrifice, had not already existed by the twelfth century, something akin to it would have had to be invented. Chivalry and the ideal of the quest were a way by which the Church could direct the violent men of the time along paths that suited its own purposes. Meanwhile sovereigns were also happy. The holy "quest" brought at least some of the most powerful sections of a disparate and self-seeking minor aristocracy to a common purpose.

Chretien de Troyes' own tale of Perceval contained not one element of Christian doctrine and the writer offered little information as to what "his" Grail might actually be. He certainly did not equate it in any way with the cup of Jesus. Nor does he show it to be the vessel used to catch the drops of blood from Jesus' body at the time of the crucifixion, as was later claimed to be the case. All of this was to follow. As a legacy of Chretien's work Church and state alike would show itself happy to adopt the Grail and its objectives as their own. But tales of the "magic cauldrons" prove conclusively that the Grail as a vessel was no new invention. It was already thousands of years old when Chretien wrote about Perceval. Because the objects that became equated with the Grail were much older than Christianity, they could not originally have had any connection with the faith. In my comprehension, there were people at large in Chretien's world who were well aware of this fact. It is almost certain that the mysterious writer Chretien de Troyes was one of them.

CHAPTER 15

The View from Avalon

Around the same time as Chretien de Troyes was composing the first of the medieval accounts of the Grail, events were taking place in England that would come to have an important bearing on later Grail legends. News was going round that the bodies of the famed King Arthur and his wife Guinevere had been located.

The King Arthur of popular imagination is a character based almost entirely on medieval ideas. More than one historian has dared to suggest that no such person ever existed. This is hardly likely to be the case however, because the name of Arthur exists through the length and breadth of Britain. It is mentioned in a number of early British documents and appears in many French legends. To put this character fully in context is difficult because Arthur lived in a period that quite rightly became known as the Dark Ages. Contemporary documentary accounts of Arthur are virtually non-existent.

Arthur, son of Uther Pendragon, is a character who has been dear to my heart since childhood. There is barely a location in either Britain or France associated with Arthur's supposed life that I have not visited. I believe that I must have read almost all the information available regarding this most enigmatic of British heroes. After years of searching, I came to understand that to tie down the genuine historical character of Arthur is impossible. The real Arthur was undoubtedly a warlord. He seems to have been a general in chief of the various Celtic factions that were trying to stem the Saxon incursions into Britain in the sixth century. There is absolutely no factual evidence that he was King of all Britain, or even all England. During his period of history, such a rank and position would have been impossible.

Undoubtedly someone by the name of Arthur did achieve

significant military success against the Saxons. He may have prevented the Germanic invaders from ever gaining control over the area that is today known as Wales. My own past research shows that many of the battles associated with Arthur and the Saxons were fought very close to the present border of England and Wales. This is especially true of the English county of Shropshire.

Arthur has to be of importance to our present search, if only because so many of the Grail legends feature him. The fact that they do may have more to do with medieval symbolism than any actual connection between Arthur and the Grail itself. There are many connections between Arthur and salt line locations, most of all in the Shropshire Welsh border. There is a latitudinal salt line at 2 degrees 51 minutes West that more or less follows the English–Welsh border for much of its length. Arthur's Battle of Baddon, which I have previously associated with "The Brython," a hill fort between Oswestry and Welshpool, was fought more or less on the salt line. This would also be true of the Battle of Bassus. My evidence shows that this took place in what is the modern settlement of Baschurch, in Shropshire.

The more northerly English town of Carlisle has also been associated with Arthur since time out of mind. Many people have suggested that the location of Camelot, Arthur's famed capital and castle, can be found in the region of Carlisle. Although some distance to the north Carlisle is very close to the same longitudinal salt line at 2 degrees 51 minutes West.

In total, the tales of Arthur are wide ranging. So many locations are included as possible sites for his life and victories that it would be impossible to suggest that all of them have salt line connections. It seems that many ancient stories attracted Arthur's name over the years. All in all, he has become the epitome of the British capacity to survive, even against fearful odds.

One of the most important salt line locations directly associated with Arthur of Britain also features strongly in Grail stories. This revered spot and resort of the New Age reveler is Glastonbury. Glastonbury Tor is a strange hill, rising from an area of much lower ground. It is situated in the southwest of England, in the county of Somerset. So significant is Glastonbury Tor that is must surely have been a place of deep and abiding mystery in prehistoric times. In those days, it rose as an island in the flooded land. Many people have suggested that this was "Avalon," the magical isle to which the body of Arthur was taken after his last battle of Camlan.

The whole concept of Arthur and Avalon may be something of a medieval invention. In popular myth, Arthur was not dead when he was taken to Avalon, but merely injured. There, it was said, he and his knights would sleep away the centuries until Britain was once more in need of him.

Whether Celtic imagery gave way to medieval opportunism it is difficult to say. Claims were made in the late twelfth century that the bodies of Arthur and his queen, Guinevere, had been located in the grounds of the abbey at Glastonbury. This monastic house stood just below the Tor. The site of this abbey has also long been associated with Joseph of Arimathea. He is said to have come to Britain after leaving Mary Magdalene, and the other Marys, in southern France. Joseph was almost certainly a real character because his name is mentioned in the New Testament. He it was who asked for the body of Jesus after the crucifixion and who supplied the tomb where Jesus would lie before rising from the dead.

Legends suggest that Joseph, a merchant, traveled to England and that, at Glastonbury, he built the first Christian church on English soil. In 1191, the monks at Glastonbury Abbey claimed, during building work, to have unearthed the bones of a man and a woman in the region of the Lady Chapel. The bodies were found at a great depth. They were buried between two ancient, inscribed pyramids. The bones were accompanied by a lead cross, which bore the legend:

Hic jacet inclitus rex Arturius
in insula Avallonis seultus.

Here lies the famous King Arthur,
in the Isle of Avalon.

At this period it was a boon for any abbey or cathedral to hold the relics of important religious characters. For this reason alone, the claims of the monks of Glastonbury have to be taken with a very hefty pinch of salt. However, the position of Glastonbury is such that the latitudinal salt line at 51degrees 09 minutes North passes right through Glastonbury Tor. The Tor stands immediately adjacent to the abbey. And here we get to the nub of the matter. Someone had taken the deliberate decision to associate Arthur with the prehistoric salt line site that also carried legends relating to the very commencement of Christianity in Britain. But this was a form of Christianity supposedly espoused by a Jew, and a man who must have known Jesus personally. The same legend regarding Joseph states that he brought the Holy Grail, the chalice of Christ, with him to Glastonbury. We should not forget that there are also legends associating Glastonbury with the first

English Church by way of the mysterious "Culdees," mentioned earlier.

Despite a natural skepticism, the expert Leslie Alcock suggests that the Arthurian finds might have been genuine.[20] It is known that the form of lettering used on the lead cross that was found with the bodies was of a tenth-century form. Such letters could not be contemporary with letters used in Arthur's own fifth- or sixth-century period. But neither were they relevant to the twelfth century, when the bones were found. Alcock suggests that the real Arthur had been buried at Glastonbury, and that subsequent building work meant demolishing the mausoleum in which he had been laid. By the tenth century, Arthur was already a popular character. When the lead cross was made to mark the grave, the monks concocted an inscription that made him into a king, which he had never been.

In the light of my own research, this explanation seems a little too convenient, but it isn't beyond the realms of credibility. Certainly, the discovery of the bones came at a most important time in the re-emergence of salt line awareness. The bones were found just three years after Chretien de Troyes wrote his first Grail story and four years after the loss of Jerusalem. No tale associating Arthur with the Grail emerged before the bodies of he and his queen were claimed for Glastonbury. Although locally popular, Arthur appears to have been a relatively minor player in British folklore until that time.

An alternative explanation for a bogus burial at Glastonbury is also trotted out regularly. It is suggested that the Norman/English King of England at the time, Henry II, arranged the whole business as a sort of public relations exercise. Rumors had been going round that Arthur had risen in Wales. In this case, the spirit of the "original Arthur" found the form of a flesh and blood character. This was Arthur, son of Geoffrey of Anjou and Constance of Brittany. Henry may have attempted to lay these rumors to rest by producing a very dead Arthur. A few crumbling bones were not likely to come back to life under any circumstances.

This possible explanation is clearly flawed. Medieval people may have been suggestible, but they were not stupid. Any attempt to equate Arthur son of Geoffrey of Anjou, and the historical Arthur was symbolic. Anyone with real influence would have been aware of that fact. The very last person who would have wanted to find the grave of King Arthur, a totally British king, would have been the Norman Henry II. Even if he had, he would surely not have wanted to discover it down in the southwest. This was far too near the Celtic heartland of Wales and Cornwall, where rebellion was always a threat.

Whether or not Arthur and his wife were laid to rest at Glastonbury, their present fame knows no bounds. Arthur will come into this story time and again, but he certainly was not associated with the Grail when the first chroniclers were working on the subject.

As Arthur and his queen were being disinterred, and immediately after Chretien de Troyes wrote his seminal work towards the end of the twelfth century, there was a sudden explosion of interest in the Grail. In the 1190s, a Burgundian writer called Sir Robert de Boron leaped into the ring with *Joseph d'Arimathie - Roman de l'Estoire dou Saint Graal*. This is a complicated tale and could well point to Glastonbury. The story deals with the Grail as a receptacle for the blood of Jesus. The drops of blood were collected by Joseph of Arimathea at the time of the crucifixion. In this story, the cup was not brought to Avalon by Joseph himself but arrived via his sister's husband, a man named Hebron. Hebron changes his name to Bron on arrival at the blessed place.

There appears to be a mixture of mythologies at work here because Bron is almost certainly synonymous with Bran. Bran is a Celtic deity and hero. It is likely that Sir Robert, either deliberately or accidentally, got the two characters confused. Once ensconced in the "Vale of Avaron," Bron takes on the guise of the "Fisher King." Here we find a character that figures in almost every Grail cycle. Bron has a family of twelve sons, the twelfth of which is Alaine. When a fabulous table is constructed to honor the Grail, or in this case "Graal," Alaine, who is celibate, takes the "Siege Perilous." The Siege Perilous is synonymous with the seat occupied by Judas Iscariot at the Last Supper. In later Grail cycles, by which time the table is in King Arthur's capital of Camelot, Galahad replaces Alaine in this seat. Like Alaine, Galahad is sexually pure.

Next on the Grail bandwagon comes a mysterious writer by the name of Wauchier. His Grail is quite different from that in the previous two stories. In Wauchier's account, the Grail is capable of feeding the assembled guests at a banquet. In some ways it appears more like a person than a simple vessel, though it also has some of the qualities of the "magic cauldrons" of old, which have come into modern storytelling as "the magic porridge pot." King Arthur appears for the first time in the Wauchier document. From this point on he is almost always present.

By far the most influential of the early Grail works is that of Wolfram von Eschenbach. This is entitled *Parizival.* It gave rise to a tradition that culminated in the musical tribute created by the composer Wagner. Wolfram's book appeared at the very end of the twelfth century. The author claimed that the work of Chretien de Troyes was incomplete and therefore of little merit. His own information supposedly came from Kyot le Province, who in turn is said to have received it from a learned man of Spanish nationality named Flegetanis. Wolfram is emphatic that Flegetanis was born of an Israelite family and that he was directly descended from Solomon.

Like almost all the writers of the period Wolfram doesn't seem entirely sure what the Grail is, or more likely deliberately hides the fact. And it is with the work of Wolfram that a fabulous female character appears in the Grail romances. Wolfram calls her "Repans de Schoye." It is she who bears the Grail, which rested on a green silk cloth. Wolfram tells us that it "... surpasses every earthly ideal," and that it is "... the perfection of earthly paradise, both root and branches."

For probably the first time Wolfram also equates the Grail with a stone. He calls this "Lapis Exillis." There are many interpretations of this phrase, for language at the time was written as it sounded and there was little in the way of established norms in spelling. The phrase could be "Lapis ex caeli," which means stone from the sky, or perhaps "Lapis Elixier" the famed Philosopher's stone of alchemy.

Wolfram tells us something about Flegetanis, the man who supplied the original material for his book. Flegetanis observed things in the starry constellations about which he preferred not to speak. These represented arcane mysteries. Flegetanis claimed that there was a thing called the Grail, the name of which he had read clearly in the constellations. The Grail, he said, had been left on the Earth by a group of angels. From time to time noble, baptized men had been called upon to guard it.

It is quite possible that, in part at least, Flegetanis was referring, in an astronomical sense, to the constellation Crater, mentioned in the last chapter but there are other clues here. Information known to that group of people I have referred to as the "Megalithic priesthood," had been preserved by them for thousands of years. It included an understanding of the salt line system and of Megalithic mathematics. As we shall see, these people were also the recipients of other practical information, which would fuel their endeavors for many centuries beyond the time of Flegetanis. Being of the line of Solomon, Flegetanis himself might also have been of the Megalithic priesthood. It is unlikely that either he, or other members of his Fraternity, would have any absolute understanding of how and where all this fabulous knowledge had emerged. Stories of it being handed down, direct from the deity, by angels, would be quite understandable.

Following, as it did, hard on the heels of the other early Grail stories, Wolfram von Eschenbach's book, *Parzival*, is probably the most enigmatic of all the Grail cycles and is certainly the work that has attracted the most attention. It carries the same mystical and magical stories to be found elsewhere. However, in the hands of Wolfram they seem to be forerunners of many belief patterns that sprang up in the years following his death. This is particularly the case with regard to Kabalism, for many of Wolfram's images seem to be Kabalistic in nature. We don't know where Wolfram was when *Parzival* was written, but it is likely that he was well traveled. All over France, Kabalistic schools were developing. Some were already well established by his time and it is noteworthy that one such school was located in Troyes. It has also been suggested that St. Bernard of Clairvaux was personally interested in Kabalism and that he had experts in the subject working in his own abbey.

Kabalism grew out of Judaism, though it was to become a mystery school of Christendom. Culled from certain sections of early Judaic thinking it represented the esoteric aspect of Jewish thought and practice. Kabalists were not unlike certain factions of Buddhism or Hinduism and they had much in common with some sects of Gnostic Christians. They believed that it was possible to achieve a "union" with the Godhead that surpassed earthly matters or indeed the material world in total. To tread the Kabalistic path meant advancing, step by arduous step, toward this ideal. Although virtually a medieval European invention, Kabalism has much in common with esoteric studies that are still popular today but it also spawned an interest in "alchemy," a more practical aspect of Kabalistic studies. Modern chemistry owes practically everything to its alchemical origins, though it is not likely that any self-respecting chemist today would be willing to admit the fact. I will deal specifically with the subject of alchemy in a later chapter.

Wolfram's stories are replete with knights who wear white tunics with red crosses on them. It is quite clear that these men are Templars. There is nothing especially extraordinary about this fact since at the time *Parzival* was written, the Templars were reaching the pinnacle of their success in Europe. Talking in allegory, Wolfram describes locations where such Templar-type knights exist. He claims that it is from this group of especially favored individuals that rulers for states all over Europe are dispatched in times of need. To Wolfram, the Grail is frequently portrayed as the magical stone. In the narrative names appear, mystically carved into the stone, though these disappear when the intended individual has read them.

Many Grail researchers have paid great attention to the details of Wolfram's stories, which appear to have been written with two distinctly different audiences in mind. In one respect, *Parzival* is the "adventure story" of its day. It would have been of great interest to learned individuals. These avid readers must have suffered from "religious indigestion" considering the deeply Christian quality of much of the reading material available to them. But time and again the writer urges the knowledgeable to "read between the lines" of his stories, in order to glean the truth of what is being said.

Since Wolfram was writing well within the timescale of the Knights Templar, it becomes clear that the Grail, whatever it might be, was somehow associated with them. As Wolfram wrote his story, the Templars still had over a century to consolidate their positions throughout Europe but when their end did come, it was fearful and, apparently, sudden.

CHAPTER 16

A Monstrous Heresy

At dawn on Friday 13 October 1307 a series of raids took place all over France. The object of this exercise was to arrest as many Templar knights as possible and to seize their lands and property across the entire kingdom. King Philip IV of France was the instigator of these events. He had managed to lure the Grand Master of the Templars, Jacques de Molay, to France, so that he too could be taken into custody at the appointed time.

Molay and perhaps dozens of other Templar knights were tortured in the most horrible ways imaginable. It was very important that Philip IV, known as "the Fair," should extract as much evidence of wrongdoing on the part of the Templar Order as he could. Philip didn't care much about impressing the Pope, for the Pontiff too was virtually a captive in France at the time of these events. But he was anxious to prove to the monarchs of other European states that his attack on the Templars was justified. This, he reasoned, would convince them to take similar actions themselves. His attack on the Templars was a calculated risk, for the institution was powerful, even beyond the confines of France. It was a risk he had obviously decided to take, perhaps for several reasons.

The charges brought against the Templars were many and varied. As a number of historians have pointed out, they may have been guilty of nothing except being the wrong institution in the wrong place at the wrong time. Leaving aside for a moment the possibility that they truly were a heretical sect, intent on destroying the Christian faith, what reasons would Philip have had for trying to wipe out the Templars altogether?

The main impetus was most likely greed. The Templar Order was extremely rich. Philip was a man of his time and it was the nature of medieval kings to store their treasure in specific locations, for use in times of war. He almost certainly assumed that the Templars behaved in the same way. By this period, the Templars had become somewhat lax in their observance of the Order that bound them. They were lavish in their entertainment of men like Philip. Their leaders dressed in fine clothes and walked through vast halls decorated sumptuously by the most famous artists of the day. Philip had observed these facts at first hand. It probably never occurred to him that the very economic methods of the Templars meant that their wealth lay wherever the next economic opportunity was to be found. Treasuries there were, but not on the scale that Philip expected. The Templars were creating a form of proto-capitalism, and that meant that the true value of Templar Inc. lay in the confidence that its clients retained regarding its power and ability to supply what was wanted, but Philip was not a Templar, and so did not understand all these facts.

The King had previously sought honorary admission to the Order. This request had been granted to certain other princes of the blood royal. Unfortunately for the Templars, Philip had been refused. This fact must have irritated such a proud man as the French king beyond belief. The thought of collecting everything that the Templars owned in terms of land, ships, goods, and treasure, might have been a significant incentive for Philip to turn on his erstwhile friends but is unlikely to have been the only reason. In the years since the final loss of the Holy Land, at the end of the thirteenth century, the Templars had become, essentially, a European based group. The Order was still growing. It represented thousands of fully armed soldiers, each with his arms and entourage, and with nobody to fight. The Templars had taken strict vows never to cross swords with fellow Christians, but how much reliance could the King of France place on a mere piece of paper?

Stories had been circulating that the Templars wanted a European country of their own. It was being rumored that they had their sights set on southern France. Philip did not rule the entire region, but he would not have wanted such a powerful army, with its own territorial objectives, sitting on his doorstep. By all surviving accounts, Philip was a suspicious, cruel, and calculating individual. Doubtless, he saw in the rest of humanity a reflection of his own nature. There is reason enough here for Philip IV to want an end of the Templar Order but what were the circumstances that allowed him to put his plans into action?

Philip picked his moment very well. Towards the end of the thirteenth century, and especially during the late 1280s, western Europe had suffered from a series of very wet years. The result had been catastrophic for farmers, of which the Cistercian Order and the Templars were the most successful example. Sheep had died in thousands for several years running. This meant that yields of wool were low. The Cistercians, who had grown lax in their ways and opulent beyond belief, suffered the most. Many of the great Cistercian houses had mortgaged up to ten years' wool production in advance to Flemish merchants. When the bad years came, they simply could not produce the goods and had to buy wool in from other sources in order to meet their obligations. In England, Scotland, and France, royal assistance was necessary to save the Cistercians from bankruptcy. This alone meant that when the Templars found themselves in difficulty, their brother monks were in no position to help them out, since Cistercian influence was at an all time low.

Added to this was a general lack of public support for both

Cistercians and Templars. In the case of the latter "as drunk as a Templar" was a saying in common usage on both sides of the English Channel at the beginning of the fourteenth century. Templars were accused of being high-handed, bullying, and self-seeking.

However, there were two other distinctly different factors that allowed Philip IV to move against the Templars when he did. The first was the election of Pope Clement V, a Frenchman by the name of Bertrand De Got. He came to power in 1305 and, under pressure from an increasingly powerful French Crown, he resided in Avignon, France, rather than in Rome. To say that he was a "captive Pope" would be to infer that his ideas differed in some way from those of Philip, which was not the case. Clement was every bit Philip's man and it is self evident that the King of France could not have turned against the Templars without the Pope's approval.

Probably most important of all, control over Champagne itself had at least nominally come to Philip as early as 1284, when he had married Joan of Navarre, heiress to Champagne. Partly because of legalities but also on account of disputes regarding Champagne with the English crown, Philip was not in a position to absolutely enforce his influence there until around 1305. It was at this time that Queen Joan died and the title to Champagne passed to the son of Philip and herself (later Louis X). Louis was too young to rule Champagne in 1305, but the coming of the title into the French royal family, together with all the other factors itemized above, signed the end of the Templar Order in France. It is impossible to believe that the Templars themselves, and especially their political and religious masters, the Troyes Fraternity, would have failed to realize this fact at least two years and probably more than a decade or more before 1307.

Historians show great surprise at the fact that the last Grand Master of the Templars, Jacques de Molay, walked into Philip's trap like a mesmerized rabbit, though the intensive research of Stephen Dafoe and myself would tend to suggest that his actions represented a deliberate strategy. We strongly believe that Jacques de Molay acted in the way he did, simply to "buy time" for the careful reordering of both Templar and Troyes Fraternity personnel and economic interests which may already have been taking place for years.

There remains a further possibility, and despite Philip IV's generally cruel disposition and overbearing personality, it cannot be ruled out. It is likely that Philip was in possession of genuine proof that the Templar Order was guilty of some heinous crime against the Church. Jacques de Molay stood accused, along with the Order of which he was the head, of specific crimes. He admitted to all the charges put to him whilst he was under torture. Of course, this means nothing. But the record shows that Philip IV and Pope Clement brought the following charges against Molay and his Order:

1. The denial of Christ and defiling the cross.
2. The worship of an idol.
3. The performance of a perverted sacrament.
4. That they were guilty of ritual murder.
5. The wearing of a cord of heretical significance.
6. The use of a ritual kiss.
7. Alteration to the ceremony of the Mass and the use of an unorthodox form of absolution.
8. Immorality.
9. Treachery to other groups of the Christian forces.

Specific evidence was heard. For example, it was testified that those seeking admission to the Order had been instructed to spit on the crucifix and to tread it underfoot. They were told concerning Christianity. "Don't have faith in this. It is too new."

It was said that the Templars had worshiped a strange bearded head, which was supposedly known as "Baphomet." Templars were accused of homosexuality, of debauchery and in fact just about every crime imaginable. Of course no reasonable defense was allowed because the Templars were guilty from the moment Philip had the idea to snare them. But even bearing these facts in mind, it still seems more than likely that the Knights Templar represented a genuinely heretical sect. Though none of the Knights remotely deserved what came to them, technically, they were probably guilty as charged by the standards of the time.

The reason that we cannot know the extent of their guilt for certain is that only a few of the Templar brotherhood would have been aware of any heretical beliefs at all. Few people now doubt that the Templar Order constituted a body not unlike a modern Masonic Fraternity. There would therefore have been a system of progressive enlightenment into the true beliefs of the institution. Of the most profound secrets, novice members would have been totally ignorant. Only the most trusted Templars, the Preceptors of countries or districts, and the Grand Master himself would have known the whole story.

Under torture, it is likely that almost any Templar would have eventually pleaded guilty to whatever charges were laid before him. But if the interrogators did not know what accusations to put, this may not have been a problem. It should also be remembered that there could have been accusations that Philip deliberately chose not to make, for his own political reasons and to safeguard a Vatican that must have known full well what real Templar beliefs and motives had been all along.

Many authors have quite fairly suggested that during the two centuries of its existence the Templar movement had mixed with a number of peoples of different religions. This was especially true in the case of Islam, with which it had excellent relations in some parts of the Near and Middle East. It is known that the Templars advocated a coming together of Islam, Judaism, and Christianity. This in itself is not too far away from some strands of Islamic belief. Followers of all these religions are declared by Muslims to be "Peoples of the Book." If we are to accept that the Templars had become a heretical sect, the Muslim association might be the most likely explanation were it not for certain facts.

The original Grand Master of the Knights of Christ and the Temple of Solomon, Hugh de Payen, had come from a longitudinal salt line location, in Troyes. Chief patron of the Templars, St. Bernard of Clairvaux, had been born on another longitudinal salt line, this time in Burgundy. The same had also been the case with many subsequent Grand Masters, though the origin of some is unknown. However, the last Grand Master, Jacques de Molay, was born in a village close to the Jura city of Besancon. This is situated on the longitudinal salt line at 6 degrees East. It is on the same salt line that first alerted Xaviar Guichard to the existence of this extraordinary Bronze Age spider's web. And if this is not proof enough in itself of a continuing thread, matters go further. The man who stood beside Jacques de Molay and who died with him on 18 March 1314 was Geoffrey de Charney, Preceptor of Normandy. Geoffrey's ancestral lands lay in central France. His family held the small town of Lirrey, which occupies both a longitudinal and a latitudinal salt line position.

These two men were roasted slowly over a carefully controlled fire in a small island in the Seine. Both could have been spared the death penalty if they had stuck to their original statements of guilt. However, on the day before their execution they had stated that their admissions of guilt had been extracted from them under torture. They recanted fully and so had to die. At no time did either man declare any love for, or allegiance to, Jesus, but neither did they declare any association with Islam. Whatever true secrets either man possessed went with them to their grave. Their ashes were collected from beneath the spit where they were burned and nobody knows where they are today.

There are clues as to the true nature of the beliefs that the highest members of the Knights Templar espoused, and to which initiates who proved worthy and capable were gradually brought. These existed from the very start of the Institution and were part of the original rules of the Order. They had been drawn up by St. Bernard of Clairvaux. The Templars never lost faith in Bernard. It is said that during his long captivity, Jacques de Molay composed a prayer to, and concerning, St. Bernard. Bernard had remained the single most important individual to Templarism for nearly 200 years.

St. Bernard of Clairvaux, presumably with the full sanction and agreement of the original Templar knights, had dedicated the knightly Order unequivocally to the Virgin Mary. All its endeavors were undertaken in her name and it was this name that they cried as they went into battle. The Templars were, from beginning to end, a Marianist brotherhood. Bearing in mind St. Bernard's own reverence for Mary, or whatever she actually represented in his mind and heart, it is likely that the original Templars, and perhaps the whole Order for 200 hundred years, maintained a common belief with Bernard.

The bearded head mentioned in the original charges is interesting, and it may represent the vestiges of a much earlier and essentially pagan belief. The Celts, in particular, had a "cult of the severed head." Examples of sculpted stone heads can be found all over the Celtic world. This head my also have related to John the Baptist, for whom the Templars had a special reverence. Even more likely is the suggestion that the bearded head could have represented the "Green Man." Effigies of the Green Man are to be seen in many Gothic churches and cathedrals. Generally speaking, the Green Man is simply a face. He is usually depicted as being composed of branches and leaves and quite often has the tendrils of plants emanating from his mouth and nostrils. Few historians now doubt that the Green Man is a hangover from the days of nature worship and, in particular, worship of the Goddess.

Of specific interest is the name that Philip's representatives said the Templars attributed to this head, namely "Baphomet." The word Baphomet has a very special meaning. As early as 500 BC Hebrew writers and scholars had begun to use a code, which has come to be known as the Atbash Cipher. A full realization of the importance of the Atbash Cipher only came to light with the discovery of the Dead Sea Scrolls. The Essene in particular used this method of hiding specific truths. The Atbash Cipher is a fairly simple substitution cipher. It was the highly respected New Testament scholar Dr. Hugh Schonfield who realized exactly what Baphomet meant when the Atbash Cipher was applied to it.

In all probability, the name Baphomet had nothing to do with the mysterious bearded head of the Templars, and the confusion may have been due to ineptitude on the part of Philip IV's interrogators. However, the word was still of tremendous importance to the Templars because once it has gone through the mill of the Atbash Cipher, Baphomet comes out as "Sophia."

Readers will recall that Sophia was the name early Christians had given to what ultimately became known as the Holy Spirit. This was the third component of the original Neolithic Trinity, as personified in Minoan Crete, and it clearly represented the Goddess.

So, let us look at the evidence again, now in full possession of all the facts. The Knights Templar was composed of, or at least led by, people who were born in salt line locations. They seem to have shared something important in common which related in some way to the old Megalithic culture of western Europe. These people from the late Stone Age and the Bronze Age had been Goddess worshipers. The Templars were dedicated to the Virgin Mary, for whom they showed what amounted to an obsession. This had also been true of their founder, St. Bernard of Clairvaux. Bernard had deliberately manipulated the Catholic Church of his day to virtually deify Mary. The Templar Order was accused of worshiping Baphomet, which we know is a code word and which really means Sophia. Sophia, in turn is early Christian speak for the Holy Spirit, often represented as a dove. The dove has represented the Goddess for thousands of years.

It seems more and more likely that the true religious imperatives of the Templars meant that, in fourteenth-century Christian terms, they were "guilty as charged." However, their accusers either did not know the true depths of their heresy, or preferred not to speak about it publicly. In my estimation, the Templars, or rather their leaders, had been and remained, throughout the whole of their existence, confirmed Goddess worshipers, ruled by a succession of salt line priests of the old Megalithic blood. The Poor Knights of Christ and the Temple of Solomon represented a two-century long manifestation of the Golden Thread. They would not prove to be the last of their kind.

CHAPTER 17

The Survival of the Grail

Philip IV's arrest of the Templars in France was soon followed by a proclamation direct from the Pope, excommunicating all Templars who would not willingly abandon the Order, and also instructing good Christian kings to seize Templar property. In fact, the reaction he received was very mixed. It is a fact that the Templars of France were doomed and many countries in Europe more or less followed the Pope's edict. However, some monarchs, for example that of Portugal, simply ignored the papal decree. In Spain the Templars changed their name and carried on much as before, whilst in Germany the Templar institution openly confronted the state in a menacing manner, and also continued to operate.

The crown of France was able to write off the massive dept it owed to the Templar Order and it gained substantially in terms of Templar land, but it never found the supposed treasuries of the Order. It was even denied possession of the Templar's huge fleet of ships, which sometime immediately before the arrests of 1307 simply weighed its anchors and literally disappeared from the pages of history. More to the point, there is strong evidence that the Templars had already taken action to counter the threat from France.

At almost exactly the same time as Philip moved against the Templars, we find small but important pockets of resistance developing in what is now Switzerland, against its ruler, the Holy Roman Emperor. Local areas, known as cantons, rose up and in a series of masterstrokes of military genius won a number of decisive battles that freed them from any outside control. It is almost certainly no coincidence that folk tales from the region talk about the peasant farmers of the cantons being assisted by white-mantled knights.

From a strategic point of view, a relocation of at least some of the Templar wealth and economic interest east, into the Alps, would have made great sense. This probably began to take place two decades prior to 1307. The Alpine terrain was beyond the influence of France and was difficult for any ruling elite to control, yet these little cantons came to own and jealously guard the only realistic routes of commerce across much of Europe. Everything about Switzerland simply screams that it was a Templar created state, or at least inspired by those who actually ran Templarism, yet historians have completely failed to recognize the fact.

It had been as early as 1291 that the three original cantons of Uri, Schwyz, and Unterwalden had agreed to band together to fight any common enemy. This pact is the starting point of what would eventually become the Swiss state. In 1315, exactly the same year as Jacques de Molay, Grand Master of the Templar Order, was being put to death in France, the three cantons struck a crushing blow against the Holy Roman Empire. On 15 November 1315, a large group of Hapsburg knights, seeking to gain control of the important Reuss valley, were utterly defeated and destroyed by the combined forces of the fledgling cantons. It is not difficult to see the guiding hand of the Troyes Fraternity at work, though clearly the organization had changed its remit.

Templar knights who fought alongside the peasants of the cantons were confronting an enemy that the Troyes Fraternity had recognized since the time of Charlemagne. This was the Holy Roman Empire, which had been responsible for the death of Dagobert II and the usurpation of the Frankish throne. Nothing could have given the Troyes Fraternity, or more properly the Golden Thread, greater pleasure than to carve a nation for itself out of the very body of an institution it hated so much. The rumored Templar state became a reality, though not in southern France. The chosen destination was high up in the Alps, in the most defensible series of natural fortresses Europe has to offer.

Events taking place in Switzerland subsequently would show it developing into a sort of state the world had not seen before and which hasn't existed since. Across over seven hundred years, despite numerous languages and radically opposing religious imperatives, the Swiss have stuck together. Personal freedoms in Switzerland are a virtual obsession and each canton still has great control over its own running. Despite the potential for disagreements and civil strife, Switzerland has prospered. It has an influence on the world well out of proportion to its size or geographic location and it owes this to several factors:

> Switzerland is and has been for centuries one of the major banking centers of the world.
>
> It has retained a strict neutrality, even through two world wars. Though it did not participate in the League of Nations and has not been an active member of the United Nations, it has a strong bearing on world events, partly through its economic strength.
>
> Switzerland was the starting point of the International Red Cross, which to this day still has the famous Templar red cross as its symbol.
>
> Switzerland is pathologically secretive. It is almost impossible to ascertain anything about its true economic might, or how deep its tendrils run into the earth of the world economy.
>
> Many of the cantons of Switzerland retain either the

THE SURVIVAL OF THE GRAIL

patee cross of the Templars on their own flags, or the Paschal lamb, another Templar device. Some cantons retain both.

For the seven centuries of its existence, Switzerland has shown itself to be the epitome of a new utopia, formed from the winding valleys and mountain passes of Alpine Europe, created and administered by those representatives of the Golden Thread who had formerly been the Troyes Fraternity. Gradually, it grew from its original three cantons to extend south as far as Geneva, straddling the borders of modern France and Italy. Although religiously tolerant to a fault, Switzerland carefully fostered the fugitive elements of the Reformation, which would spell the end of the influence of Roman Catholicism.

How much do the rulers of Switzerland today know about these matters? It is impossible to say, but the silence of Switzerland speaks legions in itself. It can be seen for a number of reasons that the Golden Thread was far from destroyed with the attack made on the Templars in 1307. In reality, the gradual demise of the Templars was also the beginning of the end of feudalism. The Templars had woven themselves so tightly into the economic fabric of Europe and beyond that simply chopping off the head of the hydra wasn't nearly enough. Philip IV's actions merely led, inexorably, to the Renaissance. Freeing itself from the iron grip of Church and state alike, society began to look for artistic freedom and scientific truth. However, this took time. And though memories of the Templars remained, there was a substantial period between 1307 and the breaking of Catholic power during which to even speak about the Order, or anything to do with it, could have meant a grizzly death. It was during these years that the stories of the Holy Grail were most important, kept alive in order to preserve the age-old truths and to pass them on to the enlightened.

The most potent of the Grail stories during this time flowed from the pen of an English writer. The circumstances of how they came to be written are themselves an object lesson in proving the survival of the Golden Thread and how it was perpetuated, long after the Knights Templar were an heroic memory.

About three centuries after the bones of the famed King Arthur had been supposedly found at Glastonbury the most famous of all the Arthurian and Grail stories were collected together. They were compiled in one exhaustive work by the Englishman, Sir Thomas Mallory. The work of this man is as important to the Grail cycles as that of Chretien de Troyes. He is probably the last of the true Grail romancers but he shares an important fact with Chretien de Troyes. Both men were salt line dwellers.

Sir Thomas Mallory's book was known as *Le Morte d'Arthur*. It appeared in 1485. Amongst the many hundreds of tales included there are some that deal specifically with the Holy Grail. Mallory's book was one of the very first to benefit from the printing process and so it became widely available. It was a bestseller in its day, and has been so ever since. Although Mallory's work is the best known of the compilations concerning Arthur of Britain and the Grail, it was written with the aid of material already available. Very little is known about the man who put this work together. It is not even possible to be specific about Mallory's place of birth. Researchers have worked hard on this problem and there are a number of contenders. They range across the length and breadth of Britain.

The wider Mallory family has prospered across the centuries

but has enjoyed an existence on the fringes of the British nobility. However, nobody of this name has ever figured prominently in political history. Despite this fact, the Mallorys were not lacking in influence. A concerted search for the writer of *Le Morte d'Arthur* proves that sections of the Mallory clan held positions of some responsibility in many parts of the British Isles – for centuries.

Some experts assert that the Thomas Mallory in question came from Chester and others claim him to have had a Welsh pedigree. One of the most frequent candidates for the authorship of *Le Morte d'Arthur* is a man who lay, breathing his last, on the borders of Cambridgeshire and Huntingdonshire in September 1470. He was named in a will that comes from about the right period. William Caxton, the first Englishman to print books, published *Le Morte d'Arthur* in late July 1485. However, he states in the preface that it was actually written in the ninth year of Edward IV. This would place the date of writing between 1469 and 1470.

Le Morte d'Arthur appeared during the Wars of the Roses, a prolonged period of civil war in England. The Wars of the Roses took place between two distinct groups of powerful barons, each supporting a particular section of the royal family. The two groups have come to be known as the Yorkists and the Lancastrians. It is known that the Sir Thomas Mallory who wrote *Le Morte d'Arthur* was a supporter of the Lancastrian cause.

Sir Thomas Mallory of Papworth was not the only knight of his name to be considered a Lancastrian supporter but at the end of the nineteenth century, he seemed a likely candidate for the authorship of *Le Morte d'Arthur*. His supposed identity as "the" Thomas Mallory in question is attributed to the research of a Mr. T. Williams. Mr. Williams wrote to the *Athenaeum* magazine in July 1896. He wished to draw the attention of readers to the fact that a Sir Thomas Mallory had been mentioned as being excluded from a general pardon declared by King Edward IV in 1468. Later, the same correspondent declared that he had found the will of a Thomas Mallory of Papworth. The date of the will roughly matched the writing of *Le Morte d'Arthur*. As a result, the connection was made. Mr. Williams had also suggested that a William Mallory had led a rebellion against Edward IV in the north in the same year as the pardon exclusions, 1468. Whilst there is nothing at all to link the Papworth Thomas Mallory with William Mallory, there are stronger connections between a William and Thomas Mallory further north. A branch of the family that came from Yorkshire was also a staunch supporter of the Lancastrian cause. For a whole host of reasons it seems very likely that this offshoot of the Mallory name supplied the Thomas Mallory of *Le Morte d'Arthur* fame.

The Yorkshire Mallorys were listed by Leland in the sixteenth century as owning Studley. This village is immediately to the north of Fountains Abbey, not far from Ripon. Studley would have been a fitting place for any book dealing with the Grail and therefore the salt line Fraternity to have been written. It stands immediately to the north of the latitudinal salt line that runs at 54 degrees 05 minutes North. Fountains Abbey, the best known and most prosperous of all the Cistercian monasteries in Britain, was close by. The abbey stood within a few hundred meters of the village of Studley. Fountains was still fully operational when *Le Morte d'Arthur* was written, since the Reformation and the suppression of the monastic houses did not take place until some decades later. Fountains had been founded with the express sanction of St. Bernard of Clairvaux and had been under his personal protection.

What might link the Yorkshire Mallorys with *Le Morte d'Arthur* is a document discovered in an old hide trunk at Ribston Manor, near Walton, itself close to Studley. In the trunk was found a copy of the French prose romance *Merlin*. The pages of this document, now residing in Cambridge, contain some words in a hand other than that of the copyist:

> Ci commence le livre que Sir Thomas Malori Chr reduce
> in Engloys et fuist emprented par Willm Caxton.

> Here begins the book which Sir Thomas Malore (Knight) translated into English and first imprinted by William Caxton.

In itself, this is proof of nothing, but another interesting discovery was made by a visitor to the library of Ripon Cathedral in the late nineteenth century. The visitor was the Rev. Thomas Frognall Dibdin, an expert on ancient books. In the library catalogue, the Rev. Dibdin took particular note of two books. These were *English Chronicle, Antw, 1483* and *Boetius Old Engl.* The two books were listed as being in folio. Dibdin and the Dean searched for the volumes. They eventually found only one, or at least that is how it seemed. What they discovered was a "forrell," which is a white sheepskin covered folio. It contained an original copy of William Caxton's imprint of Boethius, one of the earliest works to be published by Caxton. A further inspection revealed a great surprise. Bound into the back of Boethius was a copy of Caxton's *Book for Travellers*.

The discovery of these very early works of Caxton surprised and delighted both men. Nevertheless, they could not understand why these two very precious works had been bound into one book or how they had found their way into Ripon Cathedral library. It is now generally accepted that they were bequeathed to the establishment by the former Dean Higgins. Although himself from Manchester, Higgins had been for many years the Rector of Kirk Deighton. The church of Kirk Deighton is within sight of Ribston Hall. And it was in Ribston Hall that the French *Merlin* book with the strange inscription had been found.

Sir Thomas Mallory had a bestseller on his hands with *Le Morte d'Arthur*. As a result, the author would have been a valuable asset to William Caxton. It is therefore likely that Mallory's personal library contained volumes also published by Caxton around the same time as his own work. Caxton probably gave these to Mallory as a mark of respect. The books would have passed down his family until they came into the hands of Sir William Mallory of Studley. Dean Higgins undoubtedly bought them from Sir William and they ultimately found their way into Ripon Cathedral library.

There certainly was a Thomas Mallory in the Yorkshire line at about the right time in history. He was the third son of yet another Sir William Mallory and Dionysia Tempest. This Sir William died in 1475. This date makes it likely that he had been involved in the uprising against Edward IV in 1468. The refusal of a pardon for his son, Thomas, would therefore have been quite understandable. He was probably around 45 years of age in 1485, when *Le Morte d'Arthur* was published.

It was the marriage of William Mallory and Dionysia Tempest that had brought the Studley property to the Mallorys and Studley, as we have seen, was only five minutes walk from the front gate of the richest Cistercian House in Britain – Fountains Abbey.

St. Bernard of Clairvaux had been a monk for twenty years

when Fountains was first founded. It was most probably named after his birthplace of Fountainne, in Dijon, Burgundy. There is no record that St. Bernard visited England but it is known that he had a special interest in the abbey. He was a careful administrator and would have watched its evolution from a distance, with great interest. By the time Thomas Mallory wrote *Le Morte d'Arthur*, Fountains was at its zenith. Being one of the foremost monastic houses in the realm it would have possessed an extensive library. Experts in the field are quite emphatic that this library would have certainly contained both religious and secular books. It is highly likely that amongst these were the work of Chretien de Troyes and other Grail romances from the intervening period. We must bear in mind that the Grail legends had surfaced first in Troyes, France, which was the practical heart of Templarism and the spiritual home of St. Bernard, leading light of the Cistercians. Fountains owed allegiance to Clairvaux, St. Bernard's abbey, which is close to Troyes. As far as research material for the Grail stories is concerned, no library in England at the time would have been more likely to offer the works that Mallory needed for *Le Morte d'Arthur* than that of Fountains Abbey.

Presumably the Yorkshire Thomas Mallory was living at Studley when *Le Morte d'Arthur* was created. It is likely that the Mallorys kept good relations with their neighbors the Cistercians. If so, Thomas would probably have had access to most, if not all, of the research material he needed. It is therefore likely that much of the book was compiled within the abbey scriptorium itself. It is also virtually certain that this Thomas Mallory came into contact with William Caxton, the publisher and printer, at Fountains Abbey. Caxton had originally been a high-powered wool merchant. The monks of Fountains not only raised many thousands of sheep themselves but acted as agents for many other sheep farmers in the locality. So important was Fountains to the wool trade of England that Caxton is virtually certain to have visited the abbey himself on numerous occasions. The monks there could easily have introduced Caxton to Mallory, who was their closest secular neighbor. (Time and again in my research, I found "operatives" of the Golden Thread to be associated with sheep rearing and the wool trade generally, as attested by dozens of references in this book.)

Many of Mallory's tales of King Arthur have a distinctly "northern English" feel to them. For example, he identifies Camelot as being synonymous with the town of Carlisle, just across the Pennines in Cumbria. Carlisle is positioned very close to the 2 degrees 51 minutes West longitudinal salt line. The northern approach taken by the author of Le Morte d'Arthur may be further proof that the Thomas Mallory in question was from the Yorkshire branch of the family. A Mallory from much further south and west would surely have placed his Camelot in one of the more favored southern locations, such as Cadbury-Camelot.

There were many poems relating to both King Arthur and the Holy Grail already being created, or at least transcribed in the Yorkshire–Lancashire–Cheshire region at least a century before Le Morte d'Arthur was written. One of these was actually entitled "Morte Arthur." Mallory must have had access to these and it is likely that their creators placed a local slant on the tales, which is reflected in his own work. However, the finished Le Morte d'Arthur contains a high proportion of material that is of singularly French origin. Failing Mallory's own prolonged visit to, or residence in, France, this material is most likely to have been researched at Fountains Abbey.

More than one expert has asserted that Mallory is originally a Welsh name, so its survival within this part of Yorkshire would not be at all surprising. The region had been known as "Elmet." It survived as a Celtic conclave well into Anglo-Saxon times. The writer Guy Ragland Phillips suggests that it may be related to a Celtic tale concerning a race of people, known by the name of their leader, "Mailor." Mailor was a giant who belonged to a race of people the Celts believed to have inhabited Britain at the time of their arrival. It is just conceivable therefore that both the Celts, and later the Saxons, retained some superstitious reverence for the Mallorys, as being representatives of the "magical" people who had once inhabited Britain. This could explain why, with the exception of the period of the Wars of the Roses, the various branches of the Mallory family retained their ancestral seats through all the vicissitudes of English history. The Yorkshire Mallorys were certainly salt line dwellers *par excellence*, and the judicious marriage of William Mallory and Dionysia Tempest consolidated this fact.

The Mallorys may have retained bardic traditions even older than those attributed to the Celts. Certainly, there are stories concerning King Arthur that appear in *Le Morte d'Arthur* and nowhere else. Many of these are from very old sources that must be considered Welsh or pre-Welsh in origin. Thomas Mallory may well have been familiar with the Grail's earlier counterparts.

Le Morte d'Arthur by Thomas Mallory certainly wasn't the first of the Grail romances, but it remains the most complete. What is more, it appeared at the most crucial time of all, when the struggle between the Golden Thread and the repressive forces of Church and state was at its strongest. Although the Church quite naturally tried to hijack the symbol of the Grail, specifically relating it to the cup from which Jesus drank at the Last Supper, to a whole skein of people across western Europe, it meant very much more.

In closing this chapter, it is worth mentioning a further fact relating to the timing of Mallory's book. It is possible that by the time *Le Morte d'Arthur* came to print, Mallory himself was already dead. However, the existence of the Caxton manuscripts from Ripon Cathedral library appear to suggest that this was not the case. Either way *Le Morte d'Arthur* was published at a pivotal moment in English history. In the middle of 1485, when Caxton was putting the finishing touches to the book, the king occupying the throne of England was Richard III. Just three short months after *Le Morte d'Arthur* reached a ready readership, Richard was killed at the Battle of Bosworth. The English throne came to a Welshman and a Lancastrian supporter, Henry VII. Neither Mallory nor Caxton could possibly have known about these events. After all, Richard might easily have defeated Henry Tudor and retained the throne. But a knowledge of Henry Tudor's imminent arrival could easily have affected the publication date of the book.

Richard III was not a popular king in the eyes of everyone, but he was the last of the Plantaganet kings. He certainly had the same family blood as that of Godfroi de Bouillon flowing in his veins. This was the blood that belonged to the line of David and to Jesus himself. But Richard was essentially French in origin, as were all the Norman kings. Henry Tudor, on the other hand, although a man with Norman ancestry too, was at least partly of genuine Welsh blood. What Henry became, and the way his dynasty altered Britain, is a matter of fact. However, at the time of his accession to the throne of England, he must have been greeted with enthusiasm by those of true indigenous stock.

It would appear that the habit of publishers choosing the most auspicious moment to launch a book is not at all a new phenomenon. This does certainly seem to have been the case with *Le Morte d'Arthur*. Supposedly, Caxton finished his edition on the last day of July 1485. On the very next day, 1 August 1485, Henry Tudor landed in Wales with his small army, determined to wrest the throne from Richard Plantaganet. Had Mallory's *Le Morte d'Arthur* been deliberately kept back to coincide with the arrival of this "New Arthur," in Britain? Alternatively, was it rushed through the printing process at very short notice? It appears that either Sir Thomas Mallory's Lancastrian sympathies were shared by his publisher or, at least, that Caxton was an extremely astute businessman.

Some authorities have noticed that Caxton's handling of Mallory's work is clumsy, and this is offered as proof that Mallory must himself have been dead before Caxton received the manuscript. For what other reason would Mallory have allowed his book to go to press with so many mistakes. Actually, this state of affairs is quite understandable. Speed was suddenly of the essence if the book was to be available to coincide with Henry Tudor's imminent arrival. Perhaps in those last frenetic days Thomas Mallory was elsewhere. As a Lancastrian supporter he was probably happy to contribute his genius to the coming struggle, even if that genius was somewhat tarnished by clumsy publication.

The book may have been very important. Richard's fortunes swung in the balance and in the end relied almost entirely on the behavior of one family – the Stanleys. They were powerful barons, and their lands lay predominantly in the West Midlands and in the northwest of Britain. There they had many salt line manors. Their influence was predominant in exactly those locations where Mallory places so many of the Grail legends. The Stanleys had been Richard III's uneasy allies. But on the day Richard joined in battle with Henry Tudor at Bosworth, Leicester, they changed sides. It was their troops whose blows put paid to the Plantaganet line.

Sir Thomas Mallory, a descendant of the ancient "Mailor's people" was the legatee of a book replete with mistakes – but it may have helped to gain him a British king. What is more, the Tudor kings made much of their indigenous British heritage. Along with the Mallorys and the Stanleys, the Tudors most probably retained elements of the lineal Megalithic priesthood.

And if the reader still doubts either this geographical placing of Sir Thomas Mallory, or his salt line Fraternity credentials, then Caxton's preface to *Le Morte d'Arthur* might be the clincher. Caxton tells his readers that a book concerning Arthur is well overdue because he considers King Arthur to have been the first of the three most virtuous men since the birth of Jesus. The second of these he states to have been the Emperor Charlemagne, and the last and most recent – Godfroi de Bouillon. As the reader will realize immediately, we have here three characters whose lives are crucial to this unfolding story. Caxton's mention of Charlemagne was undoubtedly meant to be ironic, as all those who were party to the secrets of the Golden Thread would have instantly realized.

CHAPTER 18

From Troyes to Rosslyn

Sometime immediately prior to Philip IV's attack on the Templars in October 1307, the substantial Templar fleet disappeared from its home port of La Rochelle. Authors have suggested numerous destinations for the Templar sailors, who had clearly been given notice of what was to come. The most plausible destination for the Templar fleet, or at least elements of it, remains Scotland.[21]

There were and always had been strong dynastic connections between those who created the Templar Order and certain elements of the Scottish nobility. Hugh de Payen, who is named as being the first Grand Master of the Templar Order, is shown in historic documents to have been married to Catherine St. Clair, whose family held lands around Edinburgh. However, the St. Clairs were not originally from Scotland. St. Clair (later Sinclair) was a Norman French family, from Pont l'Eveque, a longitudinal salt line location. The family took its name from a village dedicated to a somewhat mysterious ninth-century monk and recluse, who was known as St. Clarus. St. Bernard may well have had this saint in mind when he named his own Cistercian monastery Clairvaux, which can be interpreted to mean "The Valley of Clarus."

Templar personnel could easily have found refuge in Scotland after 1307, since the rulers of the country were reticent to outlaw the Order. It has been suggested, though never proven, that Templar knights fought for Scotland against the English at the battle of Bannockburn, in June 1314. The relationship between the Templars and Scotland had been a long one. The first Templar presbytery outside of France had been at a place still called Temple, which is east of Edinburgh. The ruins of the Templar properties there can still be seen.

Meanwhile, on the west coast of Scotland, in Argyll, there are many Templar-style graves, dating to a period after 1307. Argyll has been cited as one of the most likely destinations for the fleeing Templar ships. Whether or not this story is true, there is one specific building in Scotland that is definitely associated with the Knights Templar, but which dates from a period over a century after the Templar institution had supposedly ceased to exist. This is Rosslyn Chapel, which stands a few miles south of Edinburgh.

Rosslyn Chapel is a small, architectural masterpiece. It was built between 1446 and 1486. The building to be seen today is said by some experts to be only the Lady Chapel of a much larger projected building, which would have formed a collegiate church. On almost any day of the year buses carrying passengers from all over the world alight at the end of the lane leading to Rosslyn Chapel, and with good cause. This ornate and enigmatic little building carries more clearly than almost any other location an indication of the direction Templarism ultimately took in Britain. Rosslyn Chapel is a virtual shrine to Freemasonry.

Rosslyn Chapel is built in the Gothic style, a form of architecture that first appeared in France in the twelfth century. Nobody is certain where the idea for Gothic architecture arose but it has some distinguishing features that set it apart from earlier building techniques and it hides a wealth of secrets that formed part of the Grail knowledge held by the Golden Thread. Gothic architecture is distinguished by the use of arches with pointed tops. These are known as "ogives." This form of arch is incredibly strong and is used almost exclusively in the great Gothic masterpieces to form very tall buildings, in which the arches soar, one on top of another, to great heights. Internal stresses from the walls are carried outside the building to the very distinctive "flying buttresses," allowing walls to be relatively thin, and to have huge windows, which as a result of early and exquisite Flemish stained glass makes the interior of such buildings a blaze of color.

An author who probably best understood the knowledge that underpinned the sudden rise of Gothic architecture was Louis Charpentier.[22] In his book *The Mystery of Chartres Cathedral*, he concentrated on one of the earliest of the Gothic Cathedrals. My own research added to Charpentier's observations and turned up some further interesting facts.

The town of Chartres is situated on neither a longitudinal nor a latitudinal salt line. However, it does have a strong geographical relationship with Jerusalem. Chartres occupies a latitude of 48 degrees 29 minutes North. Jerusalem is at 31 degrees 47 minutes North. This means that in a latitudinal sense, and looking at things through Megalithic eyes, the two locations are 17 Megalithic degrees apart.

Even fairly accurate estimations of the dimensions of the huge Gothic cathedrals are notoriously difficult to obtain. Charpentier measured Chartres extremely carefully, using chains, and produced results that could be checked against Megalithic models, which makes it a good case for study. Chartres was also the resting-place of a Black Madonna and was one of the preferred resorts of St. Bernard of Clairvaux.

There has been a church of some sort on the Chartres site for a very long period of time. Prior to this, by common consent, the location was sacred to our pagan ancestors. The cathedral, as we see it today, was constructed after 1194. A great fire had destroyed the previous church. The two towers that grace the present site had been built much earlier, around 1134. Strangely, these were not in keeping with the church that then stood on the site. They were geometrically in tune with the later building of 1194, so it seems as though the cathedral as it appears today was already conceived during the first part of the twelfth century. The fire of 1194, which virtually destroyed the former cathedral, was the incentive necessary to erect the present structure. It was completed in an almost unbelievable 26 years. Many authors have suggested that Chartres was Templar inspired and that they may have supplied both the money and much of the manpower to build it.

In the world of sacred architecture Louis Charpentier is famous for having made a startling find relating to both Chartres and a number of other Gothic cathedrals. He discovered the "local cubit." The local cubit is a specific linear measurement that was used on each particular site. This unit is different for each cathedral but remains constant within a specific building. Charpentier claimed that the various local cubits were not arbitrary at all, and that they had been derived in an ingenious manner. He demonstrated that the local cubit for Chartres was equal to 1/100,000th part of 1 degree of the Earth's circumference at the latitude of Chartres. Charpentier showed that there had also been a local cubit at both Amiens and Reims. These fitted the same criteria. In both cases, the local cubit was 1/100,000th part of 1 degree of the Earth's circumference at the latitude of the locations in question.

In the case of Chartres, the local cubit was 0.738 meters. Most of the measurements of the finished building conform to this measure. It had originally seemed to me that the existence of the local cubits in Gothic cathedrals made the idea of the continued use of Megalithic mathematics in their construction rather less than likely. The local cubit is based on modern geometry, of the 360-degree variety. Megalithic geometry responds to a 366-degree circle. In the case of Chartres at least it turned out my initial assumption was incorrect.

Charpentier did not content himself with measuring the cathedral of Chartres as it looks today. Rather he took it to pieces on paper, to try and understand the ideas, knowledge, and skills that went into its design. He discovered that the whole building had been planned around three geometric shapes, which he called tables. There was a square one, a rectangular one, and a round one. Everything that the finished building became was responsive to these three geometric patterns. Charpentier claimed that the first of the tables to be constructed was the rectangular one. He showed that the dimensions of this had been determined by the width of the "sacred mound" upon which Chartres stands, a mound that has probably been sacred since Stone Age times. A study of the three tables throws up some remarkable facts.

Although Charpentier could demonstrate the continued use in the finished cathedral of what he claimed to be the local cubit, this measurement of 0.738 meters is not related to the size of the geometric tables themselves. The unit used to create the tables was just over 0.82 meters.

Together with Christopher Knight and Dr. Robert Lomas, I had been able to show exactly how the Megalithic Yard had been discovered and then passed on from site to site across almost 2,000 years. The true importance of the Megalithic Yard lies in the fact that it is a logical subdivision of the Earth's circumference.

The Megalithic Yard of 0.8296 meters is strikingly close to the measurement used to construct the geometric tables for Chartres

Cathedral. Charpentier is at pains to point out that his original assessment of the 0.82 meters measure could be short of the mark by some millimeters. The reason for this is simply that the cathedral is so hard to measure accurately. The fact that a unit of measurement so close to the Megalithic Yard cropped up at all in conjunction with the building of Chartres was immediately of interest to me.

And here the puzzle really begins, because there is a close mathematical relationship between 0.82 meters and the final local cubit of 0.738 meters. A casual observation will show that 100 local cubits of 0.738 meters, is the same as 90 units of 0.82 meters. It can therefore be shown that every major proportion of Chartres Cathedral is also an expression of the Megalithic Yard. For example:

Width of choir = 20 local cubits = 18 Megalithic Yards
Length of choir = 50 local cubits = 45 Megalithic Yards
Length of nave = 100 local cubits = 90 Megalithic Yards
Length of transept = 90 local cubits = 81 Megalithic Yards.

In the case of Chartres, the intrinsic relationship between the local cubit and the Megalithic Yard seems to have been engineered into the very mathematical base that underpins the building. This must have been done at the time of the building of the new cathedral, beginning with the towers that were constructed in 1134 and the obvious conclusion is that whoever built Chartres understood Megalithic measurement.

The true "magic" of Gothic architecture is not simply expressed in one great example such as Chartres. It exists within the most basic arch upon which all Gothic buildings stand. Each and every one encapsulates aspects of ancient knowledge, made manifest in stone. The Gothic arch or ogive is made in a very specific way. The curve of the arch is created around a five-pointed star. This is the star of Venus, or the pentacle. It is shown below, together with the rose and the rosary.

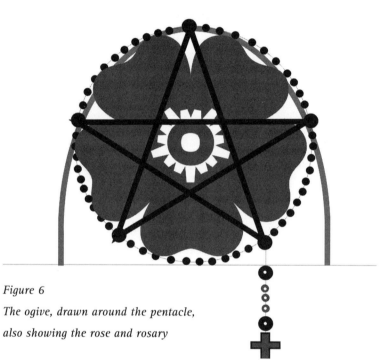

Figure 6

The ogive, drawn around the pentacle,
also showing the rose and rosary

The first known example of a pentacle is to be found carved into a standing stone on Ilkley Moor, Yorkshire, England and was probably put there between four and five thousand years ago. The pentacle itself is a good example of a geometrical device that is replete with a mixture of religious reverence and practical knowledge and so therefore typifies what I came to call "Golden Thread Knowledge."

In a previous chapter, I made reference to the fact that the pentacle represents the relationship between the Earth and the planet Venus, itself dedicated to the Great Goddess. Its form lies within the creation of the "rosary" but it has other important secrets to impart. The relationship between the angles of a pentacle betray a knowledge of what came to be known as the "Golden Mean." In medieval times, this was rediscovered by Leonardo Fibbonacci (c.1170–c.1240). Fibbonacci had been studying the reproduction rates of rabbits and stumbled on an apparently mystical sequence. The sequence runs as follows: 1,1,2,3,5,8,13,21,34,55,89,144,233,377,610 and so on. Each number is added to the previous number to create an ascending sequence that became known as the Fibbonacci Series. The relationship of each number to its predecessor settles down to a ratio of 1.618:1.

In a practical sense, this ratio had been understood for many centuries before Fibbonacci's time and had been used in the construction of buildings in Ancient Greece. The ratio is better known today as "phi." Phi is inherent in the composition of the pentacle but it appears almost everywhere in nature, from the shells of sea creatures such as the nautilus to the arms of a spiral galaxy. It is also inherent in the proportions of the human face and body. Its importance was touched on by Dan Brown in the evocative and thought provoking novel, *The Da Vinci Code*.[23]

The pentacle or five-pointed star has been demonized in recent centuries, in part because the established Church knew how important this geometric construct was to pre-Christian religion, yet it is inimical to all the great Gothic churches. The fact that those building these masterpieces were quite well aware of the relationship between the pentacle, the golden mean and the

Goddess is demonstrated in a very special way. As explained earlier, there are many examples of the ribbed ogive doorways of Gothic cathedrals and churches that have a rosebud carved into the very point of the arch. This is quite clearly meant to represent the clitoris, just as surely as these great doorways represent the vagina of the Goddess, whose womb is signified by the body of the church itself. All are tied, symbolically and practically, to the dog rose, which is capable, like the Great Goddess, of virgin birth.

Gothic architecture is undoubtedly an inspiration of the Golden Thread and began to appear during the lifetime of one of its greatest representatives, St. Bernard of Clairvaux. On more than one occasion in his life he described God as being "Height and breadth and depth and width." This declaration demonstrates St. Bernard's own fascination for numbers and sacred geometry. He was also interested in the "geometry of music," which Charpentier showed to be reflected in the ratios of Gothic buildings.

Rosslyn Chapel is an example of Gothic architecture at its best. The building is festooned with sumptuous carvings and, to the trained eye, is also a positive explosion of paganism, all of which points to the survival of Goddess worship.

Slightly behind and to the right of the altar (if indeed Rosslyn Chapel can be said to have an altar) is a fabulously carved spiral pillar, like the twisted roots of a great tree. From this emanates a riot of lively carved foliage, which wraps and entwines itself around most of the interior of the building. All of this was originally painted and would have represented a riot of color to those visiting the chapel. Particularly intriguing in this regard is the fact that some of the examples of plants, so realistically

Figure 7 Rosslyn Chapel

captured in stone within Rosslyn Chapel, such as aloe and maize, were supposedly unknown to Europeans when the chapel was built. Within this realization lies another part of the Grail secret – that of navigation.

Rosslyn Chapel was built by the Sinclair family, that same dynasty that had originally been known as 'St. Clair' and which had been allied to Templarism from its very inception. The builder of Rosslyn was Earl William Sinclair and we now know very well why examples of American plants are contained within the carvings of his masterpiece. The Sinclairs were Earls of Orkney. They had strong Nordic ties and were excellent sailors. One of their number, Henry Sinclair, set off on an epic journey in May 1398, some four decades before Columbus made his more famous voyage in 1492.

It would take him to Nova Scotia (New Scotland) and then on down the east coast of North America to the region now known as Massachusetts. At Westfield, Massachusetts there is a Templar grave, dedicated to one of Henry's knights who died in that location. A round tower was built at Newport, Rhode Island, and this has survived. The official settlement of Newport was established much later, in 1636. Records there, from four years previously, had indicated the presence of the round tower. They had suggested that a European settlement had once existed in the area.

Henry Sinclair's Nordic blood was probably an asset. According to old sagas the Vikings too had visited America. The Norman French themselves were of Viking blood, and their name actually means "Norsemen." Normans were prominent in the salt line Fraternity of the twelfth century and beyond. It is certain that their seamanship added to the success of the Templar fleet. Henry Sinclair's direct knowledge of the Atlantic sea routes was Templar in origin. Assertions have regularly been made that much of the early Templar wealth came from silver. This, it is suggested, was transported across the Atlantic from the shores of central and South America. These rumors were rife long before information relating to Henry Sinclair ever came to light.

The original Sinclair trips to America made the later journeys of Columbus and other explorers possible. An officer called Drummond was listed as being one of Henry Sinclair's officers. Drummond's grandson, John, lived for some time in Madeira. There he became closely associated with the man who would become the father-in-law of Christopher Columbus. Bartholomew Perstellow had been a friend of John Drummond's father and John himself was an intimate of Columbus. Perstellow was a past Grand Master of the Knights of Christ, which was merely a branch of the post-1307 Templar Order under a different name.

Prior to his own journey, Columbus had to prove his credentials to Ferdinand and Isabella of Spain. It was these monarchs who were to equip and finance his fleet. Columbus was in possession of certain charts. He called John Drummond before the Spanish monarchs to attest to their authenticity. In all probability the charts originated in the Drummond family. The little fleet set out under the command of Columbus in 1492. The sails of all three ships carried the red cross of the Templars and it is quite likely that Columbus himself was somehow associated with the Knights of Christ.

The foliage, carved in solid stone within Rosslyn Chapel, proves conclusively that the American continent was well understood by the Sinclairs in the fifteenth century and it seems unlikely that Henry Sinclair's journey was the first made by the family to the New World. The strong inference here is that the Sinclairs were in direct possession of Templar navigational know-how and that they were most likely simply undertaking a journey that had been commonplace to Templar sailors.

Rosslyn Chapel is suffused with mysteries. Some authors have suggested that the building is actually a copy of Herod's Temple in Jerusalem, which had been found by the first Templar knights to visit the Holy City, not long after the First Crusade.[24] It is known that there is a sealed crypt beneath the chapel and many suggestions have been made as to what archeologists might find buried within it – everything from secret documents relating to Templar knowledge, to the head of Jesus himself.

My own feeling about Rosslyn Chapel is that if any visitor wishes to see the true secrets of the building, it is merely necessary to open one's eyes and look around. Rosslyn's shape, form, and carvings show it to be a testimony to the survival of a nature-based, feminine-oriented religion, which was already thousands of years old when Christianity originated. Except for very recent additions, there is absolutely nothing to be seen at Rosslyn to indicate it was ever intended to be a place of Christian worship. What is more, the suggestion that Rosslyn Chapel is truly the Lady Chapel of what was intended to be a much bigger church doesn't stand up to scrutiny. Although there are places in which the building seems to stop abruptly, with ragged stonework and doorways that do not lead anywhere, more than one architect has borne testimony to the fact that Rosslyn Chapel was never intended to be more than it is. It would have suited the Templar, Golden Thread priests of the Sinclair family to have people "believe" their remarkable chapel would eventually form part of a true Christian church but it is, in reality, what it is suggested to be – a Lady Chapel. The Lady in question is the Great Goddess, a fact the Sinclair family understood only too well.

There almost certainly is a connection between Rosslyn Chapel and the Jerusalem Temple and I reach this conclusion for a number of reasons. Not least of these is the realization that Rosslyn Chapel stands exactly 39 Megalithic degrees West of the Jerusalem Temple. Another strong indication comes within the practices of Freemasonry, which I hope to show was the true legatee of Golden Thread knowledge from the fifteenth century onwards. Many of the rituals of Freemasonry revolve around Solomon's Jerusalem Temple and they were undoubtedly played out amongst the pillars and carved foliage of Rosslyn Chapel. The true seeker of the Holy Grail is just as likely to find it in this remarkable building, with its curious history, as if it were actually packed into some precious golden casket far beneath the floor of the chapel's unyielding granite.

CHAPTER 19

The True Nature of the Grail

Stories of the Holy Grail were a positive inspiration to the knightly classes around the time Rosslyn Chapel was being constructed, but it is likely that only relatively few individuals had any inkling of what really lay behind them. One of the most potent of the Grail romances, which was still popular in the time of William Sinclair, and certainly the most enigmatic, is one that was contemporary with that of Wolfram von Eschenbach's *Parzival* (circa 1190). We don't know much about Wolfram as a historical character, but in the case of *Perlesvaus*, we know even less. The author of this work chose to remain absolutely anonymous. He was almost certainly a high-ranking Templar knight. If we are to approach the Grail in any way, it may be through *Perlesvaus* that this is best achieved.

Like the writers of the ancient Celtic tales that comprise parts of a fascinating medieval Welsh book, *The Mabinogion* the writer of *Perlesvaus*[25] spends pages describing the nature of fighting in the medieval period. He does so with such precision and detail that one is left with the impression that the author had a detailed knowledge of the military conventions of his period. This is not history at a distance. The writer graphically describes not only the manner of fighting, but the nature of wounds sustained as a result of it. The Perceval of this tale finds himself at a castle where all the inhabitants appear to be Templar knights. All wear the Templar white tunic, and the red cross is also present. Perceval is told that he is descended from Joseph of Arimathea, though the story itself is a Dark Age, Arthurian invention.

There are many alchemical references in *Perlesvaus*, such as men made of copper. One of the Templar-type knights tells Parceval that "There are heads sealed in silver and heads sealed in lead." This extract is particularly interesting in Templar terms.

At the fall of the Templars in 1307, parts of a female skull were found in a silver reliquary in the Templar headquarters in Paris. It carried the legend. "CAPUT LVIIIM." The skull was incomplete and the bones that did remain were wrapped in white linen. The white linen was itself further wrapped in a red cloth. Although the legend carried by the reliquary has never been understood it is possible that the Templars believed these to be either the bones of the Virgin Mary or, more likely, those of Mary Magdalene. The skull and its reliquary disappeared but later representations of it show the "M" to have been of a particular form. It actually looked like ♍, which is the astrological symbol for the constellation of Virgo – the Virgin.

Aspects of king sacrifice are mentioned in *Perlesvaus*. These mesh well with the Isis myths that seem to have abounded in the deepest recesses of Templar practice. In addition, *Perlesvaus* refers to the roasting and eating of children. The accusation of this practice was leveled at the Templars in the trials after 1307. In reality, they were surely innocent of this heinous crime. However, this does smack of the legend of Dionysus, mentioned earlier in this book. The Dionysus myths were associated with a mystery cult similar to that of Isis – in this case Demeter.

Another intriguing passage from the same work seems to indicate that this transcript may have been used in part as a foundation for other accusations leveled at the Templars. In one part of the story, Perceval watches a priest beating a red cross with a staff, over and over again. The reader will recall that spitting on the crucifix and stamping it underfoot was one of the practices for which the Templars were dissolved and excommunicated.

In *Perlesvaus*, the Grail is not totally synonymous with the holy cup of the Last Supper. The writer clearly indicates that the Grail is a secret of great importance. Certainly, this secret is in some way connected with Jesus, for the Grail, on at least one level, is a kind of vision, or series of visions, some of which deal with the crucifixion. Only much later does the Grail become a chalice. Visions of the Grail in *Perlesvaus* are five in number. The first is that of a crowned king, crucified. The second image is that of a child. The third vision is of a man wearing a crown of thorns, bleeding from his forehead, his feet, his palms, and his side. The fourth image is not specified – probably for a very good reason. And the final vision is that of a chalice. What connects all these visions is a very strong light and a wonderful fragrance. All of this imagery has Kabalistic and quite possibly alchemical symbolism. It probably meant something quite specific to a certain proportion of those reading *Perlesvaus*.

Most of the Grail stories indicate that whatever the Grail might actually be, it is lineal. In other words it has something to do with a specific family or a group of people. Often characters are informed that they are "of the Grail." Since they invariably respond with surprise, it is obvious that they were not aware of this fact previously. Generally speaking the Grail, as "an object" is impossible to tie down. Perhaps the fact that the stories often revert to referring to the Grail as a chalice is most revealing. In this form, it encapsulates so much of the mystery religions and the aspects of nature and fertility that underpinned them.

Even in their Christian symbolism, there is significance to the Grail stories. Churches of the period during which these story cycles were being laid down often had wall paintings or stained glass windows depicting Jesus sandwiched between the boards of a winepress. The explanation of this habit so commonly trotted out is that Jesus is "the Vine" of New Testament speak. Supposedly, his blood is that of the sacrament, spilled to cleanse the sins of the world. But it would be just as applicable in this context to view the body in the winepress as the harvest of nature. It could be seen as the life-giving bounty of nature being pressed into the wine that would sustain humanity through the following year. It is simply a variant on the theme of "John Barleycorn," in which the barley is killed and beaten to make beer. The wine spills forth from the chalice, which is the "sacred womb." In this context, it would seem that the imagery portrayed by the Last Supper is very telling. As we have seen, it smacks more of the heart of the Vegetation god and the mystery cults than it does of any variant of Orthodox Judaism.

This alone could be the enduring message of the Grail. A yearly event played out symbolically, with Christ likening himself to the Vegetation gods of old. His resurrection is therefore synonymous with that of both Osiris and Dionysus. The missing image from *Perlesvaus*, which the author is very careful not to reveal, is almost certainly that of the Goddess herself. Through her intervention the sacrificed king does not die, since he is reborn through her. He becomes a legacy of the seed of his dead counterpart. On and on, year by year, and for eternity. If so, the images have been slightly juxtaposed, probably intentionally so. The writer of *Perlesvaus* might have wished to remain anonymous but a Church ready to punish heresy at a stroke may well have been able to track him down.

The real order of the Grail visions is as follows. The child, the scourged man with wounds, the crucified king, the Goddess, and finally the chalice, the womb of the Goddess through which the child will appear once more.

The only part of the myth that the Christian Church has managed to eradicate from this age-old story, in connection with the Christian mystery, is the presence of the Goddess. In Christian terms, it seems most likely that this role was intended to be split between the two Marys, the Virgin and the Magdalene.

In this context the widowed mother of the hero of the Grail cycles, most usually Perceval, is also understandable. Perceval is often told that he is a legatee of the Grail family. Symbolically this means that he represents the god reborn. In all the ancient story cycles, the old god must die so that the new one can take his place. This is why the widowed mother is so common in Grail stories.

The heritage of all the Grail stories lies at the heart of forgotten "initiations." The evidence that this is the case is still to be found in ancient British and Irish legends. We have seen that the Grail is, as often as not, a cup of some sort and that this imagery comes to us direct from Celtic mythology, which was almost certainly borrowing such tales from an earlier people in Britain. Once again, this brings us to the fabulous tales of "magic cauldrons."

The most complete of the early cauldron references come to us from Irish story cycles. The reason that these stories have remained intact in the Irish traditions is probably twofold. Firstly, Ireland represents the westernmost extension of Celtic penetration. It is logical to assume that the Celts populated Ireland after their arrival in the British mainland. Probably for this reason, many stories older than the emergence of the Celts as a distinct people appear to have remained more or less intact. But there is a second and more important reason for the survival of the Irish cauldron legends.

Extant in Irish literature is an acknowledgment that the island has been subjected, in remote times, to successive waves of peoples from distant shores. Robert Graves was an author who dealt specifically with these matters. Irish culture, he asserted, was influenced by newcomers from southern Spain, Thrace, and pre-Hellenic Greece.[26] These facts are no longer doubted, and particularly not the last. There are many Irish myths that find almost perfect parallels in the most archaic Greek cycles. I am personally certain, though it is impossible to prove the fact, that this was also the case with the mainland of Britain. However, further incursions of Germanic peoples, and latterly the Norman French, has purged many of these pre-Hellenic tales from Welsh legends. In the case of England, nearly all of them have disappeared. Ireland therefore remains the bastion of pre-Celtic thinking, religion, and folklore. In Ireland the magic cauldron appears regularly.

In fact all aspects and talismans of the later Grail are to be viewed in various parts of Irish mythology. This includes the Grail's power of providing food, its capacity to heal, its supervision by a beautiful woman, and its association with death and rebirth.

There was, the ancient Irish storytellers assert, a group of people in Ireland long before the Celts arrived. These people were known as the Tuatha De Danaan. They were powerful magicians and sorcerers. Some stories suggest that, forced on the defensive by successive waves of new arrivals into their midst, the Tuatha De Danaan were driven literally underground. Now they are the race of fable, the legendary people of the hollow hills. The always-superstitious Celts never failed to offer the reverence due to such learned and mystical individuals.

It is said that the Tuatha De Danaan possessed certain treasures.

Amongst these was the cauldron of Dagda. Dagda's cauldron represented the horn of plenty and as such has contributed to the Grail legends. In certain Welsh tales, Merlin had at least four such vessels. Bran, as we have seen, was also associated with the magic cauldron.

The other enduring motif of the medieval Grail cycles is the spear, present in most of the medieval stories and often seen by those glimpsing the Grail. The spear is inverted, so that its point faces the open mouth of the chalice, and it invariably drips blood into the Grail. A spear of this sort is also to be found amongst the treasures of the Tuatha De Danaan. Here it is the spear of Lug, and such weapons figure prominently in other ancient tales. Similar to the spear is the magical sword, which is one of the most enduring features of Arthurian literature. In the tales of Arthur the sword is called Caliburn or Excalibur, but it has a long and illustrious pedigree. Again, one of the treasures of the Tuatha De Danaan was a fabulous sword, known as the sword of Lug. In the Grail legends the sword is often broken, and has to be welded, or magically regenerated by the story's hero.

The association of the cauldron and the spear or sword is certainly a remnant of sexual symbolism. These objects have, with the passing of time, become the very talismans that lie at the heart of the Grail romances. It requires little imagination to see the phallic and virginal associations of the inverted spear and the Grail. This is particularly relevant when the Grail itself is a relative of the cauldron of plenty, the womb of the Mother Goddess.

In ancient symbolism swords, spears, and lightning are often interchangeable at the level of the deity. There are enduring folk themes of lightning in the late summer representing the sexual union of the Sky God and the Earth Goddess.

The main thrust of the Grail stories remains roughly similar. The hero arrives at a castle where the Lord of the land is seriously injured in the groin; in other words, he is sterile. The hero views the Grail, which is usually in the possession of a beautiful woman, and this character frequently has a Christian name that can be identified with flowers or vegetation. The vision of the Grail is often accompanied by a view of the bleeding spear. If the hero asks the correct question, "Whom does the Grail serve?," or "Whom do these things serve?," the Lord of the land, who is identified as the Fisher King, is healed. As a result, the barren land returns to fruitfulness.

In many of the romances, the hero is later told that he is related to the Fisher King and himself becomes Lord of the land. There are variations in all the Grail romances, but the pattern outlined above is a broad synthesis of most.

It is likely that the Grail stories once represented a series of stages of initiation into a mystery rite. These are likely to have been played out symbolically at the creation of a new king. They may also have been relevant when a young man of noble birth came of age. Roger Sherman Loomis in *Celtic Mythology and Arthurian Romance*[27] deals with this subject, He envisages a situation were an initiate, who must be sexually pure, is brought into a dimly lit cave. There he sees an old man, groaning on a bed. Further off is a beautiful young woman, guarding the sacred cauldron and either the sword or the bloody spear. The initiate is told that the old man is injured and sterile and that only the correct procedure can allow him to recover. When he does, the land will become fertile once again. At this point the initiate is expected to walk to the maid guarding the cauldron ask the question. "Who do these things serve?" No answer is necessary save the cheers of previously unseen watchers at the rite. With the correct questions asked the supposedly injured lord rises from his couch. The initiate is led off by the protectoress of the cauldron, the "Holy Whore" of the proceedings. Her function has been reviewed in previous chapters.

Doubtless this is only a part of the truth. Such ceremonies lie so far back in our history that no vestige of them, apart from the Grail legends, exists. It would be amazing if we did know more because a "mystery" is well named. It cannot be divulged to anyone who has not himself taken part in the sacred initiation.

Variations on this theme were doubtless associated with a symbolic death and rebirth rite. This is certainly true in the case of the Eleusan Mysteries. In these ceremonies, which took place in Eleusis, Greece, all initiates had to "die" in order to be raised to the Mystery of Demeter. Although little is known of this ceremony there is no doubt that sheaves of corn and cakes made from corn were part of the ritual. Its patroness, Demeter, the goddess of the rite, is yet another representation of the Great Goddess of Neolithic times.

There are tales from Ireland, particularly from Loch Durg, which speak of a magical cave, where aspirants were placed, ostensibly alone, for a full night. During this time they would visit the Underworld. If they returned in the morning, they were allowed out of the locked cave. If the did not emerge it was understood that they had perished and their name was never spoken again.

As to that most enigmatic character in the Grail legends, the Fisher King, there is probably a degree of genuinely Christian symbolism in his title. Jesus did, after all, say to his prospective disciples, "I will make you fishers of men." A crude picture of a fish was an early, and at first secret, symbol of the Christian sect. However, this may be only part of the truth. The gods of Irish mythology, who seem to be the counterpart of the Fisher King in the Grail stories, were invariably "gods of the sea." They are the same deities to which fishermen would have paid homage. In mystical terms, the Fisher King, with his groin injury, is the old and dying god. There can be no fertility possible because the old god has lost his potency. In many of the Grail romances, the correct question of the Grail restores the Fisher King to full health. As a result the land returns to abundance. In some of the stories, he dies within three days and the hero assumes his mantle.

Finally the all-important question remains regarding the Grail. "Whom does one serve with it?" The question is never answered directly. The reason for this silence in the romances is twofold. Firstly the answer to the question is part of the great mystery and belongs only to the initiate. Secondly, the salt line Grail romancers were responsive to a group of people who moved within the circles of the orthodox Church, but who saw its symbols in a radically different way. These writers lived in deeply Catholic societies and were understandably anxious to preserve their own lives. They also had a responsibility to fellow believers in the alternative Christianity. They knew the answer only too well but they would hardly have committed it to the written word.

"And who does one serve with it?" The Great Goddess personification of the Earth. Her consort died each year so that the world might live. In the following year she would bear the fruit of her womb, the wine of the chalice. This was the young god of spring.

This in part is an explanation of the Grail, its historical heritage, and symbolism. But it can only be a small section of the story.

Those people who kept the Grail stories alive by writing them down were aware that the Grail also represented knowledge of a more tangible and less esoteric sort. Knowledge is power and wealth – a fact that the Golden Thread recognized only too well and still recognizes to this very day. An acceptance of this fact led the Templars to create such an intricate and wide-ranging economic empire. It also encouraged the Sinclair family to maintain its contacts with the mineral-rich New World and it inspired them to build on the crumbling foundations of Templarism, something that would help to create the world we know today.

CHAPTER 20

Band of Brothers

Seen from the point of view of someone who has never encountered Freemasonry at all, the whole institution might appear somewhat bizarre. Freemasonry definitely has the overtones of a mystery religion – but a version from which the essential core has been removed. What remains are a series of moral imperatives that might appear laudable but lacking in any real spiritual imperative.

Masonic lodges are comprised of groups of men who meet on a regular basis. Any would-be Freemason must undergo a series of ceremonies before he has access to the ranks and privileges of full Masonic status. Specific tracts of obscure prose must be remembered and recited at such times. Officers of the lodge, many of whom have stylized titles, officiate in the ceremonies. The performance of these also demands specific items of clothing and they take place in carefully arranged surroundings in a room, often built for the purpose, known as a "lodge."

The three stages of initiation are known in the Craft of Freemasonry as "degrees." All of these relate in part to a semi-mythical version of the building of Solomon's Temple. The degrees are said to represent various stages of induction through which would-be stonemasons once had to pass before being accepted as "Master Masons." Freemasons recognize that the modern version of the Craft is "speculative" and that no special knowledge of actual masonry skills is necessary as a prerequisite of membership.

Freemasonry is most notable for its supposed secrecy. Actually, this is a nonsense and is a point of view that has, in the main, been dreamed up and perpetuated by a mass media that loves to suspect mystery, scandal, wrongdoing, or downright evil almost anywhere. There is little or nothing that cannot be discovered about any Freemasonic ritual in any average public library. There are certain words used in Masonic rituals that Masons prefer not to have uttered by people who are not "brothers." However, the reader may be disappointed to learn that even when these are known very well, they are not particularly illuminating to the casual observer. In short, a full knowledge of all Masonic practice is more likely to bore the interested party than to inform them in any way.

On his way to the third degree, the prospective Master Mason has to endure some fairly gruesome threats of reprisals if he ever divulges any of the secrets of the Craft. These are entirely symbolic, though as we shall see, they probably meant something more sinister once upon a time. He will also be expected, at various times, to bare one of his legs and also his chest, as well as being blindfolded. A photograph of the proceedings, rather that causing gasps of wonder, usually elicits howls of laughter from non-Masons.

To by far the largest percentage of its members, Freemasonry is little more than a fraternal social club. To most of these, the ceremonies attached to meetings are an irksome and slightly irrelevant diversion from an otherwise enjoyable meal and drink with "the lads." A small number of Masons do believe that the various ceremonies have some deep and probably highly symbolic meaning. An even tinier cross-section takes the trouble to try and discover what the Craft is really all about – if anything.

Though not a Mason myself I have studied Freemasonry very carefully. My aim has been to achieve as good an understanding as possible of the various social, historical, and perhaps religious components that comprise the Craft today. I had a head start because I am well versed in both astrology and astronomy.

These disciplines do help the researcher to gain some understanding of the rich symbolic base that underpins Freemasonic ritual.

A good knowledge of both ancient and more recent history at first seemed to be a distinct advantage to the serious student of Masonic ritual. But this soon proved to be a dubious assumption. Most of "supposed" Masonic history showed itself to be a fudge. At best, it appeared as a garbled version of pseudo history and the accumulated myth patterns of several distinct and different cultures. Anyone embarking on a close scrutiny of Freemasonry is likely to come to much the same conclusions – but first impressions can be very misleading.

To the unenlightened observer the Masonic Lodge looks like a badly arranged room filled with garish bric-a-brac. Nothing could be further from the truth. Every item of apparel, each piece of furniture, and every strange picture contains deep meaning. Some of it is biblical, much of it is cosmological, and a very small percentage is even a little sinister.

Those wishing to fully understand the intricacies of Freemasonry could do worse than studying the work of the authors Christopher Knight and Robert Lomas. In their first book on the subject, *The Hiram Key*, they sought to get to the bottom of the Craft themselves. As practicing Freemasons, they decided to discover whether the whole business was merely an eighteenth-century scam, or if it was indeed based on ancient traditions. Their discoveries are always interesting, often surprising, and sometimes unsettling.

Grand Lodge, the body in London that claims to represent by far the majority of Freemasons in England today, claims that the pedigree of Freemasonry only goes as far back as the middle of the eighteenth century. This opinion is quite understandable. If Freemasonry really does extend back to the building of Solomon's Temple, or even to the construction of the Egyptian pyramids, Grand Lodge becomes nothing more than a very modern irrelevance.

Freemasons strenuously deny that their practices are in any way "religious." In this, they are clearly at odds with the truth. A prerequisite for any would-be Mason is a professed belief in the "Great Geometrician of the Universe."" However, with this simple recognition of a causative principle of some sort, any man can become a Mason, no matter what his religious or racial background.

There is no doubt at all that Freemasonry at least predates the formation of Grand Lodge in London, which opened its doors in 1717. It was already present in England for at least a century before this time and had existed in Scotland for longer still. Grand Lodge was simply an attempt to "Anglicize" a potentially dangerous institution. The Scottish Stewart kings were ousted from England in 1688 when the Catholic James II was deposed. This dynasty, whose supporters were known as Jacobites, tried to reassert its claim to the English throne on several subsequent occasions but always failed. By 1717 England had opted for a German-born king, George I. Freemasonry had always attracted the reputation of being a Jacobite institution. However, it remained popular and in order to "sanitize" the Craft a wholly English version was created, and one that presented no threat to the Hanoverian king. Hence English Freemasonry was born. My research shows that English Freemasonry was forged from Scottish rite Freemasonry, not in London, but much further north, at a double salt line location called Castle Howard, which I shall deal with more specifically in a later chapter.

The whole subject is full of controversy and it appears that the absolute origins of Freemasonry may never be known. The most likely explanation seems to be that it was established, in something like the form we see today, by William Sinclair, the man who built Rosslyn Chapel near Edinburgh.

It is generally accepted by researchers into Rosslyn Chapel that the building contains a number of secrets that are clearly of Templar origin. The chapel was built in the fifteenth century, just over a century after the French Templar arrests of 1307. William Sinclair was the legatee of a long Templar past enjoyed by the Sinclair family as a whole. Where these "secrets" lie is open to conjecture. Perhaps, as many researchers now suggest, there are documents carefully hidden in the vaults. On the other hand, the ornate stone carvings that adorn Rosslyn Chapel could, in themselves, represent some sort of code. If this were the case, only the "knowing" visitor could make any sense of them. Some of the carvings are from Old Testament sources, whilst others appear to be mythological. Yet more defy understanding altogether.

If there was a secret locked into the fabric of the building William Sinclair obviously wished to keep it to himself. This would have been an impossibility with stonemasons crawling all over the site for years. So, it is suggested, Sinclair devised a way to maintain their silence. At this period of history, Stonemasons' guilds already existed and had done so for some time. Guilds were common in most trades. They were a sort of cross between a trade federation and a trades union. Entrance to a particular craft also meant membership of the relevant guild. Stonemasonry was one of the oldest skills of all. The origin of its guilds is lost in the mists of time well before the fifteenth century.

William Sinclair built on this natural tendency of the stonemasons to retain their skills within an ordered and carefully selected group. He effectively turned the guild into something much more mystical and exclusive. On the way, he introduced the "oaths," which condemned guild members to the most horrible and lingering of deaths if they ever divulged any of the secrets vouchsafed to them. In this manner, he made certain that specific details regarding Rosslyn Chapel would never be known by the community at large.

With the passing of time the ceremonies became ever more elaborate, and gradually detached themselves from true stonemasonry altogether. Soon there were groups of 'speculative" Masons, men who had never wielded a chisel in their lives, but who found some sort of fraternal comfort in the rituals. Royal Charters were drawn up for these first speculative lodges and the Sinclair family remained at the head of emerging Freemasonry for many decades.

Freemasonry spread across Scotland and ultimately found its way into England. Perhaps British society had lost most of the "fraternal" components that seem to be essential to any society and Freemasonry filled the void. The Craft became a magnet for the rise in interest in things archaic and esoteric that epitomized the period into which it had been born. Elements of astrology, astronomy, mythology, and early Judaism came together to form a heady mixture. It was a sort of moral and pseudo-religious cocktail that clearly appealed to the educated male mind of the period.

None of this is to suggest that even the first Freemasons were entirely the brainchild of William Sinclair. It is highly likely that their rituals and practices were based upon ceremonies that had been well known to the secretive Templars. Thus, at the very core of the Craft, we might expect to find subject matter that is genuinely very much older than the fifteenth century. This seems to be the case and Freemasonry does indeed appear to have a very ancient pedigree. It contains elements that go back to as early as 10000 BC. Since these elements are Judaic and even pre-Judaic in content, they are most likely to have found their way into Freemasonry via the Templars.

Much of the original practice of Freemasonry has been distorted and even completely changed by Grand Lodge in London. However, in the old Scottish Rite forms of the Craft enough can be resurrected to indicate the sort of practices that originally did take place. Beyond the initial three degrees of the Craft there are a confusing array of further "side arches" and "degrees" that the would-be aspirant can take – but no Mason can embark on any of these until he is a third-degree Master Mason.

In order to achieve this status he is obliged to go through a symbolic "death and rebirth" ceremony. It is generally suggested that the symbolism behind this procedure is to indicate that the aspirant has "died" to his old life and been "reborn" into the full rights and privileges of Freemasonry. This ceremony lies at the core of all Masonic practice and is common to all types of Freemasonry in the world today. The third-degree rite of Freemasonry is a direct descendant of one of the oldest forms of religious practice known to our species.

Something very similar to this ceremony certainly took place for many centuries at Eleusis, Greece, during the Mysteries of Demeter, which were celebrated there annually. These ceremonies had originally taken place in Knossos, Crete, in the Minoan period, prior to 2000 BC. Virtually identical practices were associated with Egyptian Isis worship, the cults of Adonis, Dionysus, Mithras, and a host of other deities.

Inherent in the Freemasonic version of the ceremony is the ritual use of a human skull and crossed thigh bones. These are symbols that are known to have been of particular relevance to Templarism. For this and many other reasons, it seems highly likely that the death and rebirth ceremony was culled by William Sinclair directly from Templarism. His whole invention of the Craft may well have been a deliberate attempt to keep the "essence" of Templarism alive in a society that had outlawed the Order.

The chain of Freemasonic advancement has now probably been broken. Many of the essential higher degrees that were present in Scottish Rite Freemasonry were abandoned, watered down, or deliberately altered at the time Grand Lodge in London was formed. Even the highest-ranking Freemason in England today – and possibly elsewhere too, would find it impossible to reach the eventual conclusions that might eventually have occurred to the sixteenth-century Freemason.

To the would-be Templar, advancement through the Order came stage by careful stage. It probably included secret ceremonies not unlike those once encapsulated in Freemasonry. At each successive stage, there were stories to learn, specific movements to memorize, and actions to be taken. In isolation, these would have meant little or nothing to the aspirant – they were simply necessary components of advancement. Time and again, for himself and then through leading others, the rising Templar brother would learn and recite the rituals, until they became second nature to him. So it remains in Freemasonry today. The only difference is that it seems unlikely that this journey leads anywhere these days – as it once did.

The logical conclusion seems to be that the Templar, having undergone every possible ritual, would by this time have reached an elevated status within the Order. Perhaps he would be the Master of a region or state. It is almost certain that at this time he would be given the final key – the few words or sentences that allowed him to make sense of all that he had learned across a number of years.

This is not half as preposterous as it might at first appear to be. We all carry information around with us that is learned by rote but which appears to be nonsense. I refer the reader to a little English nursery rhyme known as "Oranges and Lemons." Most British children learn the whole rhyme when they are very small. It is passed on to them by parents who have no comprehension of what the verse actually means.

> Oranges and Lemons say the bells of St. Clements.
> I owe you five farthings say the bells of St. Martins.
> When will you pay me say the bells of Old Bailey.
> When I grow rich, say the bells of Shoreditch.
> When will that be say the bells of Stepney.
> I do not know, say the great bells of Bow.

When the verse is learned, so is the tune that accompanies it. In reality, the verse and tune are a graphic description of the sound made by the bells of some of the most famous churches in London. However, the verse developed prior to 1666, at which time a great fire swept through London. Every one of the churches in question was destroyed at this time and had to be completely rebuilt. All the bells were lost, and these too had to be replaced.

It is a fact that anyone who knows the verse and its tune is in possession of a valuable piece of historical information that is now at least 350 years old. Those reading these words, who know the verse and its tune, have now been given the key to its meaning. Nothing has changed except the dawning of awareness.

If this is multiplied many hundred-fold, with stories, movements, and actions learned across half a lifetime – how much more significant might the eventual key actually be?

After a decade or more of careful research I remain convinced that this was the original basis behind Freemasonry. It represented a means by which oral traditions of a contentious and heretical nature could be passed on from generation to generation and remain intact. With this suggestion, I am on very safe ground. Even if the chain of association does remain intact, only a very few people within Scottish Rite Freemasonry are aware of the fact. These people would never admit that this is the case. Aspirants who have not yet reached the top of this particular tree still do not have the key.

Within the various ceremonies and practices we find hints that the Grail knowledge and salt line awareness was retained by at least some early Freemasons. Unlike some modern writers on the subject I remain convinced that this was the case with at least some of the people responsible for creating English Freemasonry, the same men who built Grand Lodge in London in the eighteenth century.

High up on the wall of any Masonic Lodge is a representation of a five-pointed star – the star of Venus. I have demonstrated time and again in previous chapters that this symbol is closely related to the old fertility religions based upon an assumption that at the heart of all is the "Great Goddess" of old. The astronomical patterns shared by the Earth and Venus are the first prerequisites for accurately measuring the Earth year. They lie at the heart of all geometry. Their association with "Phi," the "Golden Mean," ally them to some of the fundamental principles of physics that govern the universe. In Freemasonry the deity is referred to as the "Great Geometrician of the Universe," and a virtual obsession with geometry and cosmology is inherent in all Freemasonic ritual. Since these were aspects of Grail and ultimately Golden Thread knowledge, we should perhaps also expect to find aspects of Goddess worship present in Masonic practices.

To this day Masons refer to their own meeting place as their "Mother Lodge." It is never referred to in the masculine. The place of death and rebirth at the time of the third-degree ceremony is as surely representative of the "womb of the Goddess" as is the chamber of Megalithic tombs such as Maes Howe in Scotland or Brynn Celli Ddu in Wales. In the case of Grand Lodge in London, the architect did nothing to disguise this fact. The Lodge itself is womb shaped and is approached via a corridor that resembles a birth canal. It shares this basic design with possibly thousands of Megalithic chambered tombs across the British Isles and France.

The first English Freemasons were powerful men. They not only had the wherewithal to build Grand Lodge itself, they also named the street where it stands. To this day, it is called Great Queen Street. Early Scottish Lodges also had some telling names – for example, Mary Lodge. Of course England, by the seventeenth century, was staunchly Protestant. One of the main reasons for the formation of English Freemasonry was to expunge any

Jacobite and Catholic components that shone through the Craft.

I am in possession of a copy of a Masonic book from the Victorian period. It is entitled *Stellar Theology and Masonic Astronomy*[28] and was written by Robert Hewitt Brown. How I came by this document, I am not at liberty to say. This book deals specifically with the part astronomy and astrology plays in Freemasonic ritual. To anyone who has studied these subjects, the book makes a fascinating read, though it is of particular interest to me for a very specific reason. There are sections of the book that deal with the constellation of Virgo, to which I have referred previously. Some of these sections also hint at Goddess worship within Freemasonic ritual. Most telling is the fact that every one of these sections has been carefully scored out in the copy of the book I possess. By a happy chance, the act of photocopying the book has made it possible to read the text that has been so carefully defaced, which is not the case in the original document.

The question arises: why would anyone want to eradicate only these, specific sections? There are only a couple of possibilities that occur to me. I know that the original of the copy of *Stellar Theology* that I possess resides to this day in the library of an important Freemasonic Lodge in England. The sections relating to the constellation of Virgo and to the Goddess obviously either offended someone, or else they did not want just "any" brother Mason to read them. Why should either be the case unless the almost certainly high-ranking Freemason who defaced the book knew what the pieces of text actually implied? Having read the sections many times myself, I am certainly of the opinion that the author, Robert Hewitt Brown, understood only too well the true religious imperative that lay within Freemasonry.

A close companion to the Craft of Freemasonry, though eminent Masons might still deny any tangible connection, was Rosicrucianism. Within its mysterious origins and practices, we can find another avenue through which surviving Goddess worship has been transmitted to the modern age.

CHAPTER 21

The Rosy Cross

The earliest reference to Rosicrucianism is found around the commencement of the reign of James I of England (1603). It is now generally accepted that Rosicrucianism came about as a result of the efforts of certain German princes. These men were anxious to heap scorn on the Catholic Church as a whole and upon the Pope in particular. It was around this time that pamphlets began to appear in England extolling the virtues of a new philosophy, though one grafted upon the roots of ancient esotericism. The mythical founder of the sect was "Christian Rosenkreuz" and the primary object of Rosicrucianism was to overthrow tyrannical political and spiritual leaders and to establish a sort of "Utopia." That it was ultimately inspired by priests of the Golden Thread, there is no doubt whatsoever.

To search for the actual individuals responsible for Rosicrucianism is to set out on a journey that contains more twists and turns than an Elizabethan maze. Some authorities think that a German writer from Wurttemburg in Germany penned the pamphlets in question. His name was Johann Valentin Andrea. Little is known of Andrea, except for the fact that he was born in 1586 and died in 1654 and it is distinctly possible that we shall never fully understand where Rosicrucianism actually developed. It is telling, however, that Andrea's personal emblem was a red rose.

The Thirty Years' War in Europe (commencing 1618) saw the old hatred between Catholics and Protestants once again bringing mayhem and death to thousands of people. It also displaced many German Protestants who were sympathetic to Rosicrucian ideals. Many of these people found their way to Britain. They were assisted by the "Christian Unions," which were formed by Andrea and others with the express purpose of keeping Rosicrucian ideas and practices alive in Europe.

The Christian Unions were split into "Lodge" systems and may have been of a Masonic type nature. The arrival of these refugees into Britain could have eventually offered impetus to the rise in Freemasonry that attended the period. A fair proportion of the people in question came from Flanders. They were adept in the weaving of woolen cloth. This fact itself may prove to be very telling as our story unfolds.

Any connection between the original founders of the Rosicrucian brotherhood and sects which still carry the same name today seems to be tenuous. There are, however, plenty of people in the world who claim that a secret brotherhood of the Rosy Cross does still exist. It is suggested that this elusive faction still secretly protects the mysteries encapsulated within the original seventeenth-century ideals.

Rosicrucians clearly believed themselves to be associated with the Knights Templar. It is not beyond belief that Templars who had managed to find sanctuary in Germany or the Low Countries had somehow survived the intervening centuries as a coherent "entity." They certainly did so in Scotland. That Rosicrucian ideals should be ultimately adopted by Freemasonry is entirely consistent with what we know about the philosophy, which seems to be a natural bedfellow of the Craft.

Of particular interest is how closely some of the early Rosicrucian pamphlets, or manifestos, mirror the Grail legends. We find in early Rosicrucianism a sort of idealism, based on personal freedom of choice, that fits very well with known aspects of Templar and Grail thinking. Rosicrucians did not wish to punish the contrary beliefs of others, as did the Catholics and also many sections of the new Protestant faith. There is no doubt that it was Rosicrucianism, together with its close ally Freemasonry, that allowed the scientific discoveries (or often rediscoveries) of the period to flourish. Many of the original English Freemasons were also committed Rosicrucians.

After the first two Rosicrucian Manifestos, a longer work, entitled *The Chymical Wedding,* appeared in 1616. This was a story filled with Grail type allusion. It detailed the adventures of one Christian Rozenkreutz, a character who has much in common with the Perceval of Grail fame.

The story of *The Chymical Wedding* is told in the first person, by Christian Rozenkreutz himself. It begins with the arrival at his house, on the eve of Easter, of an angel. This heavenly messenger bears an invitation for Christian that bids him attend a royal wedding. Though shocked at the news, he gladly accepts. After a horrific dream, in which he is imprisoned and then released from a dungeon, the hero sets out on his journey. Christian must pass through a series of "gates" on his way to the magical castle where the wedding is to take place. He wears the white tunic of the Templar, with a red cross at its shoulder. In addition, he has placed four roses in his hat. He specifically states that to do so will mean he is better noticed (presumably by specific persons). Christian has had the presence of mind to carry with him bread, salt, and water. When he arrives at the divergence of four different paths, he is unsure of the correct direction. Fortunately he feeds some of his bread to a "snow white dove," which is chased by a large and aggressive raven. Christian follows the fleeing dove and soon discovers that he is on the right path. He has a compass and has been told that, no matter what byways lead from this straight track, he must continue to walk south. In my estimation, this is likely to be a salt line allusion.

Christian uses the salt to "buy" the various tokens he needs to gain entry to the magical castle. When he arrives at his destination, he meets a beautiful virgin. She remains the guide and mentor of Christian and his fellow guests at the wedding for the remainder of the story. The virgin shows a distinct preference for Christian and asks if she may have the roses from his hat.

Since all those arriving at the castle may not be worthy of attending such an important event, it is necessary for them to be weighed on magical scales. Only a handful pass the test, of which Christian is one. Those who fail, through being boastful or filled with deceit, are cast naked out of the castle. This section of the story echoes a known aspect of Egyptian Osiran religion in which the heart of a dead Pharaoh was weighed against a feather, before he was allowed to rule with Osiris in the abode of the dead.

There now follows a strange scene, in which all the royal personages present are decapitated, to the abject horror of Christian and his fellow guests. The next day the guests are taken to a mystical island, where a fantastic alchemical process is performed. This procedure is undertaken in order to recreate the "bride and bridegroom," from the distilled remains of the original bodies. Before this takes place, the guests are treated to a sort of tableau or play. They watch the performance of a drama dealing with a mysterious princess who has lost her kingdom. She is under the influence of a "Moor," which, at the period of *The Chymical Wedding*, would probably be taken to mean a Turk or at the very least someone of the Muslim faith. It was Muslims who fought against the Christians so long for possession of Jerusalem.

For a while the Princess must become the concubine of the

Moor, but she is ultimately delivered from bondage. Her kingdom is restored by the intervention of an equally mysterious prince. There seems to be little doubt that this drama is an allegorical playing out of the deliverance of Jerusalem from Muslims control by Godfroi de Bouillon at the time of the First Crusade. The princess in question is intended to represent the Holy City itself. She may also be the Goddess of the Golden Thread.

Wandering round the magical castle prior to the alchemical transmutation, Christian happens upon a sepulcher. This contains the lifeless, though perfect, body of Venus. He is told that anyone uncovering and looking at Venus has committed a terrible crime but he does not admit his transgression at the time.

Transported to the fabulous island by ship, the wedding guests now take part in the alchemical transmutation. This involves using the "essence" of the dead royals to create a large egg. From the egg springs a fabulous bird. Christian never refers to this bird as being the "Phoenix," but there isn't much doubt about its true nature. The hatched bird grows rapidly and is itself eventually sacrificed, in order to use its own essence to restore the bride and bridegroom. Only four wedding guests are present for this most sacred part of the ceremony. Christian is one of them. The remainder of those taking part are shielded from this, the deepest mystery. They are engaged in making gold, which Christian describes as a "lesser art."

With the royal couple restored, the guests return in triumph to the magical castle in twelve magnificent ships. Each of the ships carries a flag depicting one of the zodiac signs. Christian is troubled to learn that the keeper of the first gate, whom he met some days earlier, is, in reality, forced to remain at his post as a penance. He too had viewed the body of Venus. He can only be released when some other transgressor takes his place. Full of contrition, and as humble as he has been all through the story, Christian Rozenkreutz admits his crime. Already an old man, he prepares himself to become the keeper of the gate for the remainder of his life. At this time the narrative is cut short, but the final words tell us that Christian was allowed to return to his home.

A character who constantly appears during Christian's stay in the magical castle is Cupid. This impish little sprite constantly taunts the guests and the many virgins who are present. Cupid only disappears when he is angered by the knowledge that the body of Venus has been viewed by one of the guests.

There are many different themes running through *The Chymical Wedding*, but it does give us a good insight into the basic beliefs of the early Rosicrucians. It is just possible that the story is older than the early seventeenth century, because the date is mentioned several times as being 1459. This is a period contemporary with the building of Rosslyn Chapel and, very tellingly, it is also exactly 360 years after the capture of Jerusalem by Godfroi de Bouillon in 1099. Supposedly, Andrea admitted to having written *The Chymical Wedding* himself, though this is a supposition that no amount of research on my part can confirm.

So what can we glean from the story, no matter when it was truly created? Firstly, it is a tale full of alchemical symbolism. The various components at its start show that it was penned by someone familiar with the salt lines of Europe. The importance of salt echoes through a tale that is essentially of pre-Christian or only quasi-Christian origin. In fact, Jesus is rarely mentioned in the story. However, the *Chymical Wedding* does commence on the eve before Easter Day but it should be remembered that

Easter is a festival "utilized" by Christianity, not invented by it. Easter is the time of death and rebirth and of pagan origin. The *Chymical Wedding* takes place across seven days. The magical number seven appears in every conceivable form throughout the whole narrative.

We learn that the Rosicrucians believe strongly that humility is the best approach to life. We are also instructed that compassion is essential. Those who commit transgressions in the story invariably receive light punishment, or else are completely forgiven. The Grail itself is never mentioned in *The Chymical Wedding*, but there are a host of "fountains" of one sort or another. These point once again to aspects of Megalithic belief and the "underground and emerging stream" that is the probably true explanation for placement of significant sites on the salt line system. It is almost certain that an "al" was originally understood to be such an emerging stream.

The whole tale bears a striking resemblance to the performance of mystery rites, such as those of Demeter at Eleusis. *The Chymical Wedding* is, at its heart, a story of death and rebirth. At the same time, it is deeply Hermetic in nature. It serves to instruct would-be alchemists that the transmutation of base metal into gold is not the pinnacle of their efforts. Rather it leans in the direction of the "internal alchemy," mentioned elsewhere in this book. Mythology in the story is mixed and somewhat confusing. The Latin Venus and Cupid are present, though Hermes, a Greek deity, is also mentioned. There are also mentions in *The Chymical Wedding* of the mysterious Greek deity – Eros.

In the very earliest Greek myth cycles the originator of all the gods and humanity was Eros. Eros was far more ancient than Cronos, Zeus, or any of the other divinities. By the time these stories were being written down by authors such as Hesiod, Eros was somewhat out of fashion. He had become the son of Aphrodite and Ares (Latin Venus and Mars). It seems likely that this deity, or something very similar, was somehow important to our Megalithic ancestors. The birth of Eros in the most ancient story cycles contains obvious alchemical overtones.

Eros was the child of the great black bird, "Night," by her consort "the Wind." His origin was a great, shining egg. One version of the tale tells us that when Eros emerged from the egg, the material world was formed in the bottom half of the shell. The great curving arch of the sky was the uppermost part. But the Earth and the Heavens became respectively Goddess and God in their own right. From these all the other gods and goddesses would eventually spring.

In his original form Eros was not a "he" at all, but rather a hermaphrodite character. Eros is often depicted this way in the early Greek stories. Another important player in the story, Dionysus, also carried these characteristics, perhaps as a direct legacy from the old Eros. The most ancient stories tell us that Eros was a beautiful maiden at the front, and an old man to the rear. This symbolism certainly was not forgotten in late medieval times. There is a beautiful statue at one corner of the tomb of Francois II of France, which is known as "Prudence." It depicts an attractive woman in a mantled gown, who is gazing intently at her reflection in a mirror held in her left hand. In her right hand, she holds what are either compasses or dividers. But from the rear, the statue takes on a very different form. The back of the maiden's head is the face of a bearded old man. He is a serene sage, whose looks are very similar to known portraits of that ageing Leonardo Da Vinci. This statue is filled with alchemical imagery and personifies the oldest descriptions of Eros.

The presence in *The Chymical Wedding* of Cupid is interesting. It is generally accepted that the Greek Eros and the Latin Cupid are one and the same. There are differences, however, since in early Greek legends Eros predated Aphrodite (Latin Venus). Meanwhile in the Latin tradition, Cupid was the child of Venus, to Mars the god of war. The purpose of Cupid in *The Chymical Wedding* is to be a taunt to the lords and virgins present, constantly teasing them and endeavoring to create romantic intentions.

In the creation of the fabulous egg of the Phoenix the reader of *The Chymical Wedding* might be put in mind of that first shining egg from which Eros himself sprang. However, the story of *The Chymical Wedding* is so convoluted that it is difficult to understand exactly what might have been in the mind of the writer. Almost certainly, *The Chymical Wedding* is meant to be confusing. The underlying philosophy is definitely reminiscent of known, original Masonic concepts. It is a fact that a proportion of those who founded what would eventually become the United States of America were Rosicrucians. Since most of them were also Freemasons, the crossover point between the two, at least in the early seventeenth century, is quite apparent. It has been suggested that the true meaning of *The Chymical Wedding* relates to the transmutation of Old World values into those necessary to create the New World.

That Rosicrucianism owes much to the Templar Order is also obvious. Templars were using roses in conjunction with crosses on tombstones back in the earliest days of their existence. *The Chymical Wedding* plays around all these themes. It displays a continuity of knowledge and a spiritual imperative underpinning a "search for science." In truth, the development of modern science owes much to both Rosicrucianism and Freemasonry, and many of its working practices were distilled from the steaming retorts of the alchemists' laboratories.

The Rosicrucian Manifestos, and in particular, *The Chymical Wedding* of Christian Rozenkreutz, may not make specific reference to the Grail, though the rose is present at every turn. However, I believe that any student of the Grail legends must find the parallels between them and *The Chymical Wedding* so close as to make the difference academic.

It would require a lifetime of meticulous study and research to untangle the many complex themes that run through *The Chymical Wedding*. Despite this it would not take an expert to understand that Goddess worship, as well as the passing on of secret knowledge, lies at the heart of the original Rosicrucian movement. From the moment Christian, the hero of the story, encounters the snow-white dove, the symbolism within the story becomes obvious. The fact that Christian "sees" the body of Venus, is a strong indication that he has been made party to the most profound mysteries of the Golden Thread, which is why it is necessary for him to become the "gatekeeper" of the fabulous castle. The castle itself is a metaphor, symbolizing not only the religious beliefs of the Golden Thread, but also its store of very practical and extremely powerful knowledge. The more I study *The Chymical Wedding* of Christian Rosenkreuz, the deeper my understanding of the survival of the Golden Thread becomes, though this one story is worthy of a book in its own right.

The importance of the Rosicrucian movement, particularly during the seventeenth century, together with the rise in Freemasonic practice, cannot be overstated. Together, they ultimately led to the creation of something like the "New Jerusalem" the Cistercians and Templars had intended. From the crucible of Rosicrucianism and with the tools of Freemasonry, the United States of America was built.

CHAPTER 22

New Worlds for Old

Although clearly intended and planned to destroy the power of the Catholic Church for ever, the religious Reformation that took place in Europe during the sixteenth century merely served to create religious dogmas and repressive institutions of its own.

In England especially, Anglicanism soon sought to guard its own position and began to show tyrannical tendencies. Those of Rosicrucian and other "fringe" persuasions were openly criticized. On occasions, they were even persecuted for their beliefs. On mainland Europe the constant fighting between Catholic and Protestant allowed little room for a "third party" intent on pursuing a religion so old it made Christianity appear irrelevant. As a result, it must have seemed to many of the people holding to the ancient religion and values that the only way to achieve a settled life, where they could choose their own particular route to the Godhead, would be to leave Europe behind forever.

Templar-inspired voyages to the New World took place long before the more accepted voyages of mariners such as Christopher Columbus. There is no doubt regarding the journey to America undertaken by Henry Sinclair in 1398. As we have seen, this voyage encompassed not only the northern region, which would eventually be known as Nova Scotia (New Scotland), but much of the western seaboard of the present United States. The presence of the foliage of indigenous American plants, such as the aloe and the seed heads of maize, carved into the stonework of Rosslyn Chapel, bear testimony to this and probably many other journeys to the New World. In the end, even the United States Constitution would be forged from Masonic and Rosicrucian ideals. There is no doubt that the New World was intended to represent the Utopia or New Jerusalem that the Templars and the priests of the Golden

Thread had come to see as their birthright.

Probably the most famous group of travelers to the embryonic United States was the Leiden Brotherhood. Their arrival aboard the *Mayflower* is well documented and considered pivotal to the American story. The history of this group serves to illustrate very well the sort of people who forged the New World, and how they had been very much influenced by the old salt line knowledge and, almost certainly, the Golden Thread.

The Leiden Brotherhood was a group of Christian dissenters originally formed in Scooton, near Doncaster, England. This township lies in close proximity to the 53 minutes West longitudinal salt line, close to the strange village of Haxey, which is replete with ancient religious overtones. Also close by, and on the salt line, are to be found the origins of Methodism. In fact, the whole area was a hotbed of reformed religious zeal.

This part of England had always been "separate" and "different." In earlier times it was an isolated and wild place, where the flooded lowlands had formed an island of habitation along a ridge known as "the island of Axholme." A longitudinal salt line passes down Axholme and cuts through the modern village of Haxey. To this day, a strange ceremony takes place there each year on Plough Monday (close to the old midwinter festival). At this time, a ritual is enacted which speaks of memories relating to nature worship. It is known as the festival of the "Haxey Hood."

Displaced from the Isle of Axholme the embryonic brotherhood settled for a while in Plymouth before setting off for the more religiously tolerant country of Holland. There they settled on a latitudinal salt line in the historic town of Leiden. Leiden is still famed for the scientific equipment made there. Its importance in this regard goes back many centuries and shows it to be a Templar inspired city. Leiden was always a place where freedom of expression was prized above all else. Rosicrucianism flourished there.

But even Leiden could not offer these idealists the sort of society they really craved. After a few years they returned to England and hired the use of the *Mayflower*. From England, they traveled to Cape Cod, Massachusetts, also a longitudinal salt line location. Here, they landed and formed their first community.

A leading light in all of this was Edward Winslow. His family came from Kerswell, on the Great Malvern latitudinal salt line of England. His family name shows the original point of origin to have been Winslow, on the 52 minutes West longitudinal salt line, near Northampton. Winslow was one of the leading lights of the community. His family were legatees of the selfsame type of ex-Norman minor aristocracy that proliferates all through our story. The other leader was William Bradford, who came from Scooten, also on the 52 minutes West longitudinal salt line in South Yorkshire.

The time the Leiden Brotherhood spent in Holland must have brought it into direct contact with proto-Masonic brotherhoods of the early Nonconformist sort. It is very likely that at least some of those sailing on the *Mayflower* considered themselves to be Freemasons. They would have been more than familiar with Rosicrucian ideals, which were reaching their zenith at this time. The whole nature of their ultimate journey was undoubtedly affected by *The Chymical Wedding*.

The *Mayflower* set sail from Plymouth on 6 September 1620 and arrived off the coast of Massachusetts on 4 December. It is often stated that the original intention of the Pilgrim Fathers, as they have come to be known, was to join forces with a settlement in Virginia. This settlement had been established some thirteen years earlier. They were, the tale goes, driven off course by storms. In conference they decided to form their own community further north. This story is probably not true. It is known that the *Mayflower* stood off Plymouth Rock for some time. During this period members of the Leiden Brotherhood persuaded those amongst their passengers who were not of their community that they knew of a better destination than Virginia.

There is every reason to believe that the Pilgrim Fathers knew exactly where they wanted to go. This turned out to be Plymouth, Massachusetts. The site of disembarkation is located at 70 degrees 41 minutes West, which places it within 1 minute of arc of a longitudinal salt line running at 70 degrees 42 minutes West. A cursory glance at the map shows that it would be difficult to find so good an anchorage anywhere on this part of the coast that was so close to a longitudinal salt line position.

Quickly establishing a temporary base for themselves near to the shore, they struck inland. Within three days they located the site of an earlier European settlement. Odds and ends were discovered there, such as a large iron cooking pot, but there was no trace of human life. The Leiden community nearly led itself to disaster. It was pitifully badly supplied with the necessary farming implements with which to create a viable community. This was a virgin wilderness and there were few aboard the *Mayflower* with the requisite skills, even to use what implements they possessed. It now seems likely that the leaders of the expedition fully expected to find a flourishing community in the vicinity of Cape Cod. They must have been desperately disappointed to discover that it had, somehow, failed to survive. How old this settlement was and who had started it will remain forever a mystery. Even stranger is the fact that the existence of the abandoned European settlement was never mentioned again by the Pilgrim Fathers.

Little by little, Europeans strengthened their toehold on the American continent. Many if not most of the earliest settlers were of Masonic and Rosicrucian persuasion. Indeed, some of these people were encouraged to travel to the New World by none other than Sir Francis Bacon. Bacon was a man of impeccable salt line heritage, a known hermetisist and a Rosicrucian. But of course, the Rosicrucians, proto-Masons and members of the post-Templar brotherhood were not alone in seeking a new life, away from the religious and political restrictions in Europe. The new land they colonized was huge and it took time to carve out a viable nation. This did not become fully possible until some 140 years after the voyage of the *Mayflower*. By this time the Freemasons and the Rosicrucians, many as representatives of the salt line families of Britain and France, held most of the positions of influence and power. With little more than their zeal and a genuine belief in the creation of a truly democratic and egalitarian nation, these people flourished. What is more, they managed to turn the raggle-taggle collection of American settlers into an army capable of withstanding the might of a fearfully powerful Britain.

Christian Rozenkreutz, or whoever actually wrote *The Chymical Wedding*, would have been proud indeed of the first American Constitution. The story of how a desire for independence came about is well known. However, something that has not been noted until now is the fact that the list of those who led the revolt against England is replete with individuals who can be shown to have originated from salt line families in Europe. Nowhere is this more evident than in the case of George Washington. In light of the heritage of this man, and the positioning of the capital that was named after him, there can remain absolutely no doubt that the United States of America was founded upon Rosicrucian and post-Templar ideals. These were funded by people with a good working knowledge of the Megalithic mathematical principles and fuelled by their deeply Masonic connections.

Washington was certainly not alone. It has been suggested that at least 50 of those signing the American Declaration of Independence, on 4 July 1776, were Freemasons, and an indeterminate, though almost certainly large proportion, also espoused Rosicrucianism.

As an example, the family of George Washington was Norman French in origin. Originally, the Washingtons had owned an ancient manor and lands in the northeast of England. Later, for more than a century, they held Sulbury Manor, between Banbury and Northampton in central England. One could hardly conceive of a more potent salt line location than this, for it stands on the 52 degrees 06 minutes North latitudinal salt line.

George Washington's Masonic roots are well known. They may have existed in the family for a considerable period of time. Washington, northeast England, is quite close to the Scottish Border. Freemasonry of the Scottish variety found its way to this location very early. The "Stars and Stripes" of the American flag owe their origin to the heraldic shield of the Washington family. None of the other advocates of independence had better, older, or more sound salt line credentials than Washington.

The new capital of the United States, which was to bear his name, was built upon the site of an old plantation. Nevertheless, it was strategically placed, in full knowledge of exactly the same principles that had caused St. Bernard of Clairvaux to place his own abbey in the precise location where its ruins still stand in France. There is nothing remotely arbitrary about Washington DC or its positioning. It was built in full knowledge of specific geographical facts and at the express wish of surviving members of the Golden Thread.

Washington DC occupies a position 77 degrees West of Greenwich. Jerusalem is at 35 degrees 10 minutes East of Greenwich. In Megalithic terms, the distance between these two locations is so close to exactly 114 Megalithic degrees that the difference is impossible to measure. Washington DC therefore also shares a Megalithic relationship with Knosses in Crete, Eleusis in Greece, Troy in modern Turkey, Heliopolis in Ancient Egypt, Stenay in France, and Rosslyn Chapel in Scotland. In addition, it maintains the same relationship with dozens of other locations that were crucially important to the Bronze Age peoples.

Just as important is the latitudinal position of Washington DC, which is 38 degrees 52 minutes North. In Megalithic terms this places Washington DC exactly 9 Megalithic degrees north of the Great Pyramid of Cheops, and in fact the whole Giza complex. The pyramid is a structure held to be deeply significant in Freemasonic and esoteric terms.

Of course, this might all be nothing more than a coincidence. But any reader who believes this to be the case should first take a look at an American dollar bill. It contains a representation of the "'truncated pyramid," a symbol of the "Old Wisdom." This connects Washington DC with the ancient site of Heliopolis, and the Giza pyramids. Also included on the dollar bill is the "all-seeing eye" a most enduring symbol of Freemasonry. But this symbol is also closely connected to the ancient legacy of the

Old World. On the Great Seal of the United States we find the eagle, olive branch, arrows, and pentagrams. All these would be immediately recognized by occultists and Rosicrucians as enduring symbols of their art and a fair number of them relate directly to Goddess worship.

Forged from the representatives of many nationalities and across an incredibly short period of time, the United States of America represents the most powerful nation on earth. Its beliefs and ideals are not universally accepted as being truly democratic, or even "moral." Yet, for all this, to many millions of people beyond its borders the United States stands as an ideal.

It is telling that the huge statue guarding the entrance to New York harbor, undoubtedly the most important point of arrival and departure in the United States, is that of a woman. The Statue of Liberty was a gift from France. It was created by Fredric Auguste Bartholdi, a known Freemason of salt line origin in Alsace, France. It is entirely appropriate that the Statue of Liberty originated in a part of the world that had been so important to the Golden Thread in former times. However, it pales into insignificance next to the most important of the structures that adorn Washington DC, which shows conclusively that the Golden Thread was alive and well as this "New Jerusalem" was being created.

CHAPTER 23

Written in the Stars

Readers could be forgiven for making the observation that knowledge of Freemasonry, proliferating amongst the Founding Fathers of the United States, is not necessarily proof of surviving Goddess worship. I may have been able to show that the seeds of a feminine-based religion lie at the heart of Freemasonic practice, but the average Freemason these days would have no idea that this is the case, and might even be appalled by the revelation. Perhaps the same was true as the United States took its first tentative steps towards independence. In reality, there are many reasons for thinking this was not the case and that at least some priests of the Golden Thread were present and influential when the Declaration of Independence and the United States Constitution were being drawn up. Proof of the fact lies in Washington, which is, to this very day, much more than simply a capital city – its existence is the very epitome of the American ideal.

Land to build Washington was given to the new federal administration in 1791. It stood on the Potomac River and even the state of which it had originally been a part is very telling – it was Maryland. A large section of the ten-mile square – that area where the Capitol now stands, had already been known for decades as "New Troy." In reality, the land for the Capitol and the city may have been earmarked long before 1791. (Readers will recall that the very center of Golden Thread activity in Europe from the tenth to the fourteenth centuries had been Troyes, Champagne, another city named after the ancient city of Troy, in present Turkey.) In the creation and building of the Capitol, we see the very aspiration and intention of the surviving priests of the Golden Thread who quite deliberately built America.

Washington was planned by a Frenchman with noted

Freemasonic leanings, Major Pierre Charles L'Enfant, a follower of another Freemasonic Frenchman General, the Marquise Lafayette. Nobody doubts that every aspect of Washington was planned, designed, and constructed with Freemasonry at the forefront of its planners' minds, whilst the creation of the Capitol shows conclusively what the real religious imperatives of Washington's planners were.

That the capital city of the most powerful nation in the world was built on Christian precepts is dismissed as an absurdity when one learns the views of the men who were in charge of the fledgling country when Washington was planned.

Thomas Jefferson, the man who penned the American Constitution, and who later became President of the United States, is a good case in point. Some doubt exists as to his Freemasonic credentials, but none at all regarding his view of Christianity. He said:

> I have examined all the known superstitions of the world, and I do not find in our particular superstition of Christianity one redeeming feature ... Millions of innocent men, women and children, since the introduction of Christianity, have been burnt, tortured, fined, and imprisoned. What has been the effect of this coercion? To make one half of the world fools and the other half hypocrites; to support roguery and error all over the Earth.29

George Washington, after whom the capital was named, General and first President of the Unites States of America, also had very definite views regarding Christianity, even if he was more circumspect in public arenas. Thomas Jefferson once said of Washington:

> Dr. Rush told me (he had it from Asa Green) that when the clergy addressed General Washington, on his departure from the government, it was observed in their consultation that he had never, on any occasion, said a word to the public which showed a belief in the Christian religion, and they thought they should so pen their address as to force him at length to disclose publicly, whether he was a Christian or not. However, he observed, the old fox was too cunning for them. He answered every article of their address particularly, except that, which he passed over without notice.30

Washington, though obviously careful in his treatment of the subject, clearly had no religious bias, even if the religious leaders of the infant America would have wished it so.

> We have abundant reason to rejoice that in this Land the light of truth and reason has triumphed over the power of bigotry and superstition ... In this enlightened Age and in this Land of equal liberty it is our boast, that a man's religious tenets will not forfeit the protection of the Laws, nor deprive him of the right of attaining and holding the highest Offices that are known in the United States.'31

It is known that Grace was never said before meals in the Washington household and though the General accompanied his wife to church, he always abstained from taking part in Holy Communion. He strenuously fought against using the word "God," referring rather to "Providence," which he spoke of on occasion as "he" and "it," though most telling in this context, regularly as "she."

Neither were Washington and Jefferson alone in their attitude towards Christianity. Another of the important fathers of America, John Adams, is reputed to have said:

> The doctrine of the divinity of Jesus is made a convenient cover for absurdity.

Adams made his views regarding the spiritual nature of the Government of the United States abundantly clear when he signed the Treaty of Tripoli. He supervised the construction of the document himself and article 11 states:

> The Government of the United States is by no means founded on the Christian religion.

If this is not plain enough, perhaps we should hear from James Madison, another Founding Father and fourth President of the United States:

> What influence in fact have Christian ecclesiastical establishments had on civil society? In many instances they have been upholding the thrones of political tyranny. In no instance have they been seen as the guardians of the liberties of the people. Rulers who wished to subvert the public liberty have found in the

clergy convenient auxiliaries. A just government, instituted to secure and perpetuate liberty, does not need the clergy.

It would have been quite easy to fill an entire chapter with statements of this sort, for almost every one of the Founding Fathers whose names and importance have come down to us made similar utterances. It is very plain that the first four and possibly the first five Presidents of the Unites States of America were anything but orthodox Christians. Might this simply be the case because most of them were also Freemasons? After all, a devotion to Christianity is not a prerequisite of the Craft, whose members merely have to admit a belief in the "Great Geometrician of the Universe." Once again, the answer might be an emphatic yes, were it not for the fact of the existence of the Capitol building in Washington, together with the obvious knowledge and intention of those who inspired and built it.

The Capitol was designed to be the legislative and democratic seat of the United States of America. Initially conceived, as was the original conception of the entire city, by Pierre Charles L'Enfant, the Capitol stands at the elevated east end of the Mall. The site was, in L'Enfant's words, "a pedestal waiting for a monument." The architect who finally won approval for his design for the Capitol itself was Dr. William Thornton, a man of Scottish extract and a noted Freemason.

It is suggested that the floor plan of the Capitol Mall was based upon that of a Masonic temple – an east–west rectangle, attached to an unfinished triangle. In a lodge, the Grand Master would preside at the point of the triangle, which is precisely where the Capitol stands on the Mall. In essence, the Capitol is little more than a deliberately engineered temple and stands as an integral part of a street plan which is, itself, living proof of the knowledge of sacred architecture possessed by those who meticulously planned the city. Like so many buildings in Washington, the most telling aspect of the Capitol's true spiritual heritage lies in the state of the heavens at the time the corner stone was laid.

In the case of the Capitol this ceremony took place on 16 September 1793. The corner stone ceremony took place after a solemn and dignified procession, in which a number of Masonic lodges took a conspicuous part. At their head, and wearing full Masonic regalia, was George Washington himself.

The stone was almost certainly laid at midday. It is relatively simple to draw up an astrological chart for an event such as this and we can be in no doubt that to the astrologically minded Freemasons who had organized and planned the event, an auspicious chart of the heavens would be deemed necessary before the stone laying would have been arranged. In many circles astrology was still accepted as not just important, but crucial, at the end of the eighteenth century.

We are most familiar these days with personal astrology. The position of the stars and planets at the time of one's birth is said to set the seal on the sort of character a child will grow to enjoy, and is also said to play an important part in life events thereafter. Astrologers at the time of the founding of the United States of America believed wholeheartedly that any enterprise, or building, also responded to the positive and negative attributes of the time at which it was instigated. An astrologer would therefore seek the most providential planetary positions and aspects for something as important as the commencement of a building such as the Capitol. The day and time chosen are most telling. At noon on 18 September 1783, the sign of the zodiac that was immediately overhead, and therefore astrologically the most potent, was Virgo. The mid heaven (that point absolutely overhead) was 26 degrees of Virgo. The Sun, which from an astrological perspective would have to smile on such an event, was at 26 degrees of Virgo. In fact the mid heaven and the Sun were within four minutes of occupying the same position in the sky, so it is possible the cornerstone ceremony actually took place at four minutes before noon, when mid heaven and Sun would have been together, or in astrological terms, conjunct.

To any astrologer this is very telling. The Capitol building was so pivotal to the embryonic United States that it deserved the best possible "birth." Virgo, as we have seen, is indisputably the zodiac sign most sacred to Goddess worshipers. It is the sign of the Virgin. Close to the end of the zodiac sign is the constellation of Crater, and the Sun on that day in Washington was in direct contact with this most potent symbol of Goddess adoration.

Those planning the ceremony could have chosen any day, or any time within any day, to perform the necessary rites. However, they made it absolutely plain that the very azimuth of their devotions was Virgo, and with it the Great Goddess, the "Providence" of George Washington and patroness and founding spirit of this new Utopia. The Capitol is certainly a temple, and it is one deliberately built to venerate the Goddess. It was inspired by Freemasonic and Rosicrucian knowledge and was as much a legacy of the Golden Thread as any of the great Gothic cathedrals of Europe.

Taken in conjunction with a knowledge of the geographical position of Washington, and its Megalithic geometric relationships with Jerusalem, Troy, Knossos, and the Giza plateau in Egypt, there can surely be no doubt of the Capitol's true pedigree. Indeed, the entire United States of America was deliberately planned to be the latest innovation of an institution and Fraternity that was already many thousands of years old when George Washington tapped that so-important cornerstone into place. He did so under the mid-heaven gaze of the same benevolent deity whose worship had been and remained pivotal to a large and influential group of individuals. The Golden Thread now had dominion over a large percentage of the world. Financially, it pulled the strings of the western world from a series of fantastically rich banks in Switzerland, whilst the foundation of the United States would allow it to pursue its notions of commerce, religious tolerance, and democracy with impunity.

CHAPTER 24

The Golden Thread in England

Despite the apparent demise of the Templars after 1307, even in England the influence of the Golden Thread did not disappear from society. As we have seen, its presence in Scotland, by way of post-Templar conclaves and direct influence on the Scottish monarch is more evident, yet clearly it also survived within a number of the old Norman salt line families. The dynasties that had come to rule Scotland were also originally Norman and then English in origin. One royal family that had definite salt line origins was that of Bruce and it was soon followed by another, Stuart, which came to power in Scotland in 1371.

The Stuart kings, commencing with James Stuart, came south again in 1603, with James I of England (VI of Scotland). Freemasonic activity, seen in Scotland from the fifteenth century and instigated by the Golden Thread, was probably already apparent in England during the reign of Elizabeth I, the immediate predecessor of James I, but it really began to show itself when James took the English throne. English Rosicrucianism was also apparent. The thinker, statesman, and writer, Francis Bacon (1561–1628) was very familiar with what would eventually come to be known as the Rosicrucian doctrines. Bacon was an alchemist, a radical free thinker, and a man whose religious inclinations were described as being "unique" even in his own lifetime. It was Bacon who seems to have first suggested the creation of a completely new sort of society in America, though even this illustrious man, espousing the doctrines of the Golden Thread, may not have been its most important Elizabethan, English representative.

A much overlooked character, but one whose importance to these matters cannot be overstated, was Sir Thomas Gresham. Born in 1519, of a family with a distinct salt line heritage, Sir

Thomas Gresham rose to prominence as a businessman, statesman, and philanthropist. He served well in the government of the young King Edward VI of England, and later in that of Elizabeth I. Gresham was primarily a mercer and a wool trader. It was his exploits in the latter profession that first brought this man to my attention because I had learned through long years of research that so often, especially in the medieval period, wool trading and the Golden Thread were inclined to go hand in hand.

Gresham was a man of great talents, many of which he exploited in the name of England, though his real *raison d'etre* could have been quite different. He single-handedly negotiated away much of the national debt of England, which had been built up across decades of religious and political problems. In addition he was a government spy and the builder of the "Royal Exchange," an institution that was reminiscent of the Champagne fairs and which helped to put England and ultimately Britain on the economic map of Europe and the greater world. Meanwhile, Gresham and people like him willingly elevated Elizabeth, "the Virgin Queen," to a status not far short of the Goddess herself.

After a life filled with positively Herculean tasks on behalf of his nation and monarch, Sir Thomas Gresham died in the year 1579, and it is the bequests at the time of his death that are most telling. It has been assumed that Thomas Gresham was one of England's first Freemasons, and that a sort of Freemasonic Lodge was held at his large house in Bishopgate, London. Be that as it may, upon his death Gresham made a charitable gift, which ultimately led to a remarkable period in British history. Gresham established a college, which provided free lectures to anyone sufficiently interested to attend. His endeavors would eventually lead to the formation of the Royal Society and to the birth of modern science.

Somewhat after Gresham's time, England was ripped apart by a ferocious civil war, fought between King Charles I and Parliament. It is an indisputable fact that many of the Parliamentarian generals were either Rosicrucians, Freemasons, or both, for this was the period, around 1642, that Freemasonry had first arrived in England as a known and historically documented fact. However, it was not simply those fighting for Parliament who had become brother Masons because a fair proportion of the Royalist commanders were also Lodge members.

Most writers on the subject now concur with the theory that Freemasonry was especially strong within those nobles surrounding the Stuart monarchy. Charles I, whose intransigence led to the English Civil War, was the son of James I, the first Stuart king of England. There is little doubt that James I was a practicing Freemason and so it is highly likely that his son followed his inclinations.

By the end of the war the King was dead, executed by Parliament, and the country was in tatters. It was at this time, specifically on Wednesday 28 November 1660, that the first meeting of the Royal Society took place. Prior to the Civil War, a group of influential thinkers had formed what has come to be known as the "Invisible College." It comprised all manner of alchemists, astrologers, thinkers, and mathematicians, whose real agendas have never been known but the majority of whom were active Freemasons. Many of the members of the Invisible College were in possession of arcane knowledge, and it cannot be doubted that representatives of the Golden Thread were instrumental in its existence.

This institution gave the Golden Thread a greater influence in English affairs because the restoration of the monarchy in 1630 brought Charles I's much more reasonable son, Charles II, to the throne. Charles II was most certainly a Freemason himself and he had been well served by the practical advice and influence of the Invisible College whilst he was in exile. Shortly after his coronation the disparate parts of the Invisible College, many of whom had fought on different sides of the English Civil War, came together to form the Royal Society.

The Royal Society spawned some of the most brilliant scientists Britain would ever know. In its early days the most prominent of these was the world renowned Sir Isaac Newton, a man who is spoken about with great reverence in learned circles, having been called "The Father of Science." However, the real man is barely known to history. When his true biography is understood, his Golden Thread credentials are so obvious that he might as well have gone about London wearing a badge.

Isaac Newton was born in Woolsthorpe, Lincolnshire, England, in 1642. He entered Cambridge University in 1661 and was elected a fellow of Trinity College in 1667. Newton was an undoubted genius. He showed an interest in many different aspects of science though he is best known for his work in physics, specifically his discoveries in mechanics and gravity, but he also added much to the world's understanding of optics and he was an accomplished and influential mathematician and astronomer.

One of the aspects of Newton and his work that is never spoken about relates to claims he made regarding his own discoveries. Newton gathered together an extensive library and was an avaricious reader. Later in his life, when accolades were heaped upon him, Newton was quick to say about his work: "Anything

I have discovered was possible because I was standing upon the shoulders of giants."

Another fact about Newton that is rarely if ever discussed in the hallowed halls of academe is his fascination for subjects which science now dismisses as superstition and nonsense. Newton was an avid and enthusiastic astrologer and personally penned probably several million words on the subject of alchemy. He was also obsessed with the dimensions of King Solomon's Temple in Jerusalem. Newton firmly believing that if the dimensions of the Temple as described in the Bible could be truly understood, they would offer a complete understanding of physics. It is likely that the Knights Templar, actually named after the same Temple, shared this belief.

In matters of faith, Newton showed a scant regard for Christianity in an orthodox sense. He absolutely repudiated all belief in the Christian Trinity. Unfortunately, and on his own instructions, a great bonfire was made of most of his personal statements and observations, just a day or two before his death in 1727, so we can never know his "absolute" beliefs. In reality, Newton was most likely Rosicrucian by persuasion. However, it is worth reiterating at this point that the ages-old institution I have chosen to call the Golden Thread, chose to manifest itself through a number of different fraternities and organizations. This is shown to be the case as early as the Essene of the Jordan Valley, though in more recent times we can look at the Cistercian Order, the Templar Order, the ruling factions of Troyes and Burgundy, the Rosicrucians, Freemasons, and a wealth of other institutions. When the usefulness of any of them was over, the Golden Thread simply moved on – always one step ahead of those who would have gladly snuffed it out.

In my comprehension, few of those participating in any institution instigated by the Golden Thread ever even knew of its existence. Only a relatively small number of individuals at any stage were party to the true heritage of the Golden Thread or the store of spiritual and practical knowledge it possessed. I dare to suggest that Isaac Newton, either by lineal descent, or on account of his early contacts at Trinity College Cambridge, was such a person. This belief is not simply based upon the tireless work of Newton, or his "unusual" religious proclivities, but also on an event that took place during his life and the way he responded to it. His actions may have been absolutely pivotal to the direction the Golden Thread took henceforth and led, ultimately, to the world that we inhabit today.

Isaac Newton never showed himself to be remotely interested in politics, except on one single occasion. In 1685, Charles II died and was succeeded on the throne of Britain by his brother, James II. Charles, though religiously tolerant, had never attempted to restore Britain to the Catholic faith. Protestantism was firmly in command of the England Charles inherited and he was happy to leave matters that way. His brother James was very different and made it plain from the moment of his accession that he was a Catholic. From the word go, he was opposed by a large percentage of the population of Britain, though probably the most influential voice within the growing scientific community was that of Sir Isaac Newton.

It has to be remembered that from 1307 on, organizations created and controlled by the Golden Thread had been under attack from the Catholic Church. Catholicism had participated in the destruction of the Templars and had sought tenaciously to destroy the growing threat of Protestantism. Golden Thread influence in Switzerland and in other parts of Europe had fostered the Protestant faith, not because it was any more acceptable to those holding age-old Neolithic beliefs, but simply because the Protestant faith espoused a degree of freedom of thought and action, and because of its diversification. There were so many different forms of Protestants that none of them would ever stand a chance of dominating the world, as Catholicism had tried to do. Whether or not the rulers of the Catholic Church were cognizant of the "true" enemy they were fighting, they sought tenaciously to destroy Protestant Christianity.

There appears to have been a deliberate decision amongst the priests of the Golden Thread present in Britain at the time of the accession of James II, of which Sir Isaac Newton was an undoubted example. It was decided to break the power of the Catholic Church in Britain once and for all. As a result, James II was ousted and the throne was offered to his Protestant daughter, Mary and to her husband, the Dutch William, Duke of Orange. It is an indisputable fact that at this time, in 1689, plans were laid to ensure that the future royal succession could never again pass to a Catholic monarch.

Despite a very real inherent danger, should James II prevail, Isaac Newton spoke out publicly against the monarch and his bravery swayed the members of the Royal Society. The universities also followed Newton's lead, beginning an avalanche that would see the end of James II. It is possible to appreciate the full implications of the Golden Thread's decision to be rid of Catholicism on the throne of Britain for good when one observes the changes that took place at almost exactly the same time with regard to its most famous modern offshoot – Freemasonry. This introduces us to another little known but very important character from British history. His name was Charles Howard, third Earl of Carlisle.

The Howard family was one that had been of significant interest to me since the start of my research into the salt lines of France and Britain. Ancestors of the Howards had been present with William the Conqueror. They had formerly occupied salt line holdings in France and did so in England, specifically in East Anglia. However, the importance of Charles Howard, third Earl of Carlisle, only gradually became apparent. His family had long enjoyed a number of salt line holdings in England and his title, inherited from his father and grandfather, emphasized the fact, since Carlisle is one of England's most prominent salt line cities. His most significant appearance on the stage of history took place around the year 1700.

Charles Howard had been living in the very northwest of England, close to the Scottish borders. He had held several influential positions at court and, unlike many of his illustrious family, had abandoned the Catholic faith, though there is much to indicate that Charles Howard was not really a Christian at all. Around 1699, a very convenient fire destroyed a castle belonging to a close female relative of Charles Howard. This was the castle of Henderskelf, near Malton, Yorkshire, which had passed into the Howard family via a marriage with another potent Norman salt line family named Dacre. Charles Howard moved to Henderskelf and immediately planned to build a stately home on the land formerly occupied by Henderskelf. In 1700 Howard commissioned two known Freemasons, the playwright and ex soldier of fortune John Vanburgh and architect Nicholas Hawksmoor, to begin work on what would eventually be one of the finest houses in England.

Castle Howard, as it would be called, represents the most potent proof of Golden Thread survival and influence in England at the beginning of the eighteenth century. The building was constructed at the intersection of a longitudinal and a latitudinal salt line, which meet beneath the Howard family mausoleum, close to Castle Howard itself. There is nothing secret about Charles Howard's allegiance to Freemasonry, either historically, or in terms of this great house. Enormous keystones adorn all the windows and doors at Castle Howard (an important component of Masonic architecture), whilst in the grounds there is an assortment of Masonic pyramids. But this is merely the tip of the iceberg because to those who look at Castle Howard with true understanding, there are definite proofs of something much deeper. Castle Howard is a deliberately created temple of Goddess worship and probably represents the best example of Golden Thread inspired architecture to be seen anywhere in Britain.

The Great Hall at Castle Howard is a representation of the "core" of Golden Thread thinking. Here, under a massive dome, around the base of which are the twelve signs of the zodiac and the four elements, is to be found a very grand niche, containing a statue of Bacchus (who can be said to be synonymous with Dionysus in this context). Surmounting the niche in which Bacchus stands is a beautiful statue of Ceres (the Roman counterpart of the Greek goddess Demeter). Cradled in one arm Ceres has sheaves of wheat, whilst in the other she holds loaves of bread. Other statues of Ceres also adorn the Great Hall.

What makes the whole creation even more potent is the knowledge that it stands at the intersection of salt lines of longitude and latitude. There are very few locations throughout the whole of Europe that do so. The only way Charles Howard could have achieved a tighter fit would have been to knock down the ruins of the nearby Kirkham Priory, which very tellingly had also been placed on this intersection many centuries before. The preponderance of churches dedicated to St. Mary the Virgin or St. Mary Magdalene on the longitudinal salt line occupied by Castle Howard as it traverses England is staggering. If this wonderful house is not enough in itself to prove the existence of the Golden Thread, and the fact that Charles Howard was a real and important part of it, some of his other activities might set the seal on the realization.

Grand Lodge in London is the center of Freemasonry in England. It opened on 24 June 1717, an amalgamation of four existent London Lodges. English Freemasonry was a direct response to the state of the throne at the time. After the reign of William and Mary came that of another Protestant daughter of James II, Anne. When she died in 1714, the throne was offered to the German, George, the Elector of Hanover, who accepted and became George I of England and Scotland. Until that time Freemasonry had enjoyed a Scottish origin and its proponents had been supporters of the Stuart Catholic dynasty of kings. If Freemasonry was to survive in England, it had to be sanitized of its Scottish, Catholic past. This is precisely what happened. The form of Freemasonry eventually accepted in England was almost certainly "invented," by Charles Howard, third Earl of Carlisle. Special new "degrees" of Freemasonry were created, emphasizing the importance of specific English characters, such as the Anglo-Saxon king, Athelstan. These indirectly pointed to the "rightness" of the Hanoverian succession. All traces of Catholicism were eradicated from the Craft in England. To compensate, new degrees were formed to commemorate and eulogize the Knights Templar, an institution that had rarely been spoken about openly for nearly four centuries. There was a distinct paradox here because although English Freemasonry was clearly Protestant in inclination, the Templars had supposedly been the most Catholic of institutions. All these matters were heavily influenced by Charles Howard. Proof of the fact exists all over the world where the new degrees are known to this day as "York Rite Freemasonry." Charles Howard, third Earl of Carlisle was Grand Master of York Lodge at exactly the time these changes came about and was also a prominent figure in London when the English Grand Lodge was created.

Freemasonry exploded in popularity and although by the late twentieth century it would attract to itself a significant degree of criticism, it represented a force of significant subterranean power in British, European, and American society. In literally thousands of towns and cities across the western world, and on any evening of the week, new members would be inducted into what amounted to a "mystery religion," parts of which had been practiced so long that it is impossible to say with any certainty when they began. Although very few of these initiates would ever realize the fact, they were practicing Goddess worship of a type that had endured since Neolithic times. Just as importantly, they were giving the priesthood of the Golden Thread a secure, and in the main secret, base from which to operate.

CHAPTER 25

Out of the Crucible

W e might do well to consider the possible view of western society, particularly during the nineteenth century, taken by an individual visiting the Earth for the first time. Such a person may have seen the infant America, beginning to flex its economic and political muscles, its greatest harbor watched over and protected by what must be the largest statue of the Great Goddess ever created. Meanwhile, revolutionary France abounded with figures of "la belle France," a dominant matriarch, the folds of her cloak streaming around the figures of French peasantry.

In Britain, then the most powerful nation on the planet, the nation abounded with statues of Britannia, whose image adorned almost every coin of the realm and who became synonymous with Britain's great queen, Victoria. Might not such a visitor be forgiven for assuming that here was a society under the direct protection of a Goddess, who, a little investigation would reveal, had been at the forefront of humanity's adoration since time out of mind?

It is true that sexual inequality abounded, but forces were in place that would eventually eradicate, by law, all forms of sexual discrimination, leading to a society in which it would be possible for women, as well as men, to rise to the highest ranks in commerce, government, and law. This, like so much else in our societies today, was forged from the crucible of the Industrial Revolution, and I want to end this story by showing how the actions of the Golden Thread can be seen, clear and strong, in the rise of industrialization and the attendant march towards genuine democracy.

The Industrial Revolution began in Britain and, most specifically, in the scarred valleys of the West Riding of Yorkshire.

In fact the real impetus of the Industrial Revolution can be traced to one series of valleys, running back up towards the Pennine chain from the modern city of Leeds. Here, on the wide margins of the River Aire, Cistercian monks from Kirkstall Abbey, the ruins of which still guard the western river approach to Leeds, brought sheep rearing to its pinnacle.

Kirkstall was a daughter abbey of Fountains Abbey, that same foundation that had been seeded directly by St. Bernard of Clairvaux and which had been named after the village of his birth. The library of Fountains Abbey had also supplied the material necessary for Sir Thomas Mallory to complete his epic *Le Morte d'Arthur* and so bring the stories of the Holy Grail to the masses. (see chapter 17.)

Contrary to popular belief, at the time of the English Reformation, in the sixteenth century, the monks of England were not, in the main, tortured and burned when Henry VIII decided to destroy the power of the Roman Catholic Church. True, the vast majority of the monasteries were abolished and their lands passed to the crown, but by far the majority of monks received a pension and were released into society, to earn their living as they saw fit. It is not surprising that many of them chose to pursue the careers that had been important to them whilst they were still wearing the cowl. In the case of the monks of the Cistercian abbey of Kirkstall, that meant rearing sheep.

In the seventeenth and eighteenth centuries, religious conflict on the continent of Europe brought waves of immigrants into West Yorkshire, specifically from Belgium and northern France, individuals with names such as "Gaunt" and "Got." These people, known in England as Flemish, found a ready source of income in the north of England doing what they had done for centuries

– creating good, hard wearing cloth from the locally produced wool. As a result, the sheep-rearing acumen of the families of the Cistercian monks was allied to the cloth production of the Flemish immigrants. In cottages all over West Yorkshire, small-scale woolen cloth production began, based on subsistence farming and the herding of sheep on the poor uplands.

By the eighteenth century, commentators such as the writer Daniel Defoe described the valleys of West Yorkshire in terms that showed them to be the hotbed of pre-industrial endeavor. Gradually, from cottage industry to water-powered mills and then on to huge steam-run factories, the rise of the woolen cloth trade in Britain fuelled the innovations that were taking place elsewhere. New technology came along which allowed raw wool to be spun much quicker. This in turn led to innovations in weaving. The advent of the steam age allowed ever bigger centers of production to be created, until, slowly but surely Britain became the world's greatest industrial giant. Different areas of England, Ireland, Scotland, and Wales began to specialize in producing whatever local mineral resources allowed and everything came together as necessity proved itself to be the mother of invention. Meanwhile, Britain's mariners, inspired by the early voyages of Golden Thread representatives such as Henry Sinclair, traversed the globe, eventually building one of the largest empires the world has ever known.

Always, just below the surface, the guiding hand of the Golden Thread is noticeable. Nor was its presence lost on those who opened their eyes to see it. The nineteenth-century novelist, Anthony Trollope, had observed it at first hand. In one of his novels he describes a typical priest of the Golden Thread, surviving and flourishing within British society. In the book

Doctor Thorne Trollope wrote:

> ... He [Dr Thorne], however, and others around him, who still maintained the same staunch principles of protection – men like himself, who were too true to flinch at the cry of a mob – had their own way of consoling themselves. They were, and felt themselves to be, the only true depositories left of certain Eleusinian Mysteries, of certain deep and wondrous services of worship by which alone the Gods could be rightly approached. To them and them only was it now given to know these things, and to perpetuate them, if that might still be done. by the careful and secret education of their children.
>
> We have read how private and peculiar forms of worship have been carried on from age to age in families, which to the outer world have apparently adhered to the services of some ordinary church. And so it was by degrees with Mr. Thorne. He learned at length to listen calmly while protection was talked of as a thing dead, although he knew within himself that it was still quick with a mystic life. Nor was he without a certain pleasure that such knowledge, though given to him, should be debarred from the multitude.

Safe within the professions, the priesthood of the High Anglican Church, and within Freemasonry, British priests of the Golden Thread supervised the slow and often painful transition from agrarian subsistence to industrialization and from feudal tyranny to constitutional democracy. As patient as ever and with a task that never seems ended, a skein of people, with high moral imperatives and, as Trollope put it "peculiar forms of worship," continued to slowly steer the world towards that same Utopia that has always been its ultimate destination.

Even today, there is still a long way to go. Inequality, injustice, and tyranny abound in the world. The Templar objective of uniting the "Peoples of the Book" seems pitifully far from being achieved and the world often appears as dangerous and unfair as it has ever been. Cynicism abounds in western society, causing us to doubt every action and each sentiment of those we democratically choose to run our countries, yet we enjoy freedoms that even our immediate ancestors could not have guessed at.

In the necessary confines of a single book it would not be possible to offer all the evidence I have gathered which shows conclusively that the Golden Thread (or whatever it actually chooses to call itself) has been a hidden but very real guiding influence on our world for the past four or five thousand years. But there are some clues that interested readers can check out for themselves. Together with my long-suffering wife I have traveled many tens of thousands of miles, up and down the salt lines of my own native Britain and also those in France. On occasion, within salt line churches, I have seen what I have come to understand is genuine evidence of Golden Thread knowledge and survival. Any reader sufficiently interested to gain an understanding of longitude and latitude and who looks for the salt lines in their own region or country can follow in our path.

Look, especially, for churches that are placed on or very close to the run of salt lines. In particular, seek out those dedicated to St. Mary the Virgin, St. Mary Magdalene, St. John, or St. Nicholas.

Exploring the interior of such buildings, the interested visitor will sometimes see, usually in a side chapel to one side of the altar, a red light burning steadily. Generally speaking this red light, in any church, means that there is consecrated host within the building (the bread and wine used in Holy Communion). However, in the case of some churches this cannot be the case and in these instances the softly glowing light has a very different meaning.

I have seen this red light glowing on the altar of the birthplace of St. Bernard of Clairvaux, in Dijon, and in more than a dozen other French and British churches and cathedrals. From the tiniest parish church to the greatest Gothic cathedrals the red light of the Goddess flickers on, from age to age.

Should you want to see it in its most magnificent setting, visit the stunningly beautiful cathedral in Canterbury, most sacred of all English churches. There, in the undercroft, on the altar of the Chapel of St. Mary Magdalene, you will see it for yourself. It is a sure sign that "someone" in the district is a legatee of a view of life and a religious belief that is almost as old as our species.

During this most remarkable adventure I have been approached on numerous occasions by persons who have previously been unknown to me. This has usually taken place at seminars or talks that I have been asked to give. Three of these individuals have introduced themselves to me as "Michael" and all claimed to be ex-Jesuit Catholic priests. Each shook my hand warmly, told me their name and of their former spiritual calling, and then wished me good luck in my search, which they all assured me would prove to be ever more rewarding. In each case their conversations made it abundantly clear to me that they knew far more about my research than had been published or spoken about openly.

In Canterbury Cathedral I was followed closely for well over three hours after having spent half an hour in the Chapel of Mary Magdalene, explaining to a fellow researcher the significance of the red light burning on the altar. The man in question, who was always at hand, never spoke and always smiled gently when I looked in his direction. He was wearing a sash indicating that he was employed in some capacity by the cathedral. He smiled again, framed in the great doorway of the cathedral as we left and raised a hand in farewell and his smile told me that he already understood much of what I had been searching to comprehend.

I continue to receive detailed email messages from individuals who are not known to me, usually carrying snippets of information that contribute to my research and invariably these unknown contacts sign their name as Michael. When I try to reply to such emails, the server informs me that no such email address exists. On several occasions, after speaking in public, I have come across an extremely tall and intelligent American, whom I only know as Joe. Conversations with Joe have caused me to realize that he works for the United States government, though in what capacity I have no idea because he simply laughs when I ask him. Joe has furnished me with significant information about structures in America, and particularly in Washington, which to the best of my knowledge has never been published.

Amongst the many letters I have penned, in order to try and gain specific information from individuals and institutions, are some to very influential people. One in particular elicited a reply that was very telling. It came from the Hon. Simon Howard, present incumbent and guardian of Castle Howard. In my communication, I had outlined my feelings regarding Castle

Howard and the family that had built it. The reply was friendly and courteous. It admitted to none of my suggestions, but most tellingly, it absolutely denied nothing either. Though it was a written communication, I could sense the smile of the writer, as I have seen it so often on the faces of the "Michaels," Joe the American, the custodian at Canterbury, a graceful looking woman who monitored my movements in Lastingham Church, and another who never let me out of her sight whilst I was in the treasury of Troyes Cathedral, France, where the skull of St. Bernard of Clairvaux now rests in its magnificent golden reliquary. I last saw the lady in question looking at me kindly from below a statue of the Virgin. I don't know the age of the particularly statue, but it depicts the Virgin cradling wheat and loaves of bread in her arms, exactly the same as on the statue of Ceres (Demeter) in Castle Howard, England. The fact that I am being observed does not worry me and I am certainly not paranoid about the situation but I am fully aware that the Golden Thread knows me every bit as well as I am beginning to understand it.

I have to admit to feeling happy and protected in the knowledge that despite the sadness and disappointment of a world that often fails to meet our expectations of it, there is something timeless, endlessly creative, and truly loving at work within society. It has always been there.

The latest preferred name of the Goddess is Gaia, though even this name is older than anyone can contemplate. Gaia today represents our concern for the planet upon which we live, and which supplies us with all we need. At last we are waking up to the realization that through our responsibility to our Mother the Earth, we are all related in our ultimate concern for each other.

Umberto Eco, in his best-selling novel, *Foucault's Pendulum,* suggested that the continuum I have referred to as the Golden Thread is a figment of human imagination and that the only true conspiracy is the conspiracy itself. I have personally seen enough and learned enough (some of which I cannot presently divulge) to know for certain that this is not the case, as I suspect Umberto Eco is also well aware.

Despite all of this and the knowledge that the Holy Grail represents the very vagina of the Earth, which gives birth to everything living on our planet, there is much more. Gradually, and in a way I hope I have shown possible to recognize, the Golden Thread has introduced "knowledge" into the world. It taught us the Earth's dimensions and reintroduced us to a measuring system that could encapsulate time, distance, mass, and geometry as one cohesive whole – a system far more capable and yet infinitely simpler than any we use today. Through Rosicrucianism, alchemy, and astrology, we learned about chemistry and were introduced to the universe of which our solar system forms a tiny part. Scientists are very reluctant to admit the fact but their predecessors were what would today be called "occultists" and "magicians."

So where does the Golden Thread exist today? Does it continue to exert its gentle influence on the world through Freemasonry or from some unseen office in a secretive Swiss bank? Do the priests, or just as likely, the priestesses of the Golden Thread still occupy positions of influence within the world's religions? Might we discover them on the boards of multinational companies, or within the workings of that obviously Templar-inspired organization, the International Red Cross? It is impossible to say because an institution that retained and protected its true identity for millennia is hardly likely to start openly displaying its presence now.

Perhaps, even without fully realizing the fact, I have become an emissary of the Golden Thread. It is a fact that knowledge of the Goddess has had a profound bearing on my life. I can also say with certainty that a much greater understanding of what the representatives of the Golden Thread have always known about our Earth and the part it plays in the solar system is just around the corner and I can say with absolute authority that what we learn will be explosive. In the cryptic traditions of so many who have gone before I would urge those interested to watch for the Chevalier and the Cup Bearer.

In a few days I will be traveling again, this time to the Mediterranean island of Malta, where there are some Megalithic vaults I need to explore. If I am willing to listen, I might be as lucky as the hero of that remarkable novel, *The Da Vinci Code*, the author of which, Dan Brown, has also clearly "felt" the unseen hand of our common Mother touch his cheek.

> For a moment, he thought he heard a woman's voice
> ... the wisdom of the ages ... whispering up from the
> chasms of the earth.32

Megalithic Geometry and the Phaistos Disc

In order to understand Megalithic geometry it is first necessary to recognize that there is nothing "natural" about the form of geometry with which we are familiar today. It might appear that there "have to be" 360 degrees to a circle, with each degree representing 60 minutes of arc and each minute comprising 60 seconds of arc but this is merely a convention, first used in Sumer. How and why it came about is another story. It was adopted by the Ancient Greeks and that was enough to ensure that we still use 360 degree geometry today.

My research shows that an earlier form of geometry used by humanity was slightly different. In this system all circles were seen as being essentially the same as that created by the Earth traveling around the Sun. The Earth's yearly journey takes 365.25 days. The nearest whole number of days to this would be 365 days, but this is impossible to split into anything like equal segments for months. In any case, because of a peculiarity regarding the way we view dawn, to any naked-eye observer there appear to be 366.25 days in each year, so a year of 366 days is more practical. Such a year can be split into twelve months, alternating at 30 and 31 days.

If the year is 366 days in length, then on the great circle of the Earth's journey around the Sun, we might consider each day as a "degree" in the circle of that journey. From the point of view of the Earth-bound observer the journey appears to be that of the Sun through the signs of the zodiac, but it amounts to the same thing.

For a multitude of reasons I had been exploring the possibility of a 366-day year and a 366-degree geometry for some years, though evidence of its actual existence did not arise until I began to study the Phaistos Disc, a curious little artifact found in Crete and which is known to date back to at least 2000 BC.

The disc is made of baked clay and is double-sided. On one side of the disc, the side I have chosen to call side A, there are 123 hieroglyphics, placed within a spiral in groups. On side B of the disc we find 119 hieroglyphics, also in groups and within a spiral.

Understanding what the Phaistos Disc might actually "say" is virtually impossible. We have no knowledge of the Minoan language and unless we find some sort of "Rosetta Stone" to give us reasonable clues, interpreting any message the disc has to offer is likely to prove impossible. However, my interest in the Phaistos Disc was based not upon what it might say but rather what it could do.

After weeks of staring at a reproduction of the disc, I began to

The Phaistos Disc Side A

The Phaistos Disc Side B

realize that if the hieroglyphics were to be seen as simple counters, therefore ignoring any linguistic meaning they might have, the Phaistos Disc became a powerful calendar and geometric calculating machine, but one based on a year of 366 days, and circles with 366 degrees. Undoubtedly, the Phaistos Disc is a multi-faceted device and I cannot pretend to fully understand all of its capabilities, but I do now understand at least some of them.

A full and detailed analysis of my work on the Phaistos Disc can be found in my book, *The Bronze Age Computer Disc.*[33] It took 190 pages to explain my discoveries regarding this curious little device, so to replicate all my findings again here would be unnecessary and tedious. Basically, I realized that the Phaistos Disc allowed those using it to understand the necessary compensations to turn the ritual Minoan year of 366 days into the true solar year of 365.25 days. (Just as we use leap year days to achieve the same objective.) Using the symbols as counters, with 123 days on side A being counted off for every symbol on side B, the period of time covered by the disc was 14,637 days. At the end of the spiral on side A there are three dots, which I took to represent three extra days to be added to the disc's total, bringing it to 14,640 days, which is the same as 40 years at 366 days. The three dots are not really necessary, since the disc is perpetual, but nevertheless the makers of the disc put them there as an aid to understanding the disc's true purpose.

It is within the endless rounds of 123 days that the clue for calendar rectification is to be found. Four such cycles equals 492 days. If, at the end of 492 days, one day were to be removed from the 366-day ritual year, the true solar calendar would be achieved. Without any other compensation than this (one day removed every 492 days) the 366-day calendar of the Minoans would have remained in tune with the true solar calendar for well over 4,000 years before any other compensation would have to be made. The calendar compensations appear at a particular time every 1.34 years and form a pattern that anyone conversant with the study of astrology would readily understand.

"So why," the interested reader might ask, " did the Minoans use increments of 123 days and not simply ones of 492 days?" The answer is that calendar compensation is only one of the tasks this amazing little calculating machine is capable of undertaking. It also allows anyone using it to establish what degree of a particular zodiac sign the Sun will occupy at any time of day, on any day – ever! In addition it shows an understanding of a unique form of trigonometry and also relates to the relationship of the Earth, and the planets Mercury and Venus. It may be capable of much more – the search continues.

Allied to the Megalithic Yard, discovered by Professor Alexander Thom in his careful surveying of Megalithic monuments in Britain and France, the Phaistos Disc shows itself to be an instrument fully in tune with a 366-day ritual year, which appears to have been a widespread European, Neolithic convention. This form of year was understood by people of undoubted mathematical skill; they clearly comprehended trigonometry and had a full knowledge of the physical dimensions of the Earth.

The Salt Lines of the World

Below, interested readers will find the expected position of all the latitudinal and longitudinal salt lines that cover the Earth. These are based on Xaviar Guichard's estimation that the prime meridian of the salt line system was equivalent to the modern 6 degrees East of Greenwich. All longitudinal salt lines are 1/366th part of the Earth's circumference apart, whilst there are 91.5 equally spaced latitudinal salt lines between the equator and the poles.

Latitudinal Salt Lines

0 degrees 59 minutes North

1 degree 58 minutes North

2 degrees 57 minutes North

3 degrees 56 minutes North

4 degrees 55 minutes North

5 degrees 54 minutes North

6 degrees 53 minutes North

7 degrees 52 minutes North

8 degrees 51 minutes North

9 degrees 50 minutes North

10 degrees 49 minutes North

11 degrees 48 minutes North

12 degrees 47 minutes North

13 degrees 46 minutes North

14 degrees 45 minutes North

15 degrees 44 minutes North

16 degrees 43 minutes North

17 degrees 42 minutes North

18 degrees 41 minutes North

19 degrees 40 minutes North

20 degrees 39 minutes North

21 degrees 38 minutes North

22 degrees 37 minutes North

23 degrees 36 minutes North

24 degrees 35 minutes North

25 degrees 34 minutes North

26 degrees 33 minutes North

27 degrees 32 minutes North

28 degrees 31 minutes North

29 degrees 30 minutes North

30 degrees 29 minutes North

31 degrees 28 minutes North

32 degrees 27 minutes North

33 degrees 26 minutes North

34 degrees 25 minutes North

35 degrees 24 minutes North

36 degrees 23 minutes North

37 degrees 22 minutes North

38 degrees 21 minutes North

39 degrees 20 minutes North

40 degrees 19 minutes North

41 degrees 18 minutes North

42 degrees 17 minutes North

43 degrees 16 minutes North

44 degrees 15 minutes North

45 degrees 14 minutes North

46 degrees 13 minutes North

47 degrees 12 minutes North

48 degrees 11 minutes North

49 degrees 10 minutes North

50 degrees 9 minutes North

51 degrees 8 minutes North

52 degrees 7 minutes North

53 degrees 6 minutes North

54 degrees 5 minutes North

55 degrees 4 minutes North

56 degrees 3 minutes North

57 degrees 2 minutes North

58 degrees 1 minute North

59 degrees 1 minute North

60 degrees 00 minutes North

60 degrees 59 minutes North

61 degrees 58 minutes North

62 degrees 57 minutes North

63 degrees 56 minutes North

64 degrees 55 minutes North

65 degrees 54 minutes North

66 degrees 53 minutes North

67 degrees 52 minutes North

68 degrees 51 minutes North

69 degrees 50 minutes North

70 degrees 49 minutes North

71 degrees 48 minutes North

72 degrees 47 minutes North

73 degrees 46 minutes North

74 degrees 45 minutes North

75 degrees 44 minutes North

76 degrees 43 minutes North

77 degrees 42 minutes North

78 degrees 41 minutes North

79 degrees 40 minutes North

80 degrees 39 minutes North

81 degrees 38 minutes North

82 degrees 37 minutes North

83 degrees 36 minutes North

84 degrees 35 minutes North

85 degrees 34 minutes North

86 degrees 33 minutes North

87 degrees 32 minutes North

88 degrees 31 minutes North

89 degrees 30 minutes North

90 degrees 00 minutes North
(Southern Hemisphere lines are
identical.)

Longitudinal Salt Lines

0 degrees 53 minutes West	27 degrees 26 minutes West
1 degree 52 minutes West	28 degrees 25 minutes West
2 degrees 51 minutes West	29 degrees 24 minutes West
3 degrees 50 minutes West	30 degrees 23 minutes West
4 degrees 49 minutes West	31 degrees 23 minutes West
5 degrees 48 minutes West	32 degrees 22 minutes West
6 degrees 47 minutes West	33 degrees 21 minutes West
7 degrees 46 minutes West	34 degrees 20 minutes West
8 degrees 45 minutes West	35 degrees 19 minutes West
9 degrees 44 minutes West	36 degrees 18 minutes West
10 degrees 43 minutes West	37 degrees 17 minutes West
11 degrees 42 minutes West	38 degrees 16 minutes West
12 degrees 41 minutes West	39 degrees 15 minutes West
13 degrees 40 minutes West	40 degrees 14 minutes West
14 degrees 39 minutes West	41 degrees 13 minutes West
15 degrees 38 minutes West	42 degrees 12 minutes West
16 degrees 37 minutes West	43 degrees 11 minutes West
17 degrees 36 minutes West	44 degrees 10 minutes West
18 degrees 35 minutes West	45 degrees 9 minutes West
19 degrees 34 minutes West	46 degrees 8 minutes West
20 degrees 33 minutes West	47 degrees 7 minutes West
21 degrees 32 minutes West	48 degrees 6 minutes West
22 degrees 31 minutes West	49 degrees 5 minutes West
23 degrees 30 minutes West	50 degrees 4 minutes West
24 degrees 29 minutes West	51 degrees 3 minutes West
25 degrees 28 minutes West	52 degrees 2 minutes West
26 degrees 27 minutes West	53 degrees 1 minute West

53 degrees 0 minutes West	83 degrees 30 minutes West
54 degrees 59 minutes West	84 degrees 29 minutes West
55 degrees 58 minutes West	85 degrees 28 minutes West
56 degrees 57 minutes West	86 degrees 27 minutes West
57 degrees 56 minutes West	87 degrees 26 minutes West
58 degrees 55 minutes West	88 degrees 25 minutes West
59 degrees 54 minutes West	89 degrees 24 minutes West
60 degrees 53 minutes West	90 degrees 23 minutes West
61 degrees 52 minutes West	91 degrees 23 minutes West
62 degrees 51 minutes West	92 degrees 22 minutes West
63 degrees 50 minutes West	93 degrees 21 minutes West
64 degrees 49 minutes West	94 degrees 20 minutes West
65 degrees 48 minutes West	95 degrees 19 minutes West
66 degrees 47 minutes West	96 degrees 18 minutes West
67 degrees 46 minutes West	97 degrees 17 minutes West
68 degrees 45 minutes West	98 degrees 16 minutes West
69 degrees 44 minutes West	99 degrees 15 minutes West
70 degrees 43 minutes West	100 degrees 14 minutes West
71 degrees 42 minutes West	101 degrees 13 minutes West
72 degrees 41 minutes West	102 degrees 12 minutes West
73 degrees 40 minutes West	103 degrees 11 minutes West
74 degrees 39 minutes West	104 degrees 10 minutes West
75 degrees 38 minutes West	105 degrees 9 minutes West
76 degrees 37 minutes West	106 degrees 8 minutes West
77 degrees 36 minutes West	107 degrees 7 minutes West
78 degrees 35 minutes West	108 degrees 6 minutes West
79 degrees 34 minutes West	109 degrees 5 minutes West
80 degrees 33 minutes West	110 degrees 4 minutes West
81 degrees 32 minutes West	111 degrees 3 minutes West
82 degrees 31 minutes West	112 degrees 2 minutes West

113 degrees 1 minute West

114 degrees 0 minutes West

114 degrees 59 minutes West

115 degrees 58 minutes West

116 degrees 57 minutes West

117 degrees 56 minutes West

118 degrees 55 minutes West

119 degrees 54 minutes West

120 degrees 53 minutes West

121 degrees 52 minutes West

122 degrees 51 minutes West

123 degrees 50 minutes West

124 degrees 49 minutes West

125 degrees 48 minutes West

126 degrees 47 minutes West

127 degrees 46 minutes West

128 degrees 45 minutes West

129 degrees 44 minutes West

130 degrees 43 minutes West

131 degrees 42 minutes West

132 degrees 41 minutes West

133 degrees 40 minutes West

134 degrees 39 minutes West

135 degrees 38 minutes West

136 degrees 37 minutes West

137 degrees 36 minutes West

138 degrees 35 minutes West

139 degrees 34 minutes West

140 degrees 33 minutes West

141 degrees 32 minutes West

142 degrees 31 minutes West

143 degrees 30 minutes West

144 degrees 29 minutes West

145 degrees 28 minutes West

146 degrees 27 minutes West

147 degrees 26 minutes West

148 degrees 25 minutes West

149 degrees 24 minutes West

150 degrees 24 minutes West

151 degrees 23 minutes West

152 degrees 22 minutes West

153 degrees 21 minutes West

154 degrees 20 minutes West

155 degrees 19 minutes West

156 degrees 18 minutes West

157 degrees 17 minutes West

158 degrees 16 minutes West

159 degrees 15 minutes West

160 degrees 14 minutes West

161 degrees 13 minutes West

162 degrees 12 minutes West

163 degrees 11 minutes West

164 degrees 10 minutes West

165 degrees 9 minutes West

166 degrees 8 minutes West

167 degrees 7 minutes West

168 degrees 6 minutes West

169 degrees 5 minutes West

170 degrees 4 minutes West

171 degrees 3 minutes West

172 degrees 2 minutes West

173 degrees 1 minute West

174 degrees 0 minutes West

174 degrees 59 minutes West

175 degrees 58 minutes West

176 degrees 57 minutes West

177 degrees 56 minutes West

178 degrees 55 minutes West

179 degrees 54 minutes West

179 degrees 6 minutes East

178 degrees 7 minutes East

177 degrees 8 minutes East

176 degrees 9 minutes East

175 degrees 10 minutes East

174 degrees 11 minutes East

173 degrees 12 minutes East

172 degrees 13 minute East

171 degrees 14 minutes East

170 degrees 15 minutes East

169 degrees 16 minutes East

168 degrees 17 minutes East

167 degrees 18 minutes East

166 degrees 19 minutes East

165 degrees 20 minutes East

164 degrees 21 minutes East

163 degrees 22 minutes East

162 degrees 23 minutes East

161 degrees 24 minutes East

160 degrees 25 minutes East

159 degrees 26 minutes East

158 degrees 27 minutes East

157 degrees 28 minutes East

156 degrees 29 minutes East

155 degrees 30 minutes East

154 degrees 31 minutes East

153 degrees 32 minutes East

152 degrees 33 minutes East

151 degrees 34 minutes East

150 degrees 35 minutes East

149 degrees 36 minutes East

148 degrees 37 minutes East

147 degrees 38 minutes East

146 degrees 39 minutes East

145 degrees 40 minutes East

144 degrees 41 minutes East

143 degrees 42 minutes East

142 degrees 43 minutes East

141 degrees 44 minutes East

140 degrees 45 minutes East

139 degrees 46 minutes East

138 degrees 47 minutes East

137 degrees 48 minutes East

136 degrees 49 minutes East

135 degrees 50 minutes East

134 degrees 51 minutes East

133 degrees 52 minutes East

132 degrees 53 minutes East

131 degrees 54 minutes East

130 degrees 55 minute East

129 degrees 56 minutes East

128 degrees 57 minutes East

127 degrees 58 minutes East

126 degrees 59 minutes East

126 degrees 0 minutes East

125 degrees 1 minute East

124 degrees 2 minutes East

123 degrees 3 minutes East

122 degrees 4 minutes East

121 degrees 5 minutes East

120 degrees 6 minutes East

119 degrees 7 minutes East

118 degrees 8 minutes East

117 degrees 9 minutes East

116 degrees 10 minutes East

115 degrees 11 minutes East

114 degrees 12 minutes East

113 degrees 13 minutes East

112 degrees 14 minutes East

111 degrees 15 minutes East

110 degrees 16 minutes East

109 degrees 17 minutes East

108 degrees 18 minutes East

107 degrees 19 minutes East

106 degrees 20 minutes East

105 degrees 21 minutes East

104 degrees 22 minutes East

103 degrees 23 minutes East

102 degrees 24 minutes East

101 degrees 25 minutes East

100 degrees 26 minutes East

99 degrees 27 minutes East

98 degrees 28 minutes East

97 degrees 29 minutes East

96 degrees 30 minutes East

95 degrees 31 minutes East

94 degrees 32 minutes East

93 degrees 33 minutes East

92 degrees 34 minutes East

91 degrees 35 minutes East

90 degrees 35 minutes East

89 degrees 36 minutes East

88 degrees 37 minutes East

87 degrees 38 minutes East

86 degrees 39 minutes East

85 degrees 40 minutes East

84 degrees 41 minutes East

83 degrees 42 minutes East

82 degrees 43 minutes East

81 degrees 44 minutes East

80 degrees 45 minutes East

79 degrees 46 minutes East

78 degrees 47 minutes East

77 degrees 48 minutes East

76 degrees 49 minutes East

75 degrees 50 minutes East

74 degrees 51 minutes East

73 degrees 52 minutes East

72 degrees 53 minutes East

71 degrees 54 minute East

70 degrees 55 minutes East

69 degrees 56 minutes East

68 degrees 57 minutes East

67 degrees 58 minutes East

66 degrees 59 minutes East

66 degrees 0 minutes East

65 degrees 1 minute East

64 degrees 2 minutes East

63 degrees 3 minutes East

62 degrees 4 minutes East

61 degrees 5 minutes East

60 degrees 6 minutes East

59 degrees 7 minutes East

58 degrees 8 minutes East

57 degrees 9 minutes East

56 degrees 10 minutes East

55 degrees 11 minutes East

54 degrees 12 minutes East

53 degrees 13 minutes East

52 degrees 14 minutes East

51 degrees 15 minutes East

50 degrees 16 minutes East

49 degrees 17 minutes East

48 degrees 18 minutes East

47 degrees 19 minutes East

46 degrees 20 minutes East

45 degrees 21 minutes East

44 degrees 22 minutes East

43 degrees 23 minutes East

42 degrees 24 minutes East

41 degrees 25 minutes East

40 degrees 26 minutes East

39 degrees 27 minutes East

38 degrees 28 minutes East

37 degrees 29 minutes East

36 degrees 30 minutes East

35 degrees 31 minutes East

34 degrees 32 minutes East

33 degrees 33 minutes East

32 degrees 34 minutes East

31 degrees 35 minutes East

30 degrees 35 minutes East

29 degrees 36 minutes East

28 degrees 37 minutes East

27 degrees 38 minutes East

26 degrees 39 minutes East

25 degrees 40 minutes East

24 degrees 41 minutes East

23 degrees 42 minutes East

22 degrees 43 minutes East

21 degrees 44 minutes East

20 degrees 45 minutes East

19 degrees 46 minutes East

18 degrees 47 minutes East

17 degrees 48 minutes East

16 degrees 49 minutes East

15 degrees 50 minutes East

14 degrees 51 minutes East

13 degrees 52 minutes East

12 degrees 53 minute East

11 degrees 54 minutes East

10 degrees 55 minutes East

9 degrees 56 minutes East

8 degrees 57 minutes East

7 degrees 58 minutes East

6 degrees 59 minutes East

6 degrees 0 minutes East

5 degrees 1 minute East

4 degrees 2 minutes East

3 degrees 3 minutes East

2 degrees 4 minutes East

1 degree 5 minutes East

0 degrees 6 minutes East

1 Jacquetta Hawkes, *Dawn of the Gods*, Chatto and Windus, London, 1968.

2 Knight and Lomas, *Urel's Machine*, Century, 1999.

3 Alan Butler, *The Bronze Age Computer Disc*, Foulsham, 1999.

4 Xaviar Guichard, *Eleusis – Alesia*, Paillart, 1936.

5 Leonard Shlain, *The Alphabet Versus the Goddess*, A12
rkana, 1998.

6 The Old Testament of the Bible, Samuel 2:22-25.

7 The Old Testament of the Bible, 1 Kings 11:5.

8 Barbara G. Walker, *The Woman's Encyclopedia of Myths and Secrets*, HarperCollins San Francisco, 1983.

9 Morton Smith, *Clement of Alexandria and a Secret Gospel of Mark*, Harvard University Press, Cambridge, Mass., 1973.

10 James Robinson, *The Nag Hammadi Library in English*, Harper and Row, San Francisco, 1981.

11 Lynn Picknett and Clive Prince, *The Templar Revelation*, Bantum, London, 1997.

12 Michael Baigent, Richard Leigh, and Henry Lincoln, *The Holy Blood and the Holy Grail*, Jonathan Cape, London, 1982.

13 Robert Graves, *The White Goddess*, Faber and Faber, 1999.

14 Laurence Gardner, *The Bloodline of the Holy Grail*, Element Shaftsbury, Dorset, 1996.

15 Michael Baigent, Richard Leigh, and Henry Lincoln, *The Holy Blood and the Holy Grail*, Jonathan Cape, London, 1982.

16 *Domesday Book*, Introduction by Geoffrey Martin, Penguin Classics, London, 2003.

17 *Carmina Gadelica*, edited by Carmichael and McInnes, Floris Books, 2001.

18 Alan Butler and Stephen Dafoe, *The Templar Continuum*, Templar Publishing, Belville Canada, 2000.

19 Louis Charpentier, *Mysteries of Chartres Cathedral*, AB Academic Publishers, 1980.

20 Leslie Alcock, *Arthur's Britain*, Penguin Books, London, 1971.

21 Michael Baigent and Richard Leigh, *The Temple and the Lodge*, Jonathan Cape, London, 1989.

22 Louis Charpentier, *The Mystery of Chartres Cathedral*, Avon, London, 1980.

23 Dan Brown, *The Da Vinci Code*, Transworld, London, 2003.

24 Christopher Knight and Robert Lomas, *The Hiram Key*, Century, London, 1996.

25 Nigel Bryant (ed.), *The High Book of the Grail*, D. S. Brewer, 1996.

26 Robert Graves, *The White Goddess*, Faber and Faber, London, 1948.

27 Roger Sherman Loomis, *Celtic Mythology and Arthurian Romance*, Academy, Chicago USA, 1997.

28 Robert Hewitt Brown, *Stellar Theology and Masonic Astronomy*, publisher and date unknown.

29 Letter to William Short, a friend and colleague.

30 Thomas Jefferson, quoted from *Jefferson's Works*, Vol. iv., p. 572.

31 George Washington, Letter to the members of the New Church in Baltimore, January 27, 1793.

32 Dan Brown, *The Da Vinci Code*, Bantam Press, London, 2003.

33 Alan Butler, *The Bronze Age Computer Disc*, Quantum, London, 1999.

SELECTED INDEX